The End of Public Execution

The End of Public Execution
Race, Religion, and Punishment in the American South

Michael Ayers Trotti

The University of North Carolina Press CHAPEL HILL

© 2022 The University of North Carolina Press
All rights reserved
Set in Merope Basic by Westchester Publishing Services
Manufactured in the United States of America

Library of Congress Cataloging-in-Publication Data
Names: Trotti, Michael Ayers, author.
Title: The end of public execution : race, religion, and punishment in the American South / Michael Ayers Trotti.
Description: Chapel Hill : The University of North Carolina Press, [2022] | Includes bibliographical references and index.
Identifiers: LCCN 2022022447 | ISBN 9781469670409 (cloth) | ISBN 9781469670416 (paperback) | ISBN 9781469670423 (ebook)
Subjects: LCSH: Executions and executioners—Southern States—History. | Public executions—Southern States—History. | Capital punishment—Southern States—History. | Discrimination in capital punishment—Southern States—History.
Classification: LCC HV8699.U6 A448 2022 | DDC 364.660975—dc23/eng/20220601
LC record available at https://lccn.loc.gov/2022022447

Contents

List of Tables vii
Acknowledgments ix

Introduction 1
Re-centering

CHAPTER ONE
A Camp Meeting at the Gallows 8

CHAPTER TWO
Beyond Executions of African American Men for Murder 34

CHAPTER THREE
Shooting the Sheep-Killing Dogs 57
Racism in Southern Punishment

CHAPTER FOUR
Counting the South's Legal Executions 82

CHAPTER FIVE
Uncivil Executions 103

CHAPTER SIX
Make It a Secret Silent Monster 128
Executions in Private

Afterword 161

Notes 169
Bibliography 235
Index 247

Tables

2.1 Executions for crimes other than murder or rape in southern states, 1866–1920 42

4.1 Number of legal executions, 1866–1920, by state 85

4.2 Executions in regions outside the South in the 1890s 88

4.3 Comparison of Espy and Hearn/Laska executions in Counts, 1866–1920 89

4.4 Comparison of Espy and Hearn/Laska executions in rates, 1866–1920 91

4.5 Overall and African American counts and rates of 1890s executions in Virginia and Georgia 92

4.6 Comparison of Espy and Hearn/Laska executions in rates for African Americans, 1866–1920 95

4.7 Comparison of Espy and Hearn/Laska executions in rates for whites, 1866–1920 97

5.1 Executions and lynchings of African American men for sexual infractions in counts and rates in the 1890s 119

5.2 Comparison of Espy and Hearn/Laska executions for sexual crimes, 1866–1920 121

6.1 Major state votes for changes in execution 140

Acknowledgments

For help in finding materials, thank you to the staffs at Cornell's Olin and Law Libraries, the Ithaca College Library, the Newspapers and Periodicals reading room of the Library of Congress, the Library of Virginia, the Virginia Historical Society, the Southern Historical Collection and the North Carolina Collection of the University of North Carolina, Chapel Hill, and the Morton Library (with its gargoyle of my father) of the Union Presbyterian Seminary in Richmond.

For financial and logistical help in pursuing this project, thanks to Ithaca College's (IC's) School of Humanities and Sciences for the Robert Ryan professorship, as well as to IC's Provost's office, to the Virginia Historical Society, and to Christopher Swezey, friend and home-base during my trips to the Library of Congress. Students provided important help on this project, particularly Priyam Banerjee and Cosmo Houck. I required a variety of spaces to complete the writing: Cornell's A. D. White Library, a park bench on Cayuga Lake, and many local coffee shops: The Shop (now gone), the Press Café, Ithaca Coffee Company, and Gimme Coffee. The Constance Saltonstall Foundation for the Arts repeatedly provided lovely spaces for me to write with the focus that I otherwise only dream of having.

I thank the many readers who helped to strengthen this work. Much of the manuscript at some point or another over the last thirteen years has been aerated through the capacious minds of the Chapterhouse Beer&History Writing Group: Michael Smith, Robert Vanderlan, Aaron Sachs, Derek Chang, and Jefferson Cowie. Other readers of portions of this work include Amy Louise Wood, Elaine Franz, Kidada Williams, Donald Mathews, Randolph Roth, Fitzhugh Brundage, Bruce E. Baker, Robert Tinkler, Gavin Campbell, Seth Kotch, Dennis Downey, Grace Elizabeth Hale, Vivian Bruce Conger, and Jonathan Ablard. Comments and responses from two presentations at the Southern (2006 and 2014) were very helpful, as were responses to a paper presented at the 2011 St. George Tucker Society Meeting. Anonymous readers offered very important feedback as well, both for the book manuscript and for two articles related to this work that appeared in the *Journal of Social History* and the *Journal of American History*. The editorial staff of the University of North Carolina Press helped me correct many flaws and inconsistencies, as did the proofreading of my sister, Beth Schneir. Thanks to you all.

As I wrap up this project, I am conscious of how my work is dependent upon a range of less direct and tangible benefits from the wider society. My many treks to the Library of Congress were sped along by investments in Amtrak and the DC Metro system. My employment and my own education would not have been possible without significant investments by Ithaca College, the federal government, and the states of Virginia, North Carolina, and New York. We have set up a society in which schooled, middle-class people like myself can work with the assets of our society to carry projects like this to fruition, and I thank those responsible for the decisions over the course of generations that have made that possible, even while I reflect on how so many within our communities lack the means and schooling to similarly deploy society's assets to their own ends.

As with anything I do, my lifelong partnership with Christine has been the foundation of my life and therefore my work, and the love of our daughter and our son has given me joy in the midst the darkness of the topic I study here. Support from David Frahm and from friends and family of all sorts and spread out across North America have been essential to grounding me, allowing me to complete this project.

THE DEATH, RACISM, AND HORROR at the heart of this project wore on me in significant ways in the course of this project, particularly as real-life challenges faced my family. My father was ill through the first half of my work on the project, and his death in 2013 so filled me with pathos that I could not bear to look at my thousands of documents about death for more than a year thereafter. Two years later, my mother, even less expectedly, passed. I simply did not have the requisite margin to allow me to focus on this deathly project. I tinkered. For some time.

My father and my mother gave me hope, and their spirits as they struggled with each of their illnesses and with each of their passings demonstrated both how important these human moments of transition are and how to accomplish them with grace and a startlingly inspiring amount of complaisance. In their lives and in so many ways, they gave their children (and others around them) a foundation of love and support upon which to build. There is no one my father did not wish to call "brother," and no one my mother did not offer a smile to.

THIS BOOK, A HUMBLE OFFERING on a disturbing topic that it is, is dedicated to them: Joan Thompson Trotti and John Boone Trotti, southerners in blood and bone, born from the mountains of Virginia and the Carolinas in the midst of the Great Depression, reminding us in the lives they lived that so much in the South stands far apart from the history, charted here, of racism and violence. There is also sweetness, a striving toward a better world, and a humble walk with God. There is also grace.

The End of Public Execution

Introduction
Re-centering

> When murderers are executed as murderers, and not lionized by the people; when they are no longer allowed to pose as heroes on the awful death-trap, and to harangue the populace to their hearts' content, there will be fewer of them called upon to mount the gallows.
> —*Atlanta Constitution*, 7 June 1891

DANFORTH'S DROP.

AUGUSTA HANGS A MURDERER IN ARTISTIC STYLE.

The Victim Refuses the Proffered Drink of Whiskey and Went to His Death Sober—The Last Scenes.

Augusta, GA, September 4—(special)—Frank Danforth, the murderer of Lizzie Gray, his wife, was hanged today at 12:28 o'clock. The execution was in private, and took place in the jailyard, in the presence of several hundred witnesses. There was an immense throng of negroes on the outside, and men and boys were perched on the housetops and trees. Among the crowd who got up on the high jailyard fence and viewed the execution were many white women, who unflinchingly stood the test of their courage.

Exactly at 12 o'clock, Sheriff P. J. O'Connor, with his deputies, and Messrs. Henry Campbell, Calvin Sego and Ed Pritchard, entered Danforth's cell, where Revs. C. T. Walker, Lyons and Goodwin were sitting singing most fervently religious and devout hymns.

"Stand up, Frank," Sheriff O'Connor commanded. Without a tremor or the least nervousness, the murderer arose and listened to the death warrant. While the preachers were singing and praying, Danforth rocked to and fro in cadence with the music, testified his belief in salvation by ejaculating expressions indicative of the greatest contrition. His favorite expression was "None but the repentant can be saved."

—*Atlanta Constitution*, 5 September 1891

Covering two generations and the 1,200 counties of the South, this investigation of capital punishment after the Civil War centers on the shift from legal public executions—complete with religious services viewed by thousands—to executions behind walls in the South of the late nineteenth and early twentieth centuries. As in the *Constitution*'s report of the execution of African American Frank Danforth, this transition was complex; even the word "private" in the report above requires interpretation, for hundreds were in view of the execution despite the jail's walls. The South's punishment regime was combined with the South's vibrant African American religious culture in these moments, yielding a complicated picture of racism, of salvation, of hope, of punishment.

Punishments are meant to do more than to reprimand individuals; the death penalty in this era was both retribution for the missteps of the condemned and a violent lesson particularly for those who were perceived to be a criminal class: here is what happens to those who violate the laws. Before 1850, legal executions in the South were performed out in the open in front of thousands; the last legal public execution in the South (and nation) occurred in 1936. In between, the South witnessed important shifts in the use of capital punishment, in the place of religion at the gallows, in the ideology of race and of gender, and in the notions of what whites in the South considered sufficient punishment and retribution.

I came to this study armed with the norms held broadly in the field, only to find the evidence from more than 1,300 execution reports at the heart of this study confounded them: that executions rose as lynchings declined, that public execution was considered a harsher form of punishment (and more like a lynching) than an execution performed in private, and that Black criminals were more commonly executed publicly than white ones. These things were not so. The dynamics of civility and a rising middle class sensibility that are so prominent in the scholarship of the North and West in terms of the changes in capital punishment did not fit the realities of the South in the nineteenth century, a region so distinctive in its history of violence, race, politics, punishment, urbanization, industrialization, demography, and more. The North, the West, and the South all moved to privacy in executions; that does not, of course, mean that they did so in the same ways or for the same reasons. As the most violent region, the one using the death penalty the most, and the one so fundamentally riven by racial difference, it would be odd indeed for the South not to be distinctive in terms of these shifts in capital punishment.

The execution reports in southern newspapers shifted my understanding of the nature and the place of public executions and of private ones (chapter 6) in the South's punishment regime. They taught me how important religion was to this story (chapter 1), that the numerical trends of executions were less helpful than I had presumed (chapter 4), if still important. Some of the most compelling evidence would involve storytelling and the ideology of racism (chapter 3), which could be no surprise: the issues of race and punishment were clearly in mind from the beginning of this project, and they remain central. But joining them by the end of my work on this book is gender, both in terms of masculinity and in terms of the inclusion of women in the audiences of public execution and their exclusion in private ones. It turns out that the years between the end of Reconstruction and the start of the violent 1890s are vital to this study, and that class matters not just in terms of policing a perceived criminal class but also in terms of religious culture. By putting legal executions at the center of study rather than at the margins, new relationships are revealed between a range of themes in southern history.

Among those themes, this project emphasizes how fundamental was southern white fear to the fifty years after the Civil War. As with most panics and mass hysterias, the concerns of southern whites about the future of southern Blacks had some relationship to reality, but it was a reality viewed in a fun-house mirror of racist twists and exaggerations. Incremental improvements in African American lives were viewed through the fever dream of white supremacy and judged against an inheritance and a memory of total white control. After all, almost every tool of control available to proponents of southern white supremacy was eroding in the late nineteenth century, starting, of course, with slavery's dungeonful of punishments dramatically ended by an invading and occupying army, capped by constitutional amendments eliminating whole realms of southern life and law. But changes also included the rise of African American voting, literacy, mobility, gun ownership, property ownership, and more. "New issue Negroes" in the wake of the Civil War were simply not appropriately keeping to what most southern whites insisted was their place. "New issue Whites," in contrast, maintained the same attitudes and expectations of the old order, having inherited all of the antebellum ideas of the naturalness of complete white domination. They had created a panoply of violent tools of control under slavery, and when stripped of them, they re-created new forms of control in the late nineteenth century. At the same time, the success of the violent white efforts to reconquer the region from Republican regimes during

Reconstruction taught this new generation the utility and the feasibility of lethal white action.[1] The dissonance between a white-supremacist vision of what should be natural and a world failing to comport with that vision is fundamental to understanding everything in this study and perhaps everything in these generations after the Civil War.

While not the subject of this study, lynching haunts this book, for the *legal* use of death as a penalty was related to extralegal killings (chapter 5). Neither are the new or expanded punishments of imprisonment, convict lease, and chain gangs the subjects of this study, though these elements of the New South's punishment regime are likewise important contexts here. The elements of control deployed by southern whites in this era of fear and change were multifold.[2]

This study interrogates how the South's punishment regime appears when the *legal* use of the rope is made central. This focus on legal execution in the South—and the move from public to private execution—adds most to the history of capital punishment in the United States, which largely— bizarrely—has engaged little with the history of the region, despite it being the part of the nation to use the death penalty the most for more than two hundred years. The few works that engage with the South have tended to focus more upon a later era and miss many of the dynamics at work in the late nineteenth century. In that, this study is charting new territory.[3] That the South's history of capital punishment tells a story distinct from the one we tell about the death penalty in the North is particularly important, adding a crucial layer to our understanding of punishment, violence, and race.

For growing numbers of whites in the late nineteenth-century South, legal, public execution was failing to sufficiently cow the southern Black population, and this perceived failure offers vital insights into the rest of the violence of this era. In the half-century after the Civil War, 80 percent of those legally executed in the South were African Americans. From a distance, the public nature of southern executions appears to be yet another means of terrorizing and humiliating African Americans, a legal analog to lynching or to the slavery-era display of severed heads on pikes as lessons to other would-be Black criminals.

But a closer look reveals important complexities in the history of public executions in the South, and that is what this study is centered upon, telling the story of how southern, legal executions changed their nature in this period. One of the most important complexities is how the religious services at the gallows undercut the official narrative of these moments being chastening or cautionary, teaching the underclass a lesson. Instead, they more often became celebrations of the penitent saved, with African American voices leading the public celebration. Executions had contested meanings: they were moments of justice, of state power; but they were also moments of religion, exceptional moments that transcended normal life. The South's transition away from public execution reveals the slow march of civility less than it adds yet another aspect to our understanding of Jim Crow segregation and the elimination of African American authority from the South's public life. A growing white distaste for this public, religious ritual impelled state after state in the South to end public execution in the decades following the white reconquest of the South after Reconstruction. The prospect of African Americans convicted of rape or murder publicly proclaiming their innocence (sometimes) as well as their salvation (almost always) to thousands of emotionally charged Blacks and whites—"I'll meet you all in heaven!"—became anathema to many white southerners.

In this way, this study is in conversation with much more than the scholarship of racial violence and the law, for capital punishment intersects with many sides of southern history. These moments at the gallows were likewise moments of religious expression, and this work contributes a chapter to the study of African American religion in the South.[4] Historians far too often sideline religion or interpret it as ahistorical rather than a dynamic force itself in our past; here, religion mattered. Capital crimes and the appropriate punishments for them were discussed by public figures who were defining the nature of white supremacy and the South's order, and so this work connects to the intellectual history of the South as both white and Black leaders sought to shape the public perceptions of this racial order.[5] These moments on the gallows likewise were framed in terms of gender, and in multiple ways: women were in the audiences of public executions, a few women were executed themselves, and some executions of men were for sexual crimes.[6] With these areas of study—religion, gender, and the ideology of race—the findings here support, extend, and elaborate on arguments already to be found in the literature, allowing evidence from the gallows to add a few dozen pages to each of these scholarly discussions.

From one perspective, this study is quite narrow, seemingly: simply investigating 1,300 isolated and odd moments of lethal retribution and public religious theater, placing them in the context of the developed scholarship of several subfields of southern history. Yet it is often just in such repositionings, such glances askance, that new elements come into view: fresh connections that foster insights into the wider story of the South's history. And the adjustments in perspective offered by this focus on legal executions yield robust results. Much was at contest in the era of Jim Crow, white supremacy was not secure, and in moment after moment, year after year, Black southerners were the center of attention of large white and Black audiences, upon the stage of the gallows and proclaiming their faith and thereby their authority. I leave this study much more convinced of the vulnerability of white supremacy, of the everyday battles required to sustain its artificial privilege, and of how the extremity of horrifying lynching must be interlocked with white southerners' fear-filled perceptions of the weakness both of their punishment regime and of their justifications for it. I also leave this study more convinced of the distinctiveness of the South's history and that the national story of capital punishment is incomplete without further consideration of this region that has used the death penalty the most.

By incorporating the nature of, changes in, and arguments over capital punishment into our wider understanding of the South, we see the landscape of racial violence in the postbellum period afresh. The South's revivals at the gallows reveal public executions to be subversive moments in a violent era. When private executions were mandated at last in the South, it was another victory for Jim Crow segregationists who desired to eliminate all traces of public Black authority, not to mention all massive mixed-race and mixed-gender crowds in public spaces.

Mounting the platform was more than the sheriff and the condemned; with them was a minister. The audience was not just a crowd there to chasten the malefactor; it was a congregation of whites and Blacks who joined in the singing of hymns. Even the gallows had become contested terrain, with a service performed before crowds and with African Americans leading that service, as with Frank Danforth's "private" execution in Augusta in 1891 that began this introduction:

ON THE SCAFFOLD

Courageously he mounted the gibbet and stood calmly upon the trapdoor, and after his legs were tightly tied together with a strong rope the sheriff asked him if he had anything to say.

"Yes, sir," he said to the Sheriff, and then turning to the crowd, spoke out in an audible tone as follows:

"Of course, friends, gentlemen and ladies, one and all, I have made my peace with God on this earth. He has forgiven me for my sins. O Lord, yes! O He has made me rich and pure in the spirit of the Holy Ghost, and I am going home to my Savior. That is all I have to say."

The service on the scaffold was then commenced. Rev. Barnes read a chapter from the Bible and Rev. Walker closed with prayer. While services were going on Frank kept up singing out, "They can kill my flesh, but not my soul."

At 12:16 the rope was put around his neck, the knot resting under his left ear. At 12:27 the black cap was tied over his face by Deputy Campbell. The ministers, the sheriff, and his deputies, and last Frank's brother-in-law, Rev. Calhoun, shook his hands, bade him good-bye and came down from the gallows. His last words, spoken while the black cap was over his face, were:

"I am going home to Jesus."

AND HE WENT.[7]

CHAPTER ONE

A Camp Meeting at the Gallows

> There is a fountain fill'd with blood,
> Drawn from Immanuel's veins;
> And sinners, plunged beneath that flood,
> Lose all their guilty stains,
> Lose all their guilty stains.
>
> The dying thief rejoiced to see
> That fountain in his day;
> And there may I, though vile as he,
> Wash all my sins away.
> —Traditional Hymn

> A short address was made by parson Hays, colored; the hymn, If I must die, oh let me die in Jesus, was sung, which was followed by a prayer by parson Crow, colored. During the singing the pathetic voice of the condemned man [Isam Kapps] was heard above all others when it came to the verse commencing If I must die oh let me die in peace with all mankind. At the close of the hymn Kapps stepped on the center of the trap and addressed the immense concourse for ten minutes. . . . Continuing for three minutes in an enthusiastic strain, he bid all farewell. His arms and legs were pinioned, the black cap drawn over his face, and with the words "Oh Jesus, I come this evening," the trap was sprung and Kapps was launched into glory.
> —*Galveston Daily News*, 8 May 1880

Public executions in the South were religious rites as well as state-sanctioned capital punishment. They were visible, contested moments of punitive power *and* of sanctification. From the perspective of the state, the purpose of an execution was more than to end a criminal's life; it was also to demonstrate vividly to the wider public the costs of criminality. Punishment is designed to be punitive (against a particular lawbreaker) but also preventative (a warning to avoid crime).[1] And in the South, "since there is this widespread belief that prison sentences are not effective deterrents to [African American] crime, there is a tendency, periodically, to single out a Negro for hanging—

to make a lesson of him that the community will not soon forget."[2] In theory, displaying such an execution in public before a crowd of thousands might further stress that message to the wider community: here, before you all, is what happens to a murderer.

But public events cannot be so easily controlled by the state, particularly when the state's representatives were not the only authorities atop the gallows. In the Protestant-dominated South, an execution required the presence of religious leaders, for a soul was about to leave this world of sorrow to be judged by God. This religious ceremony at the public gallows fundamentally shaped the nature and experience of these events, and in a direction askew from, or even countervailing, the state's punishment goals.

Christians believe that every one of us is a sinner, as we are all spiritually frail and beset by temptations in this imperfect world, and most Protestant faiths stress how we all deserve our destiny to be damnation. It is only the grace of God that saves any of us—flawed vessels that we are—from that eternal punishment. Evangelical denominations particularly stress how this grace is not earned or deserved, not based on one's place in the world or even one's actions, saintly or sinful. Grace is given: a miracle. This fundamental tenet of Christianity—a belief even more central, perhaps, to the evangelical Protestantism dominating the South (including African American churches) than to most—is no less true for those sinners who found themselves on the gallows. In the light of a religion steeped in both the universality of sin and the hope that any repentant and devout soul might be blessed by the miracle of God's grace, it is important for every sinner, at the end, to have a chance to embrace the Lord and to ask for forgiveness. "The wages of sin is death." But that is not the end of the scriptural passage: "but the free gift of God is eternal life in Christ Jesus our Lord."[3]

What made the religious significance of execution days still more stark was the fact that the Christian tradition offered countless examples of parallel moments: a history filled with blood and sacrifice, including the sacrifice of the son of God, echoed in a holy sacrament, first offered by Jesus to his disciples: "Take, eat, this is my body . . . drink of it, all of you; for this is my blood of the covenant, which is poured out for many for the forgiveness of sins."[4] The Gospels then describe how even the son of God found this world full of tribulations, and he died bleeding on a cross, killed by the state out in the open and beside common criminals, to save us from our sins. The story of the early church is likewise strewn with martyrs and those suffering in service of God's work on earth. Suffering, sacrifice, sin, and grace were woven into the most central beliefs, stories, and sacraments of the evangelical churches of the South as well as into any funeral service of Christians. In public executions, the ministers and the condemned made these powerful touchstones of Christianity the central elements of their services.

In that way, public executions were not mere moments of punishment; they were moments of prayer and even of celebration: a sinner coming home to Christ, leaving this flawed world to find a place in heaven. Public executions had a liturgy of sorts, a set of standards and expectations that most condemned embraced. And the messages in these public performances of faith were among the most multilayered in this era of white supremacy, for while a Black man (four-fifths of the South's legally condemned were Black) was dying for his missteps, he was also claiming before a crowd of hundreds or thousands to be going to heaven, to be forgiven, to be in God's loving hands, willing and (often) happy to be moving on from his difficult life through Christ's grace to a paradise in God's many-mansioned home.

The scholarship of racial violence in the South, when it has addressed public execution at all, has tended to treat it as something of an analog to lynching. This is giving far too much weight to the government's goals in terms of punishment, presuming that their plans for a chastising punishment regime were fulfilled in practice. For a tremendous number of white and Black southerners, religion was central to their lives and to their understanding of the world; to them, the secular authorities on the scaffold (the sheriff and guards) in no way displaced the authority of God's ministers who stood on the scaffold as well. The sheriff might be on the stage in front of the congregation, and he might release the trap, but the representatives of the ultimate authority, to many in the crowds assembled, would be the ministers of God who led the congregation in prayer and hymns and urged the poor sinner to repent. One was acting merely in the moment, performing a human task; the other was guiding a soul to eternity by doing God's work.

The historical record reveals that these moments of public execution were much more (and much different) than mere expressions of state power, for they were also some of the most public moments of African American authority in the late nineteenth century, proclaiming their faith before huge mixed-race and mixed-gender crowds. And they were centered as much upon grace and hope as they were upon crime and punishment. Generations later, southern African American religion would be the backbone of the civil rights movement, and a generation before these moments, whites framed religion as a potentially dangerous commodity needing to be contained and controlled under the slave regime in the antebellum South. There are many such moments in American history defined in part by religion; this is another. Religion played a critical role in offering a radical break with the states' conception of justice and punishment in the midst of the Jim Crow South and before crowds of thousands. "Radical" might have more than one meaning in that last sentence: in amount (a "drastic" break) but also in nature (a role that subverted the white South's goals in punishment).

At many times and in many ways, whites have sought to discount the humanity of African Americans. Some might believe they had no soul, and many might find solace in the thought that they were not really Christians: that their attempts at religion betrayed an inability to truly live up to the teachings of Christ. If so, society might bear less responsibility for them, as they fell outside the bounds of true faith. African Americans clearly rejected this idea, insisting upon their Christianity, the sanctity of their souls, and their equality in the eyes of a just God.[5] In that way, religion was of fundamental concern to the Jim Crow South, and religion expressed before large multiracial crowds, still more so.

Until the turn of the twentieth century, the norm for executions in the South was the hanging of a Black man, an event as public as the sheriff and the state laws would allow, and religion was at the heart of the events on the scaffold in front of a large "congregation." Chapter 2 fills out our understanding of these moments by investigating categories of executions at the margins around this norm. But this chapter centers on the very heart of the matter: the public, religious execution experience that was the norm in the South of the late nineteenth century.

The South's "Hempen Harvest"[6]

With the region's long history of both violence and capital punishment, execution day was not a rare event in the South, and well into the Gilded Age, the South's executions remained public. Overall, public execution—hangings in open spaces in full view of any who chose to attend—was most common up to the early 1880s in the South. Starting in the early twentieth century, private executions clearly predominated: these were in some way behind a barrier (but still might involve a large crowd) or in the bowels of a penitentiary (several states began centralizing their executions under state authority and/or using electrocution; both tended to be definitive end points to any public features in executions). Even in the early twentieth century, a scattering of public executions persisted in the South.[7] In between, in the twenty years from the mid-1880s to the middle of the first decade of the 1900s, private executions outnumbered public ones, but a tremendous mixture of trends made this an uneven and slow transition. The Georgia hanging of Danforth in the introduction is an example of this mix of public and private. This mixture included a large number of executions with the actual hanging behind a barrier of some sort, but with quite a crowd and all of the theater of the gallows, including its religious dimensions, in public before the drop.

When the condemned man was Black, the audience that congregated around the scaffold was likewise largely Black. "Three thousand people witnessed the spectacle," reported one newspaper in 1893, "and we are informed that cotton picking was entirely suspended for three days in four counties. The negro field laborers for many miles around Mount Vernon went there the day before the execution and camped out."[8] Dozens of articles from across the region merely estimated the numbers in the crowd at a hanging, adding "mostly colored." Dozens more described the crowds of "every hue," and still more refrained from any such general conclusion of the crowd's racial proportions, but described a prominent African American presence.[9] Perhaps as telling are the ways these papers report this as a commonplace, as expected: executions in the South were not events reserved for white audiences.[10] They were performed before mixed-race crowds, and when the condemned was Black, the crowd was often overwhelmingly African American.

The role of the sheriff and his men in these executions, though central, took only a few minutes: reading the death warrant, affixing the cap and noose, tying arms and legs, and dropping the trap.[11] But the period of anticipation before the drop could last more than an hour. While the nature of these moments varied, a pattern in the proceedings was so common that it became understood and expected; white papers regularly expressed tired familiarity when reporting Black executions, peppering their brief descriptions with "of course" or "as usual."[12]

What the papers proceeded to describe as so commonplace was, in essence, an African American camp meeting at the scaffold, a religious ceremony ushering a repentant sinner's soul to God's embrace. These sources reveal moments of active and public roles for African Americans in an era when they had few such opportunities. From a perspective focusing on the state's goals for capital punishment, these religious ceremonies might seem superficial, a sheen covering the deadly acts of the state.[13] But placing African American religion at the center of our view and acknowledging how, for Black congregations, "Biblical stories offered them ways to narrate their own story" and how they saw themselves as a chosen people who had prayed and prophesied over emancipation and these prayers were answered, the central importance of religion in these moments becomes obvious and even inevitable.[14] What else could it be but central?

In these ceremonies, the condemned man might speak at length to the white and Black crowd but particularly to the assembled African Americans. The condemned, according to one report, "asked all the colored people to gather on the north side of the gallows where he could talk to them."[15] Another noted that the hymn was "sung principally by the colored people."[16] Several reports note a condemned man refraining from speaking unless he saw friends there: one replied to the sheriff's query about having a statement that "if any of his friends were present he did," and another "recognized a colored friend upon the wall surrounding the jail, and then asked that the cap be removed so that he could say something."[17] Several reports merely note that the condemned was particularly speaking from the scaffold to the African Americans in the audience.[18] These moments at the gallows were not, then, performances for the benefit of whites.

Facing his certain death, the prisoner occupied an unusual position in this moment: almost like a seer, he was granted attention he may never have had in normal life.[19] His words had authority, at least of a kind, for they were death-words, the last he would speak when nothing but the truth was worth saying, and nothing but God's judgment awaited him. This was vividly demonstrated in the 1893 execution of a Black murderer in Louisiana when asked if he had anything to say:

> "I'm gwine home to Jesus," was the response in stentorian tones, and the spectators fell back in dismay.
>
> "I tell you, my brothers," he continued. "I am going home; yes, I am going home, and he says: 'Take ye no fear, for he that believeth in me shall have everlasting life.' But I tell you must believe, and if you don't believe, you will be damned!" and here the speaker's voice again rose high and shrill as he leaned far out over the railing; his eyes glittered and again the spectators gave an involuntary shudder and fell back.
>
> No matter how absurd it may seem, when a man who is about to face his Maker cries out in warning, and the death light glitters in his eye, his words are heeded. Not a sound broke the stillness of the prison when the echo died away.[20]

The duration of a condemned man's speech varied greatly, depending on the man as well as the generosity of the sheriff.[21] It was common for sheriffs to allow convicts to "have their say to their hearts' content," for the sheriff too was on display, and this moment afforded him an opportunity to demonstrate his paternal regard for the community. This latitude could result in a "harangue" lasting an hour or more in some cases; in others the convict might speak five minutes or not at all.[22] "He asked for one hour in which to make his speech," wrote the *Atlanta Constitution* about Dick Townsend, African American convicted murderer. "This was granted, but he scarcely spoke five minutes. His talk was similar to the speeches delivered on such occasions, was mixed up with chant songs and advice to his hearers to take warning at his fate."[23]

Some convicts overtly drew upon the expectation of a camp meeting: "I am glad to see dis large congregation here," began one in his speech on the scaffold; another, Bible in hand, said he was "ready to open the meeting."[24] At times, reports show the condemned to be in a religious ecstasy, repeating phrases in "a sing-song tone, beating his feet in time" about "going home" or to glory, or going "to sleep to awake in his father's house of mansions."[25] If claiming innocence, the condemned would tend to blame no one, and declare his assurance that he was going to heaven. If admitting guilt, he would typically blame liquor, bad company, bad women, and/or the devil, would enjoin his brothers and sisters to steer clear of these, and would, again, be sure of his forgiveness and his home in heaven. The mood of convicts varied significantly: from so weak they had to be helped onto the scaffold to full of brash bravado. But often their tone was of happiness, of troubles at an end, trials of this world over, and looking forward to the next life.[26]

White papers made particular note of occasions when African American condemned strayed from the religious enthusiasms that were so common. "It is an incident of this tragedy that this negro walked to his death with all the fortitude and calmness that could be expected of a martyr. There was no bravado about him, no exultation, no hysterics, no pretended bravery. There were none of the frenzied religious accessories that are often seen on such occasions."[27] Another report likewise emphasized the religious trend by offering an exception to it: "Unlike the average negro who meets his death in this manner, he did not claim to have a through ticket to the world above."[28]

In a rare treatment of the gallows in an African American paper, John Mitchell of the *Richmond Planet* interviewed in 1905 two prisoners condemned to die the following day.[29] Just as white papers reported, religion was central to Mitchell's article as he quoted liberally from the condemned: "I am looking to Jesus for the hereafter. I have a soul to be saved. . . . My prayers are: Let His will be done. If anything comes, I know it to be His will. If anything don't come, I know it to be His will. I have packed my trunk. I have the time marked upon the board." The second prisoner said similar things:

"'I stand in this way,' he said. 'I once was lost, but now am found. My troubles have been very heavy, but I seem to be comforted now. I am satisfied I shall have a resting place. I believe to my heart that I have been forgiven.'"[30]

Frequently, the public religious ceremony at the scaffold was preceded by a religious meeting inside the prisoner's jail cell. Some newspapers reported that the singing and praying went on for hours or even throughout the night before the execution, with multiple ministers preparing the condemned for his judgment day. "He was awakened yesterday morning shortly after 5 o'clock by a delegation of colored people headed by three ministers. . . . They sang songs and exhorted at the top of their voices until 7 o'clock."[31] "Shortly after awaking, and after the outer cell doors were opened, they began to sing hymns. Their voices, as they sang the old, old, hymns, in that peculiaration [sic] which belongs only to the Southern negro, echoed down the aisle of the jail, and was heard in the Court-yard green."[32]

On occasion, newspapers printed crowd reactions to the prayers and hymns emanating from the scaffold, emphasizing how a wider community—not just the convict and his minister—viewed the execution in religious terms. "A woman in the front row interrupted the proceedings by emitting scream after scream, and others took up the cry. The cries were not of anguish, but of happiness and religious fervor, such as one hears at a negro camp meeting. Officers forced the woman to desist and the affair proceeded."[33] Another condemned man "launched into a sing-song kind of style. The negroes commenced saying 'amen,' 'Glory be to God.' The crowd commenced swaying backward and forwards, negro women shouting, and several fainted. The commotion would doubtless have become very great but just as [the convict] Wimbush was at the full height of his voice and the excitement commenced to increase, Father Colbert exclaimed, rather excitedly, to Wimbush, 'Hush, sir; say not another word! You are talking foolishness. You must die a Catholic and not a Methodist.'"[34] More often, the coverage in white papers was more brief and generic: "The negroes seemed greatly affected by Daniel's oratorical effort and moaned and groaned as he talked," or that a condemned's speech was punctuated by "loud shouting by the negro women in the crowd, which continued until the body was cut down."[35]

The gendered nature of these events might be as important as the fact that they were racially inclusive: this was a public event that men, women, and children might all attend. At least one teacher dismissed his school to allow students to attend.[36] As it was a political, judicial, and punishment event, the inclusion of women and children would seem out of place. Women could not vote or serve on juries, and if tender topics threatened to be aired in the course of a trial, judges might clear courtrooms of women spectators: the unseemly was not for them. But when seen as a religious service, executions would be a natural place for the whole community: why would any religious rite be held for men alone? If women rarely faced execution, they regularly attended public hangings in the South, just as women constituted a prominent portion (often a majority) of southern congregations, Black or white. If ministers were male, the churches nevertheless provided ample spaces for African American women, both as participants in the congregations and in auxiliary roles in church governance.[37] While most observers wrote about women being active participants in the "congregation" of a gallows crowd, on the scaffold at one Florida execution were four women (and two ministers) there to support the condemned in his last moments.[38]

This is not an inconsequential point: public executions were perceived and experienced in terms of both race *and* gender. White papers might link the disorderly, emotional outbursts at the services at the scaffold to the women in the audience, often with an appalled tone. The *New York Times* called these outcries "the most deafening and unearthly religious yells it is possible to imagine, from the throats of at least a thousand horror-stricken negroes. The women especially showed great excitement—some of them shouting 'Glory! Glory!" and even rolling upon the ground in their frantic demonstrations. . . . [The condemned's] colored sisters really thought they were helping him on the road to immortal bliss."[39] The mixture of genders and races—both together—in the audiences at the gallows charged these events even more.

Many reports mention the crowd reacting to the drop itself, the precise moment when the sinner's life was over and his judgment came due. "When the drop fell there was a great moaning and shouting among the crowd, which seemed to be considerably worked"; "the negroes . . . echoed his every groan, and at 1:18, when the drop fell, they broke into loud weeping and louder groaning."[40] In at least one execution, music was planned to see the condemned through: "As the trap was sprung, the holiness band began to sing and entertained a large crowd with prayers, speaking, and singing until the body was cut down."[41]

These were moments at the scaffold where two worlds met. In an era in which Blacks and whites were increasingly living apart, working segregated from one another, learning in race-specific schools, amusing themselves in separate institutions, and worshiping in segregated churches, this was a moment when they were together in a crowd. Moreover, this mixed crowd centered on a Black man and his ministers. The nature of this meeting of Black and white could play out in a number of ways depending on a range of unique circumstances: the crime, the passions aroused, and more. If the punishment regime was working well, surely some crowds gathered at the gallows to condemn a malefactor despised for his crimes, yet there are few sources in the historical record that yield evidence of this attitude.[42] An exception was the condemned advising the crowds to steer clear of bad company and bad liquor. This was common at the gallows and would be a conservative element of the message from the scaffold that authorities would appreciate.

But African Americans did not necessarily share with whites the view that a Black man condemned by white authorities must be guilty of his crimes or (even if they believed him guilty) deserving of his fate. The rampant prejudices in the entire judicial process from the police to the scaffold were likely to make southern blacks see a condemned man as a martyr and his death as something more akin to a sacrifice.[43] "The colored people, and indeed, many of the whites, commented on what was transpiring" as the law sought "examples or rather victims from among the poor, the lowly, and the ignorant. Only negroes, they said, were hung in Louisiana. . . . The poor negro, brought up in ignorance, the companionship of poverty and vice, who had nothing to guide him but his instinct or his passion was made to suffer the extreme penalties."[44] This persistent sense of injustice could color the African American perception of even those hangings when the guilt of the condemned was beyond dispute; it predominated if many questioned the justice of the conviction.[45] It is hard to imagine that African Americans in many execution crowds were convinced that justice was unfolding before them. There is even less evidence of Blacks viewing somberly an execution as a stern lesson.

Instead, in the overwhelming majority of instances, African Americans appear to have gathered at the gallows to witness and celebrate the rise of an innocent soul or that of a sinner now repentant and embracing the true faith.[46] Religion offered a powerful way to frame the challenges facing African Americans at this time. At the very least, religion gave solace and neutralized some of the terror of a hanging.[47] But religion at the gallows could mean much more. One condemned man, Bible in hand, said he had made his peace with God, but warned, "Whenever you see any men who go to the jury box to convict a man of something he did not do, will you look at the Book? You know what God says, 'Vengeance is mine, and I will recompense it.' God is going to hold all of you accountable." This condemned man did not receive the pardon he thought his due, and closed with "I did get a pardon, though, from Jesus, where Gov. Buckner must go for one finally."[48] Like Frank Danforth, quoted in the introduction, others spoke of how limited was the power of the state: "My soul is saved. They can't take that. They can take my life, but my soul is the sweetest thing I've got and it will go to heaven."[49] "You are a good many people here; look at me and see," said another condemned man. "I have sinned against the law and God has forgiven me for it, forever and eternity. God is more than man, but man makes the laws; there is nothing but sin in this world."[50]

The state might desire capital punishment to be chastening and inhibiting, but the African American crowds and even the condemned men standing before them with ropes around their necks rarely experienced public executions that way. Many African American condemned were drawn to the public nature of capital punishment: John Williams "fairly danced up the steps of the scaffold with a light and airy step, bounding to the platform in three jumps and bowing to the crowd," and John Thomas began his gallows oration with "I am proud to have such a large audience present."[51] George Washington fostered suspense when a reporter interviewed him: "'I'll tell that at the hanging,' he said in anticipation of a public hanging."[52] After claiming he had a "through ticket to cross the River Jordan," a man condemned for murder philosophized about his execution: "Some men are born to die a natural death; others to be killed, and others on the scaffold, and . . . 'thank God,' he was one of the latter."[53] Another said that he was a soldier in the Union army "but bless God, I am now a soldier of the cross. . . . I am perfectly satisfied and willing to die. O people, if you only had my feeling how happy you would be."[54]

These sentiments should not be surprising, for they are the straightforward responses of people steeped in the evangelical faith of southern African American Christianity. Miles Thompson, convicted of rape and murder, took this sort of talk even further when he said on the gallows, "Hold the children on your shoulders so they can see me die. Take warning. I am like Christ on the cross."[55] "Hurry, hurry," chided another while standing on the trap, "Let me see my Jesus."[56] A Texas man likewise requested the execution be public, and another in Arkansas faced his death "with a benediction upon his lips and a smile on his face."[57] In a surprisingly wide array of ways, African Americans throughout the South used the religious authority they had in the late nineteenth and early twentieth centuries to reframe these moments of punishment into rites of sacrifice and expressions of faith. The nature of the evangelical denominations in the South helped them considerably in this effort.

Religion in the African American South

Religion could operate in a variety of ways at the gallows, for there were thousands of individual executions that unfolded each in its own way, and there are many different interpretations (from conservative to radical) of the Bible and Christian teaching. If this chapter charts the norm (the largest trend evident in the historical record of public execution), that should not imply that religion played a uniform role in every circumstance. In particular, there was an evolution in the minds of white southerners in terms of the effects and utility of religion at the gallows. Especially early in the postwar era, many whites *wanted* African American condemned to "get religion," and some scholars have interpreted that as the whites seeing such an execution as sanctioned by God.[58] If a condemned man were to "make peace with God," that act would work in "symbolically absolving the white community of any guilt" and signal the condemned's acceptance of white power in society. Perhaps more important still were the practical reasons for white sheriffs to promote religion among the condemned: a confession might identify other culprits who could be apprehended.[59] An even simpler explanation is the fact that so many whites likewise shared the fundamental tenets of evangelical Christianity.

More broadly, many whites in the South longed for religion to play a conservative role in African American communities, but with emancipation, they lost their grasp on the spiritual lives of southern Blacks. Whites would often stress those Bible passages that tend in a conservative direction; particularly common was an Ephesians passage about servants obeying their masters. "The white preachers don't give the whole scripture," according to one escaped slave in the antebellum era; Black congregations filled out the picture of God's word by adding passages about suffering and others about God's love and salvation.[60] Before the Civil War, most ministers were white, including those on the gallows; they could frame the moment as they thought most appropriate. Not so, after the war: now, it would be African American ministers choosing scripture and hymns and praying for the condemned. If religion can be conservative as well as liberating, what is most striking is how rarely the historical record after the Civil War shows gallows services to hew to this sort of conservative message.[61]

Religion in the South was more complex than differences between white and Black. Like many white observers, middle-class Blacks had a different way of worshiping than the vast majority of southern evangelical Blacks who most often were subject to legal execution in the South. These more educated and respectability-focused African Americans tended to see the emotionalism, the lack of educated clergy, and the stress on faith rather than on a moral code as elements of persistent primitivism and even the perversion of religion. If whites blamed these failings on the innate savagery of Blacks themselves (see chapter 3), middle-class African Americans blamed them on the horrors of slavery and oppression and what the position of Blacks in America taught the ignorant in the Black community. To them, these elements of religion in the South were in need of reform.[62] For decades, educated Black ministers and middle-class congregations (a very small portion of the South's Black churches) were at odds with much of Black religion in the South.[63] Where the congregations were more evangelical and lower class, they tended to win in this contest, pulling recalcitrant, (over)educated ministers into line to exhort in the style they demanded.[64] And it was rare that a gallows crowd witnessed a middle-class African American man hanging for a crime; the vast majority of condemned were lower class and evangelical.

Whites as well as middle-class African Americans in the late nineteenth-century South might look down on the religious enthusiasms of the mass of African American evangelicals, but members of Black evangelical congregations considered themselves to be as good Christians as their "betters"; indeed, they were convinced of their superiority. Faith was something they *had*; they did not require any tutoring from the upper classes.[65] They saw middle-class African American services as drained of meaning ("style is crowded all the grace out of religion," in the words of one African American evangelical contemporary): dry services both devoid of spirit and divorced from what they saw as the early church traditions of spontaneity, simplicity, and purity.[66] White churches had all these faults plus the dramatic failing of white attempts to use religion to justify white oppression and prejudice.[67] After white preaching in the antebellum era, slaves would often gather themselves to have "real meetings." "It ain't enough to talk about God, you've got to feel him moving on the altar of your heart."[68] After the Civil War, those "real meetings" became the heart of thousands of new, separate Black churches where "real religion" could thrive.[69]

The scripture justified this view of their own churches embodying the ideal of Christianity. In his Sermon on the Mount, Jesus preached that the poor were blessed "in spirit, for theirs is the kingdom of heaven," that the meek "shall inherit the earth," that "those who hunger and thirst for righteousness shall be satisfied."[70] Of all the peoples of the earth, who better represented the devout Christian—poor, hungry, thirsty, and meek—than southern evangelical African Americans in the late nineteenth century?[71] The son of God was talking to them, showing that they are among the chosen peoples of the world: "Blessed are those who are persecuted for righteousness' sake, for theirs in the kingdom of heaven. . . . Blessed are you when men revile you and persecute you and utter all kinds of evil against you falsely on my account. Rejoice and be glad, for your reward is great in heaven, for so men persecuted the prophets who were before you."[72] The apostle Paul reiterated and reinforced the importance of this interpretation in his letter to the Romans: "We rejoice in our sufferings, knowing that suffering produces endurance, and endurance produces character, and character produces hope, and hope does not disappoint us, because God's love has been poured into our hearts through the Holy Spirit which has been given to us."[73] Christ himself suffered, as African Americans of the South did and as did the early church followers of Jesus, and if wisdom comes from suffering, so might God's grace come to African Americans who were devout believers even in the face of persecution.

The church centered the South's Black community from the earliest moments after the Civil War. One of the first actions of Blacks was to leave white-controlled churches and to form their own, a post-emancipation religious revolution. Within ten years of emancipation, most Blacks worshipped separately from whites, a quick development shocking and disturbing to the white South.[74] For African Americans, that new center to their communities consisted of the evangelical denominations of the Methodists and especially the Baptists.[75] It would be almost unimaginable, therefore, if religion failed to be a vital element of the public execution of African Americans, when a soul rises to judgment. The ministers, condemned, and crowds in attendance simply translated the sacred culture of African Americans to the public and charged context of capital punishment, a translation that had dramatic implications.

The most noted element of both gallows ceremonies and Black religious practice altogether was their emotional enthusiasm. African American religion in the South emphasized an intuitive connection to God, a passionate experience of religion that could include shouting, chanting, singing, calling out, dancing, and more, as congregants felt bodily the presence of the Lord.[76] This was faith, expressed. Just as at revivals, the services on the gallows could include chanted sermons, emotional catharsis, and call-and-response from the audience, not to mention the embrace of new members of the faith into the fold: in this case, the condemned, repentant sinner committing or recommitting himself to Christ.[77] These extravagant emotional outbursts gave physical expression to the conversion experience and being overwhelmed by one's faith, the "Holy Spirit operating upon the heart."[78] The love of God overflowed their bodies and could not be contained or restricted. For devout African Americans, such effusions signified the authenticity of faith and the close connection between an individual and the sanctifying spirit; proof, perhaps, that the Holy Spirit was alive in this frail vessel.[79]

This emotional style of worship was founded in scripture, passages that spoke of the overwhelming importance of faith. For those participating in the effusive camp meetings of the Great Awakening, for evangelical Christians of any era, and for most African American congregations in the South, having the Holy Spirit working through the individual in the course of church ceremonies was considered to be adhering to worship as the Bible described it in the earliest days of the church. The second chapter of the Acts of the Apostles tells of the moment, at Pentecost, when the twelve disciples met after the resurrection of Jesus. This was when they began to gain followers, when the Christian church, in a sense, began to grow. This experience at Pentecost was not rational, calm, or learned; it was a physical expression of the Holy Spirit taking over the disciples to such an extent that observers were bewildered, with one mocking the disciples by saying "they are filled with new wine."[80] What happened to the disciples? "And suddenly a sound came from heaven like the rush of a mighty wind, and it filled all the house where they were sitting. And there appeared to them tongues as of fire, distributed and resting on each one of them. And they were all filled with the Holy Spirit and began to speak in other tongues, as the Spirit gave them utterance."[81] Peter responded to the confusion of the onlookers by explaining the death and resurrection of Jesus, and how "being therefore exalted at the right hand of God, and having received from the Father the promise of the Holy Spirit, he has poured out this which you see and hear."[82] When asked by the crowd surrounding them what they should do, Peter replied in the way that evangelical Christians like these southern African American congregations took to heart: "Repent, and be baptized every one of you in the name of Jesus Christ for the forgiveness of your sins; and you shall receive the gift of the Holy Spirit. For the promise is to you and your children and to all that are far off, every one whom the Lord God calls to him."[83]

This commitment to Christ was found in the sacrament of baptism, but perhaps even more in what most evangelical Christians considered to be the key moment in an individual being saved: the conversion experience of publicly taking up this commitment. At these moments, evangelical Christians succumbed to emotion, to the power of the Holy Spirit. For most congregations, this was an experience that required preparation, for it was a stark and convulsive moment of real change in an individual's life, a necessary precondition to any hope for heaven in the afterlife.[84]

For these reasons, conversion was the crux of the faith in these churches. One's devotion, one's faith, was the key in the African American sacred cosmos, pushing most other elements of Christianity to the margins: the chastising Old Testament God or a focus on good works, for instance. Not that African American churches lacked these elements; rather, they were not as stressed, nor were they the elements of faith that resonated most deeply with the typical congregation of evangelicals. Allison Davis found in her analysis of the Black church several decades later that an "emphasis upon eternal punishment in hell-fire was much less strong than that placed upon salvation and eternal joy. . . . The powerful emotional release of 'salvation,' and the full catharsis from sin, suffering, and fear granted to the repentant are the aims of the service; not the moral castigation of the sinner."[85]

When a congregation wanted to "get happy," that meant hymns of suffering and a pastor who could lead them through the turn from moaning in their acknowledgment of their sinfulness to the overflowing joy of the knowledge that God's forgiveness and salvation awaited them.[86] Here again, scriptures were a guide: "Since all have sinned and fall short of the glory of God, they are justified by his grace as a gift, through the redemption which is in Christ Jesus, whom God put forward as an expiation by his blood, to be received by faith. This was to show God's righteousness, because in his divine forbearance he had passed over former sins."[87]

That prospect of salvation charged religion with power for African Americans. In a world of abundant suffering, evangelical Christianity offered the hope of equality before God and the hope of transformation in the next life. This belief in God's grace simply offered a new way to interpret the world, a model of being chosen that made so many of the cruelties and injustices of the world around them simply and powerfully irrelevant: property or riches, color of skin, educational attainment, family connections.[88] Or perhaps even more than irrelevant: the injustices facing African Americans could be seen as evidence of being chosen by God. Faith, devotion, and a commitment to believing in God's love were within reach of all: the poor were exactly as deserving (or more deserving) of redemption as the rich.[89] This possibility of receiving God's grace was, for some believers and evangelical denominations, something more akin to an *assurance* of grace: in Peter's words, "You *shall* receive the gift of the Holy Spirit."[90] In a line reminiscent of speeches of condemned from the gallows, African American visitors to one congregation testified that "they were not afraid of death, because 'if you live right, you don't have to worry about dyin',' and they were ready to die tonight. All knew they were saved."[91]

This assurance received still more support with the combination of the story of exodus with the transformative history of the end of slavery, leading many southern African American Christians in the late nineteenth century to think of themselves as a chosen people, destined for the providence of God in the next life, as Peter promised, if not in this.[92] This belief in redemption might resonate particularly powerfully in southern Black communities because it mirrors more traditional African beliefs that life and death are not so separate, that those who have gone before will be there to guide those who pass, and that after death, the world of spirits will be "free of difficulty, injustice, birth, and death."[93] The radical potential of religion in general (and particularly in the moment of the gallows) was not lost on whites in the South; there is some evidence that antebellum whites feared having slaves attend executions.[94]

This focus on individual salvation was in that way radically egalitarian: the low and the high are equal in God's eyes, and it is not that anyone earns or buys or is born into the promise of salvation.[95] More radically still in this moment in the South, white and Black become brothers in Christ.[96] This emphasis on the egalitarian elements of Christianity in evangelical religion had several important consequences in terms of institutions and styles of worship. It meant in particular that southern Baptists did not stress the importance of intermediaries between the individual and God: learning was not as vital for ministers in these churches compared with other denominations, for the measure of a good minister was faith rather than schooling, as well as the fact that an individual's salvation depended on oneself alone; or better, it depended on God's grace.

Baptist churches likewise offered local control and autonomy. These churches, particularly in the rural South, were the most tangible and important physical presences built and owned by African Americans.[97] Importantly, the congregations were in control of them: ministers received an annual call in many denominations, and any who did not serve the desires of the congregations found themselves replaced. More immediately, filling the collection plate might prove more difficult if a minister did not fulfill the expectations of his flock. Far from a rigid and centralized hierarchy, southern evangelical churches were dominated by the authority welling up from the congregations themselves.[98] In other words, it was not only the theology of evangelical religion that could be empowering; the very act of gathering together in common purpose and with authority over their religious lives was a strong influence on the self-image of many devout African American southerners.

Churches were *homes* for African Americans in the late nineteenth-century South. They were important in centering the community, in providing a framework for collective action.[99] At the very least, they offered a sacred culture that assuaged the pain of suffering in this era; at most, they offered a theology of equality, justice, and salvation that could incubate a growing sense of self-worth and authority that Blacks might wield. Indeed, white repression had the unintended effect of underscoring the parallels between African American experience and the history of the early church, emphasizing the worthiness of Black Christians who were so beset in the South.[100]

The most powerful religious reference at the gallows would be to Christ's own public execution, and while specific comparisons between the condemned and Jesus crucified on the cross or to early church martyrs were not common in reports of executions, they were not unknown. One condemned asked to be hanged at the same hour as Christ was crucified, and others said they were to "die like Jesus" or "like the apostles of the Lord did."[101] "I am willing to be sacrificed as an offering," said one, and another's minister said, "You have the consolation of knowing that the Savior of men died as you are dying today. He died as a criminal under the sentence of the land, and bore as great a shame as man could bear and tasted the deepest trouble."[102] Another condemned, when reciting the Apostle's Creed, "when he came to the words, 'suffered under Pontius Pilate,' he interpolated the words with 'just like we are going to suffer now.'"[103] Yet another simply said, after protesting his innocence "in a quiet, cool way," that "Christ had hung upon the cross and that he was no better than Christ, that he trusted all to the Lord."[104] If most did not go so far, it was the norm in public executions of African American men to invest their deaths with religious significance, and the religious texts that supported gallows services deepen this significance still further.

Theology at the Gallows

That African American evangelical Christianity would be in evidence at the gallows is commonsensical: why would this central element of African American life be absent here? But that common sense does not mitigate the radicalism of these moments: transposing redemption and salvation into the context of punishing murderers and rapists was a dramatic statement, and many of the particular hymns, prayers, and Bible passages further emphasized that. Most reports of executions merely mention that the religious ceremony was observed or generically said something about prayers and hymns. But occasionally, the reports mention not only what the condemned said on the scaffold but also something more specific about the texts of the ceremony. This scattering of evidence suggests the substance of the religious messages that could center the services at the scaffold.[105]

The hymns, central elements in the ceremonies at the scaffold, tended to emphasize these themes of sin and redemption. More than one report, in fact, called the religious portion of a public execution a "song service."[106] A condemned woman sang rather than spoke her last words: asked if she had anything to say, "she came forward and, stretching wide both arms, sang, rather than spoke, something like the following, which she repeated again and again: 'Thank God. I bid you all good-bye. Farewell, farewell to you all. Thank God! I'm going to my long home. I want you all to get a lesson from Barbara. Farewell.'"[107] Other condemned men wrote their own songs while awaiting execution. One that the condemned sang from the scaffold was called "Three Friends," who were God, the jailor, and the sheriff, as he was thankful for the way he had been treated while in jail.[108] Another was written in the days before the hanging and given to the local press to publish with their coverage, and an African American paper, the *Huntsville Gazette*, obliged:

> Jesus, the Savior of Sin,
> He freed my soul
> and took me in.
> Roll on, sweet moments of time,
> And let the poor prisoner
> Go home, go home.
>
> I can tell, to sinners around
> What a dear Savior that I've found.
> I am going to lay on my crown,
> Roll on, sweet moments of time,
> And let the poor prisoner
> Go home, go home.
>
> Sing, oh! Sing ye holy band,
> For I've a home in the promised land.

I say to you, ye sinner man
I hope to meet you in the promised land!
Roll on, Roll on, sweet moments of time,
And let the poor prisoner
Go home, go home.[109]

Although most execution reports merely mention that hymns were sung without naming them, at least 107 different hymns were mentioned in execution coverage. Fourteen of them were mentioned more than twice in execution reports, with the hymn that opens the chapter mentioned by name the most: on fifteen occasions, "There Is a Fountain Fill'd with Blood" was listed by name.[110] Others mentioned in more than five reports were "And Am I Only Born to Die" (nine times) and with eight mentions each, "Jesus, Lover of My Soul" and "Nearer My God to Thee."[111] None of these hymns were particularly written for the moment at the gallows, and the references to death, sin, and blood refer to more universal understandings of the fate of humanity: the inevitability of death, the sinful nature of all men, and how Jesus's sacrifice—his blood (not the condemned's)—redeemed sinful humanity, allowing for God's grace to save us.

Hymns were joined by scripture reading and prayers, which newspapers at times printed. God's word from the Bible was at least as powerful as hymns, having still more religious authority. Forty-three specific Bible passages were listed in the newspaper coverage of executions.[112] Almost half (nineteen) are from the Psalms, and most of the rest are from a wide variety of passages from the gospels. Eight passages are mentioned multiple times in execution reports, with the Lord's Prayer (Mathew 6:9–13) mentioned thirteen times.[113]

What were the messages in the Bible passages and hymns from the gallows? A few Bible passages focused on justice and how sins are paid for. Man is helpless and doomed ("I am reckoned among those who go down to the Pit"), his life is short and full of sin ("who can bring a clean thing out of an unclean?"), and God is not pleased ("by thy wrath we are overwhelmed").[114] A similarly chastening tone can be found in hymns like "And Am I only Born to Die," as well as "And Must I Be to Judgment Brought." These are hymns and Bible passages that the state might readily approve of, for they are severe, focusing on God's judgment for every misstep, how we should live without sin, emphasizing that hell or heaven weighs in the balance.

But those messages of judgment and sinful wretchedness were rare. Many more hymns and Bible passages at executions—paralleling the tendencies within the African American church overall—reflected the egalitarian view of all humanity redeemed by Christ's sacrifice: "The blood of Jesus cleanseth from all sin," and "If I must die, let me die with hope in Jesus's blood."[115] As one condemned said: "Death brings all men level, the dull, the wise, the reverend, and the sinner."[116] "Men are all a vain hope," quoted one minister from the Bible, but the Lord can save us despite our failures and corrupt natures. "They have all gone astray, they are all alike corrupt."[117] Many of the hymns plumb these depths of sorrow here on earth: "The world is dark and drear, I feel so alone; Beset with sin and fear, I sigh and moan," "all our sins and griefs to bear," "nothing but sin have I to give, nothing but love shall I receive."[118]

In paradise, God will "wipe away every tear . . . and death shall be no more;" all will be made anew.[119] Hymns regularly centered on this hopeful vision, often in the context of worldly suffering: "Hide me, O my Savior, hide, Till the storm of life is past," "I suffer my threescore years, till my deliverer come, and wipe away his servant's tears, and take his exile home." Many of the messages in prayers, Bible passages, and hymns were "Lord, I am sin— but thou art love."[120]

This hope for a better world springs from the sacrifice of Jesus, saving us from sin, and most refer to this in generic ways: "Our hopes we owe to Jesus' dying love."[121] In this era more conversant and comfortable both with death and with blood, other passages refer more graphically to God's sacrifice of "the blood of his own son"; another refers to the stoning of Stephen, as he called out to the Lord, asking for forgiveness for those who wronged and murdered him.[122] A passage from Luke is still more radical in terms of being quoted from the scaffold, describing the persecution and crucifixion of Jesus, and Jesus saying to the two criminals beside him on Calvary Hill, "Truly, I say to you, today you will be with me in Paradise."[123]

Sacrifice and suffering, so central to the reality of African Americans in this era, were also central to Christian theology. This world was a place of persecution, martyrs were all about them, and through Christ, sacrifice led to salvation.[124] As one condemned said from the gallows, "It is a heap of trouble to live. It will only be painful for a moment. Then I have not many friends and I do not see much happiness for me, even should I live to an old age."[125] How will I be received by God? One hymn answered with "Just as I am—poor, wretched, and blind."[126]

Perhaps more than any other sentiment, being saved—redeemed—was at the heart of many of these hymns and passages, just as it was the heart of evangelical Christianity. These passages stress the power of God to cleanse ("Wash me thoroughly from my inequity, and cleanse me from my sin!") and redeem ("Forgive us our debts," "Deliver us from evil"). This is a picture of a caring God guiding us to eternal life ("God sent his son into the world, not to condemn the world, but that the world might be saved through him").[127] And what lies before us is "a land of pure delight" where "death is a gate to endless joy."[128] "We're marching thro' Immanuel's ground to fairer worlds on high" is a beautiful Christian sentiment to sing; what makes it more pointed is the context in which it was sung. Singing that hymn at the hanging of an African American convicted murderer in Georgia in the last decade of the nineteenth century makes for a more charged message.[129]

To a secular society, these might seem to be merely ideas put into play in such a moment: a religious patina (a "standard script" of sanctification) upon the deadly action of the state.[130] Imagine for a moment that this was so, that these rituals at the gallows were rote. Saying these words, valuing the souls of African American sinners, would still be a challenge to white supremacy. But why make such an assumption when the South was full of devout Christians, and the church was the central institution of the African American community? In 1881 Tennessee, Black ministers petitioned the governor for a respite, not to challenge the death sentence but in order to give the condemned time to prepare for his death.[131] These concepts were not small matters to believers; they were at the root of the lives they built. In a world so cruel, the hope of Christ's message had particular power, and the religious element of an execution raised the event to a more exalted plane of faith, far above mere secular authorities.

It is important that hymns, prayers, and exhortations from the ministers present amplified the religious content of the condemned's claims, validating and even making more universal his hopes to repent and be saved. Except when the condemned was Catholic: unlike Protestant ministers, the Catholic clergy discouraged any theater at the gallows beyond quiet, simple contrition.[132] The public professions of faith from Protestant condemned were reinforced and given sanction by a prayer from a minister, or from more than one (one convict had eleven in his cell before his execution), along with the singing of hymns, often with the crowd joining in.[133] "The hymn was sung in the same wailing tune, and the effect produced by several hundred negro voices can better be imagined than described," wrote one white observer.[134] An execution of two condemned men in Murfreesboro, Tennessee, in 1880 was not out of the norm when it was prefaced by a succession of four Black ministers who led the crowd of 10,000 in a hymn ("And Must I Be to Judgment Brought?"), a prayer, another hymn ("My Lord, the Appointed Way"), and another prayer, followed by lengthy statements by the prisoners.[135]

While most white commentary on the services at the scaffold were brief, like that above, at times they narrated the nature of the prayers of the ministers just as they did the words of the condemned. Again, their treatment could be varied, from mocking to respectful, as when the *Atlanta Constitution* wrote how thousands were silent as a "beautiful prayer" rose from "the lips of the black minister":

> Oh, God! Thou hast promised that Thou wouldst be a shelter in every storm. Come and shield this poor man in this extremity. If the cup of bitterness may not pass from him speak to his soul and say that thine own son did drink it and that Thou lovest those who suffer. When he goes through these deep waters may he feel beneath his feet the rock of thy salvation, and about his neck the arms that lifted Peter from the waves. Through their tossing and their danger lead him safely and bring him to the other shore. Oh! Thou friend of the friendless, to whom shall he turn but unto Thee? Thou has promised comfort in sorrow and peace in pain. Be with him now and to the end that he may be with Thee where the wicked cease from troubling and the weary are at rest.[136]

At the scaffold were women calling out and an African American man who shouted, "You see Jesus on de cross! He say its finished. He say it suffice. Glory!" Hundreds sang a hymn before the prisoner told the sheriff he was ready.[137]

The presence — and often participation — of a crowd/congregation in this moment deepens the importance of these messages still further. The condemned were not alone on the gallows in front of these crowds, making claims to salvation and standing in Christian penitence amid a sea of hostile strangers. These were local hangings with local crowds, and those crowds were often filled with people the condemned knew and with devout believers there to help shepherd him to the other side. In this way, religion was not just an individual's set of beliefs; it was rather something acted out in the presence of other believers, a community built by common faith and action.[138] Many reports stress the participation of the audience at the gallows, that this was a communal service: "A vast chorus of colored voices joined" and "a large portion of the crowd joined in the singing."[139] Even crowds outside the walls in a private execution might participate: "Occasionally the voice of the preacher within could be heard giving out hymns, which were taken up and sung with religious fervor by those outside."[140] In some cases a more organized musical effort was involved, as when "the Christian Association sang the remaining verses of the hymn 'Why should we start and fear to die?'"[141] It was rarely a lone Black man on a public stage making the claim to be redeemed; it was more often an African American man, his ministers, and his community making, endorsing, and celebrating that claim.

When at the 1883 execution of rapist Joe Young in Richmond, Arkansas, the condemned sang "Amazing Grace" before a "throng of people, many of whom were colored men and women . . . who sympathized with the condemned," surely the devout crowd meant it, felt it, when they "echoed every groan" of the condemned.[142] And when a condemned called out that he was ready to go, that he had sinned and was paying the price, that he was sure God forgave him and he was headed home, why would we question his sincerity? And when the trap fell, and women in the audience were reported to scream and faint, they were steeped in a religion of enthusiasm: calling out, dancing, and *feeling* the grace of God was the very nature of true religion. Calling out was merely an expression of that faith, translating their experience of religion more generally to a public moment at the gallows.

THE RELIGION AT THE GALLOWS was no liberation theology, no religious radicalism, no call for revolution. Yet the egalitarianism of religion meant that these hymns, prayers, confessions, professions of faith, and Bible passages were a challenge to white supremacy nonetheless. The hymns were a part of the shared heritage of the nation, elements of the hymnody of American Christendom for generations before this period. And, of course, the Bible passages were a part of a still deeper shared heritage. The condemned and his ministers were staking a claim, then, to universals, and transporting them into the charged atmosphere of capital punishment, where white authorities were killing yet another Black man.

As important, the simple fact of having thousands listening to the public, religious authority of Black ministers and a condemned sinner's own testimony was subversive. The very presence of African American public authority in these moments had significant meanings—though very different ones—to both African American and white witnesses in the crowds or congregations. What had been white religious authorities on the scaffold in antebellum times were now Black authorities ministering to the condemned and preaching before mixed-race congregations. Black churches were the first and largest African American efforts on their own behalf after the Civil War, and so religious authority held a special place in the community. To whites at the time, these religious authorities might be honored as sincere or they might be dismissed, as African American religion was so often dismissed: that these were generic Christian references haltingly understood by a childlike race.

But to African Americans, this theology could invest this moment with something much more powerful. At most, a sheriff's authority was over a body, the physical world around us. But the authority claimed by the condemned and his ministers concerned the eternal soul. The ministers spoke of mainstream Christian principles, but by making their pronouncement in this setting—by placing the condemned's murder or rape within the frame of sin, temptation, repentance, and God's grace—these principles became more pointed. A crowd singing the hymn that opened this chapter ("There Is a Fountain Fill'd with Blood") to a man condemned for rape, who, according to the hymn, might have "all his sins washed away": this was not the message the state sought to emphasize.[143] And that so many of these hymns and prayers were about the sins *of us all* and how God's grace can claim any of us: this is among the more egalitarian elements of Christianity, an antiauthoritarian strand of theology publicly pronounced in a moment when the civil officers were trying to demonstrate their authoritarian power.

Several convicts expressed displeasure when they found that they would be executed within jail walls rather than before a crowd. The law required Wash Fletcher to be hanged in private, but "he wanted a million people to see him hung, and wanted to make a speech to them."[144] Having an execution in public did not tend to make the moment more horrible for African American condemned men and the crowds that gathered; the congregation at the gallows made the moment more meaningful. Or, perhaps better: it shifted the nature of what the moment's meaning was. At its most brazen, it could even make such a moment into a critique of justice and white supremacy, creating implicit or explicit connections to the tribulations of Jesus and early church martyrs and referencing the injustice of this flawed world. The presence of women at these public moments of violence and punishment emphasizes the importance of religion there: this was a public space still (for a while) open to women, if in supporting roles in the crowd/congregation.

The lesson of the typical public execution in the South in the late nineteenth century diverged from the conventional ideal of punishment that crime does not pay and those guilty of the worst crimes will pay with their lives. Far from being a lingering element of rough justice in a slowly modernizing South, the norm for public executions, infused as it was with religious meanings, displayed a rich, rare moment of African American public authority. Instead of stern justice, the lesson at least as prominent in these moments was that the worst criminals that whites could imagine African Americans becoming—murderers and rapists—might be saved in Jesus's enfolding arms with God's grace if they would earnestly, honestly repent. Public executions in the South became an inversion of the goals of white authorities: the focus on the salvation of the sinner turned the event into a celebration of the Good Death of the penitent saved.[145] If rarely couched in radical terms, the simple act of publicly and communally valuing the souls of African Americans bit into southern white supremacy.

This chapter explores the norm for public executions after the Civil War, but not all executions were of Black men for murder. What of executions outside of that norm? What insight does the contested ideology of race and punishment shed upon these moments? How and why did this norm change around the turn of the twentieth century? The balance of this book investigates these questions.

CHAPTER TWO

Beyond Executions of African American Men for Murder

> "I want to read the 59th and 60th verses of the 7th chapter of Acts of the Apostles, which tells of an old man who was mobbed and what he said before Christ." He read the verses and continued: "I am proud that I can look upon this audience and say this is the happiest part of my life on this earth. . . . In conclusion, I want to say," he said, "I am ready to die. I am willing to die. God wants me to come home. I am going home."
> —JESSE JONES, white man condemned for murder, at the gallows, *Arkansas Gazette*, 7 December 1895

The most common execution experience in the late nineteenth-century South was of an African American man (82 percent of all condemned) convicted for murder (86 percent of all executions), an event as public as the laws allowed, and invested with a sacred purpose of celebrating a fallen sinner's recommitment to Christ, including the words of the condemned himself and prayers from minister(s), as well as hymns sung by those gathered. But those were not the only executions in the South. Between 1866 and 1920, juries also condemned white men (17 percent of the South's condemned) for murder and, somewhat less often, both white (4 percent of those condemned for this crime) and Black men (95 percent of those condemned) for the crime of rape (which was 9 percent of all executions), and Black men for attempted rape (2 percent of all executions). Even less often, juries condemned Black men to death for other crimes (3 percent), or Black women (only nineteen in total, less than 1 percent of condemned), or, most rarely, white women (only twice) for murder and accessory to murder.

The norm for executions explored in chapter 1 would mean less if these executions were quite different, and one might imagine a logic for differences: that these crimes or criminals, being out of the ordinary, fostered unusual interest or drew distinctive crowds. Executions of Black men for more minor crimes (such as burglary) might foster more outrage in Black communities that would result in novel storylines in the press and/or different crowd behaviors than if they had been accused of murder. Likewise, one might imagine that executions of women would be much more conflicted events for crowds and newspaper writers. Or that executions of whites would have distinctive crowds, crowd behavior, and storylines in the press compared with the executions of African Americans.

Only in terms of whiteness do any of these hypotheses find supporting evidence in the historical record. And even the white condemned—so often drawn from the poorest social strata of the South—were typically portrayed in ways similar to the Black condemned, simply with more column inches devoted to them: white society cared more about the white condemned and therefore enriched the stories they told about them. But they seldom told a story of crime and punishment very different from the story of the public executions of Black men for murder.

In that way, exceptions to the norm of religious public executions were extremely rare even when the *categories* in the execution (executing women, whites, or Black men for crimes other than murder) were themselves more exceptional. Even in terms of rape, the crime that whites obsessed over, there were about a dozen instances of violence at execution days, but otherwise the hundreds of legal executions for sexual crimes were likewise civil affairs with religious services at the gallows. This chapter looks from multiple perspectives beyond the norm, and that reorientation allows us to get a fuller picture, one that confirms how important whiteness was and how white womanhood in particular had protections in this era that others were not given. But most importantly, it emphasizes just how important—commonplace—the religious ceremonies at the public gallows were.

Execution Days When the Crime Was Rape

The crime of rape became central to the defense of white supremacist violence in the late nineteenth century. Lynching was based in the "stern underlying principle" rooted in the "basic passions of humanity," wrote Thomas Nelson Page: "the determination to put an end to the ravishing of their women by an inferior race." "Twenty-five years ago," he continued, "women went unaccompanied and unafraid throughout the South. . . . To-day, no white woman, or girl, or female child, goes alone out of sight of the house except on necessity; and no man leaves his wife alone in his house, if he can help it."[1] William Hannibal Thomas wrote that the African American's "imperious sexual impulse, which, aroused by the slightest incentive, sweeps aside all restraints in the pursuit of physical gratification," was "the main incitement to the degeneracy of the race"; that the race's "male members have an inordinate craving for carnal knowledge of white women"; and that "lynching will stop when they cease to commit heinous crimes."[2] Rebecca Latimer Felton made one of the most-quoted formulations of this connection between sexual fear and lynching: "If it needs lynching to protect women's dearests possessions from drunken, ravening human beasts, then I say lynch a thousand times a week if necessary."[3]

Scholars have undercut all of these claims, interpreting this passionate outpouring of fear and racism as a rationalization for white violence rather than a relationship based in reality, just as African American writers like Mary Church Terrell noted at the time.[4] In their analysis of ten states in the South, Stewart Tolnay and E. M. Beck found that only about one-third of lynchings included even an *allegation* of "sexual norm violations"; the most prominent alleged offence was murder.[5] Others have found similar proportions, from Ida B. Wells in the 1890s to recent studies of individual states' lynching.[6] Moreover, we can safely assume that even when allegations of rape were made, some would be either false or mistaken. After all, white southerners were eager to classify even consensual sex between a Black man and a white woman as rape. Given the power that the charge of rape conferred on whites intent on violence, there might be an even more general pressure toward deploying this charge in situations where it would be useful for whites but where no basis for the charge existed at all.[7] Certainly the many gallows speeches claiming innocence suggest the possibility.

Given the white South's near obsession with Black-on-white rape and how it served as the central pretext for lynching, what was an execution day like when men convicted of rape were hanged legally? The answer is telling: no different from executions for murder. Mostly.

If rape was rarely far from whites' thoughts when it came to extralegal punishments, at least by the turn of the century, that did not mean that most African American men accused of rape were lynched. Some were never prosecuted; of those who went to trial, some were acquitted; of those convicted, a majority received prison sentences. In addition, at least 421 southern men were executed legally for the crimes of rape, attempted rape, or rape and another crime between 1866 and 1920.[8] Legal execution for the crime of rape was a southern phenomenon. In the twentieth century, the only states with the possibility of the death penalty for rape were the twelve states of the South under consideration here, along with the border states of Maryland, Missouri, and Oklahoma and the western state of Nevada.[9] A few northern states had ended capital punishment altogether by the Civil War, and the rest of the states outside the South reserved death as a penalty for murder in the first degree. Interestingly, in the antebellum era, most of the South was in line with these national trends by punishing rape with prison rather than death—as long as the accused man was white.

The South legally hanged *men* for the rape of *women*; there are no women in the Espy file condemned for sexual crimes, and I have found no evidence of any man being condemned for a sexual crime against another man.[10] In punishing for sexual crimes, race mattered: whites were rarely legally executed for rape (or lynched for it). This was particularly true in the Deep South: from 1866 to 1920, no whites were legally executed for sexual crimes in Alabama, Mississippi, or South Carolina.[11] In that span, only twenty-six white men in the other nine states of the South were legally executed for sexual crimes; at least 386 African American men were.[12] That amounts to 92 percent of all legal executions for sexual crimes being of Black men; this is almost the percentage of African Americans among those who were lynched for sexual infractions (95 percent).[13]

One might imagine that southern whites would be particularly opposed to the public, African American authority embodied by the camp-meeting experience at the gallows when the condemned had been convicted for the crime that whites used to justify lynching. Yet most executions for rape follow the same pattern as for murder. Are these legal executions so "normal" because any rape charge that aroused white passions ended in a lynching instead of the legal noose? Surely this must be so in some cases: with some accused men wrested out of the legal system altogether, the remaining legal cases for sexual crimes would have a disproportionate number that aroused less outrage.

While it might make sense to imagine that the passions of both whites and Blacks would be more often boisterous in sexualized cases like these, particularly given the psychosexual obsessions so often layered into the white rhetoric on race at this time, the historical record rarely supports that connection. In fact, out of the more than 350 cases of legal execution for sexualized infractions in the South between 1866 and 1920, only thirteen yield clear evidence of a lynching-like execution scene. But that is only the execution scene; this dramatically underplays the fears and passions such cases could awaken in the minds of whites. Much of the evidence of a "lynching-like" experience in the justice system would occur *before* the execution—conflict at arrest, in court, in the speed of the judicial process—and might therefore be invisible to the sources that anchor this study. These cases might still be seen as something akin to a "legal lynching" even if they ended with a civil execution day.[14] These elements of disorder before execution days are vital to understanding the relationship between lynching and the legal process, but this study of executions simply offers less illumination of them.

The fact remains that legal executions for rape were *not* typified by being disorderly or rough affairs. The tone of coverage tended to be just like in executions for murder. Many were tiny articles that reported little more than that an execution occurred. They were short enough that including one in its entirety does not burden this paragraph:

HANGED FOR RAPE

Hattiesburg, Miss., Aug. 5 — Jose Perryman, the young negro who criminally assaulted Miss Mellie Walters, near Eastabuchie, on May 21, was hanged here to-day at 1:30 P.M. In seventeen minutes after the drop he was pronounced dead. Death resulted from strangulation. About 2000 people witnessed the execution, which took place in the courthouse yard. This was the second legal hanging in this town.[15]

Many more reports in papers were three or four paragraphs long (perhaps one-half column of print in the newspapers of the day) and were somewhat more descriptive—giving a brief account of the crime or trial and saying briefly what occurred at the gallows—but in no way adding to any sensation. Rather, they present as finishing off a story of crime in the locality. Many others were still longer, perhaps a column of the front page and a bit more carried over into the interior of the paper. These were the most common sort of execution report for these crimes, and they tended to parallel executions for murder: religion on the gallows, I'll see you all in heaven, all in front of crowds of Black and white.[16]

On those occasions when newspapers explored executions for the crime of rape more thoroughly, the reports tended to be like those in chapter 1 as well: giving the hymns and printing the prayers of the ministers or the words of the condemned, say, or something of what the crowd asked of the prisoner on the gallows. Or perhaps outlining more thoroughly the crime committed or the pursuit of the condemned and his trial. The most thorough newspaper coverage was of executions that became notorious, and two of them were in Kentucky: the first private execution in that state in 1880 earned the print of almost the entire front page of the *Louisville Courier-Journal*.[17] And the hanging of Rainey Bethea in front of more than 10,000 in 1936 (the last public execution in the nation) included a long story and two photographs in the *Louisville Courier-Journal* and even more in the *Louisville Times*: four photographs, a reproduction of Bethea's handwritten will, and six different articles.[18] One of the most through treatments of African American religion at the gallows in a white southern paper was at the execution (for rape) of Alexander Terrell in Houston in 1897. In more than a column of print, the *Galveston Daily News* quoted the condemned and ministers, gave Bible verses and multiple hymns from the religious service held in the condemned's cell, and then continued at the scaffold. Acknowledging his guilt and absolving the jailer from the duty the law forced upon him, Terrell ended by saying, "I want you all to rejoice with me. I can meet it as bold as a lion. I am not afraid to die. . . . Jesus, be with me. Farewell to you all."[19]

Rape was a flashpoint in the racial dynamics of this era, and in some cases, accusations of rape fostered lynchings as well as a few instances of mobs of whites at the legal gallows. But most accusations of rape, if not ending in acquittal or a term in prison, resulted in an execution day no different from those for murder.

Execution Days When the Crime Was neither Murder nor Rape

Within the South, not only did states have death as a possible penalty (at the discretion of the jury in most states) for other crimes than murder and rape, but many southern states actually employed the gallows for them, if rarely. This is one of the most notable, categorical ways that the South's punishment regime differed from that of the rest of the nation. But this distinction needs to be kept in perspective, for few were actually hanged for these crimes. Of the 2,740 executions listed in the national list of executions called the Espy file between 1866 and 1920 in the South, only ninety-five of them (3.3 percent) were for crimes other than murder or rape.[20] More complete than the Espy file (but only covering six southern states) are the lists from Daniel Hearn and Louis Laska, and if they found more executions in general than in Espy, few of those "new" executions were for crimes other than murder and rape, and what they found were proportional with what were already in the Espy file: one further execution for robbery, three for arson, nine for attempted rape, and eleven for burglary.[21]

Jury discretion was key in these crimes: a means of continuing the southern penchant of punishing not just for the crime but also for who the criminal was. In the antebellum era, a crime might earn one penalty for whites (a term in prison, say), another for free Blacks (death), and yet another for slaves (death or transportation out of the state). With postwar constitutional amendments, these distinctions in the law were no longer possible: all persons born or naturalized were citizens; citizens cannot be denied "life, liberty or property, without due process of law"; and states must provide "equal protection of the laws." Among the many dramatic changes with the end of slavery was a transformation of criminal codes throughout the South. In Reconstruction, the criminal codes shifted to reflect the new colorblind requirements of the constitutional amendments after the Civil War, then shifted again with reconquest by white Democrats in the 1870s, this time to reimpose the expectations of the white ruling class in the South that the system of justice should make distinctions between different people regarding crime and punishment.

The new laws would be constitutional; the new laws would embody the prejudices whites had come to expect in the antebellum period. These were not mutually exclusive goals, and they extended to the use of capital punishment. Jury discretion in assigning punishment would be constitutional, at least under a strict reading of the Constitution, because all accused criminals faced the same statutes, which were not written with reference to race. In these same years, southern states followed a similar trend by rewriting other laws (vagrancy, for instance) to allow for terms in prison, or, increasingly, for terms in a convict lease system, the South's new form of forced labor.[22] All of this is in addition to the wide discretion of white officials in control of who would be charged and what the charges would be. In the words of one scholar, "southern justice was designed after the Civil War as an intricate system of entrapment."[23]

Jury discretion in terms of crimes earning capital punishment allowed (white) juries to make what distinctions they would, including punishing African Americans (but rarely whites) with the death penalty for a range of crimes. In Virginia, for example, burglary after the war was punished "with death, or in the discretion of the jury, by confinement in the penitentiary for not less than five nor more than eighteen years."[24] This expansive range of punishment—with no mention of race specifically—allowed laws to pass constitutional scrutiny while also allowing juries to decide for themselves who should be given the death penalty.

In the use of jury discretion in punishment, the South was innovating. Not only did most states of the South add capital punishment (in the discretion of jury) to prison terms for a variety of crimes beyond rape and murder, this jury discretion became the norm in the South for all crimes, including in rape and murder cases. With murder, the South led the way: the first four states to introduce jury discretion for murder were from the South, as were seven of the first ten states. By the turn of the twentieth century, only Arkansas, Virginia, and North Carolina among the southern states failed to allow juries to determine whether a convicted murderer would be imprisoned or hanged.[25]

This is an issue where state boundaries matter a great deal, for states wrote their laws differently. Some had numerous crimes earning the death penalty, while others punished more crimes with prison (or convict-lease) terms. If all had more expansive capital punishment regimes than was the norm in the other regions of the country, that does not mean each southern state expressed this lethal trend in the same way, or that those laws stayed the same over time. As important, actual executions were quite rare for non-murder/non-rape crimes that might be on the books in a given state.

All southern states had laws after Reconstruction to allow death as a possible penalty for the crimes of murder in the first degree, rape, and treason.[26] That is just about the extent of the capital crimes for fully half of the southern states. Arkansas, Florida, Kentucky, Mississippi, Tennessee, and Texas had few other crimes that could earn death as a penalty by the 1880s.[27] And in terms of actual executions, these states reserved the death penalty for murder and rape. In the entire period from 1866 to 1920, the Espy file lists only a single execution for a crime other than murder or rape in Florida, Tennessee, and Texas and none for Arkansas, Kentucky, and Mississippi.[28]

If race plays an outsized role in any discussion of capital punishment, that is particularly true here. Four of these six southern states with very few capital crimes on the books (Arkansas, Kentucky, Tennessee, and Texas) had the four smallest percentages of Blacks in their population among southern states.[29] A wider (national) context parallels this trend: all four of the northern states to abolish capital punishment in the nineteenth century had minuscule African American populations.[30]

The other half of the South had more extensive lists of crimes that could earn the death penalty, and some of them deployed it for these crimes with regularity. These crimes included arson, burglary, robbery, attempted murder, and attempted rape (table 2.1). Three states (North Carolina, South Carolina, and Virginia) account for more than two-thirds (84) of the 119 executions for crimes other than murder and rape.[31] Alabama, Georgia, and Louisiana likewise had death as a penalty for crimes other than murder and rape, but in practice, assigned death as a penalty for them less often. Not only do states with more African Americans tend to execute for these crimes, but it also appears that the older and more established southern states tend to deploy the death penalty as a possible punishment for a wider array of crimes, and southern frontier states (including Texas, Florida, and Arkansas) tend not to.[32]

TABLE 2.1 Executions for crimes other than murder or rape in southern states, 1866–1920

Crime	Number of Executions	States Executing for the Crime (and no. of executions)	Notes
Accessory to Murder	4 Espy	Florida (1) Virginia (3)	A rare crime to earn death penalty. All executed for this crime were African Americans, and two of the four were women.
Arson	16 Espy (+3 H/L)	Alabama (3) Georgia (1) S. Carolina (9 +1) Virginia (3) N. Carolina (+2)	This was most prominent early, with all executions before 1894 and most in the 1880s. Three of the six whites executed in the South for non-murder/non-rape crimes were in Alabama for this crime.
Attempted Murder	2 Espy	Louisiana (2)	Only two cases in 1882 in Louisiana for this crime—surprising, given the long list of executions for attempted rape below. Both were Black men.
Attempted Rape	41 Espy (+9 H/L)	Georgia (1) Louisiana (6) N. Carolina (3) S. Carolina (14 +4) Tennessee (1) Virginia (16 +5)	The largest (and most widely employed) category of offense earning death after murder and rape. Executions for this crime appeared later in the era (after 1895), with Virginia (1890s) and South Carolina (1910s) introducing legislation to make it a capital crime and using it often thereafter. Two in Louisiana and three in North Carolina were listed in Espy file as "Burglary–Attempted Rape." Only Black men were condemned for this crime.

TABLE 2.1 (continued)

Crime	Number of Executions	States Executing for the Crime (and no. of executions)	Notes
House-breaking/ Burglary	14 Espy (+11 H/L)	Louisiana (1) N. Carolina (13 + 10) Georgia (+1)	This is mostly a North Carolina category of capital crime; given the gendered nature of the home, it is likely that there is a sexual danger element of the crime of "housebreaking" in this era. Three of the six whites executed in the South for non-murder/non-rape crimes were in North Carolina for this crime.
Rioting	2 Espy	Georgia (2)	This is a single execution of two Black men in January of 1892 in Georgia.
Robbery	16 Espy (+1 H/L)	Alabama (6) Louisiana (1) N. Carolina (2 +1) Texas (1) Virginia (6)	A broadly shared, if rare, crime to earn the gallows. All of the condemned for this crime were African American men.

Note: Hearn and Laska's additions to the Espy file are in italics and parentheses. Espy file; Hearn and Laska.

Death is the harshest penalty, and these crimes were not the harshest crimes. It would make sense that African Americans might be more offended by death as the penalty for a burglar and act accordingly, creating a very different execution moment. Or death as a penalty for such a crime might indicate heightened passions among the whites in the region. It is important, then, that newspaper reports of these executions for non-murder/rape crimes were not notable in being qualitatively different from those evaluated for murder. Some of these executions were public, some private, and some had qualities of both, just as in executions of murderers. Some of the stories, particularly when the condemned was white or when there were multiple condemned executed on the same scaffold, were involved, several-column stories, sometimes with images. But most of the stories were short, few were sensationalized, and they did not seem to draw more attention in terms of crowds, rescue attempts, military guards, or in any other way than did executions for murder. What the *Raleigh Observer* termed the "Chapel Hill Burglars," for instance, received only about one-third of a column even though there were three of them and the "mixed crowd" at the execution numbered an estimated 10,000. They failed to confess, remaining "stout in their denial of the crimes, and proclaimed and protested their innocence" and "expressing a hope of salvation." "Louis Carlton spoke fifty minutes. He denied his guilt and said that he was going straight to Jesus."[33] Another article, despite it being "perhaps the first execution for highway robbery in Alabama," was only one-quarter of a column. In this pseudo-private execution, the sheriff "admitted forty or fifty negroes" to witness the hanging (including the victim of the robbery), not to mention those witnessing the hanging from windows of surrounding buildings. The hanging included African American preachers singing two verses and chorus of a hymn, but the condemned did not speak.[34]

The clearest pattern in these executions concerns race. Almost no whites faced the death penalty for *any* of these crimes: three white men in North Carolina for housebreaking and burglary (two in one event in 1879; the other in 1902), and three others in one arson case in 1884 Alabama.[35] No whites were executed in the South in this period for the crimes of accessory to murder, attempted murder, attempted rape, robbery, or riot. The discretion offered to (typically white) juries in regard to these crimes, in practice, meant a continuation of the antebellum tradition of whites facing one set of penalties and Blacks another. This is, of course, only an exaggerated example of a wider theme: racial discrimination through choices of prosecutors and through jury discretion likewise flourished in the application of the entire criminal code, including chain gangs and lengths of prison terms.

These rare executions for crimes other than rape and murder are exceptional in terms of their overwhelming use against African American convicts as well as in their divergent uses in different states. But even here, the two largest categories of crimes southerners were actually executed for—attempted rape and burglary—are closely related to the sexual crimes treated above. Burglary involved breaking into a house, a private space and one that is the sphere of women. It seems likely that there could be a gendered and sexualized element to many of these cases as well: a threat to the home is a threat to its women. But more than in this general or philosophical linkage to sexual crime, intruders in these spaces were often literally threatening to the women whom they found there. Particularly in North Carolina, where death as a penalty for attempted rape was not on the books, death for burglary might have stood in for that crime.[36]

Executions for these crimes seem to have functioned (culturally, ideologically, rhetorically, as evidenced in the press coverage) in ways similar to the more common executions for murder and for rape. None of the executions for crimes other than rape and murder that I've found in the historical record were particular fraught events. These might be "exceptional" crimes in a strictly categorical sense, but the only meaningful way that they diverged from norms was in the fact that most of these crimes ended in death only for African American men. If all of the history of capital punishment is skewed in that direction, it is most skewed in terms of these more minor crimes.

Execution Days When the Condemned Was a Woman

Women played an important part in the changing nature of execution in the South, most often by being a part of the audience-congregations at the public gallows and then being excluded from the small audiences attending private executions. Women were also themselves condemned to legal execution in the South, but rarely. Between 1866 and 1920, twenty-two women were legally executed in the South, less than 1 percent of the region's overall condemned.[37]

Almost half of the southern states in this era executed no women at all, according to the Espy file's data on capital punishment: Arkansas, Florida, Mississippi, Tennessee, and Texas. The states less reticent to execute women were the most settled states of the eastern seaboard, which, in turn, emphasizes how frontier states (Texas, Arkansas, and Florida) were among those not executing any women. Another way to characterize the distribution of these exceedingly rare executions is to note that the states executing the most women were among the southern states that used capital punishment the most overall. Four of the five states that executed no women were four of the five states that deployed capital punishment the least overall.[38]

Nineteen of the twenty-two women executed between 1866 and 1920 were African Americans, two were white, and the historical record is unclear in terms of race for one. Out of these twenty-two executions, I have been able to find newspaper reports for twenty.[39] Executions of women were almost all early in this period. Only one was after 1896: the South's single electrocution of a woman in the era (the first woman electrocuted in the South and one of the first in the nation), Virginia Christian in 1912.

Women were given the death penalty only for the crimes of murder or accessory to murder; twice the crime was by poisoning, and twice it was infanticide. In six of the twenty that I found on record, the execution was not merely of the female condemned, but rather a woman executed along with her male accomplices in murder (in five of those cases, for the murder of her husband).

The nature of these moments varied as widely and in roughly the same ways as the execution stories of men. Five were clearly public executions, with thousands in attendance; nine were clearly behind walls, but with crowds gathered outside the walls; three were more of a mixture, with barriers involved, but also some of the theater of public execution with interactions between crowds and those on the scaffold; for one, the reporting was unclear. These proportions of public and private are not out of keeping with the trends for executions of men before 1896. Only two white women were executed in the South in this fifty-five-year period, and that is fewer than we would presume, as approximately one-fifth of executions in this era overall were of whites.

As one might expect, the coverage of executions of women takes note of gender, but in a wide variety of ways. Most of the stories of women being executed, as with executions overall, were covered with matter-of-fact dispassion, with three earning bare one-paragraph mentions that give very few details of any sort, and most of the rest earning something like a column of descriptions of the scene and crime.[40] What is most notable in this collection of cases, in fact, is how they *don't* stand out in terms of gender; the event, though rare, tended to be consistent with the norms.

In these stories, the gender of the condemned was noted, but the standard for evaluating the moment seems to be roughly the same. As with men, reporters appear to evaluate the condemned in terms of manner, emotion, and strength of character in this difficult last moment. With men, they might call it being manly in the face of death, but the expectations remained similar for women: are they needing help to walk to the noose or walking with a firm step? Crying and looking ashen or composed and singing a hymn? And, especially, did they confess? The tone of reporters seems more impressed by women holding themselves together—expecting them to fold in the face of this trauma—but they are not, otherwise, judging women condemned by a different measuring stick. Caroline Shipp, for instance, "displayed courage rarely seen in women" while on the scaffold.[41] Even the case of a young Black woman who was condemned for murdering another woman out of jealousy over the affections of a white man who lived with the condemned and had several children with her—surely quite the sensational, interracial story for this era—earned but one column of description of the circumstances of the crime.[42]

Compared with those of African American men, the executions of African American women were about as often public, about as religious, about as long in terms of reports in the press, and using a similar tone and focus for the stories. A great crowd gathered to see Margaret Harris hanged, for instance, "principally negroes from the towns and stations along the line" of the train from Atlanta to the gallows. "There were a great many women among the crowd and they evinced as much curiosity to see the revolting sight as the men, many of them sitting near the gallows for two and three hours so as to get an unobstructed view."[43] Others mentioned the condemned, as in executions of men, wishing the crowd well and assuring them that they will see each other in heaven.[44] In more than one "private" execution, the surrounding walls, houses, and rooftops were full of people trying to get a view of the execution.[45] These are all commonplace elements of execution days in this era for men as well.

Only a few executions of African American women earned somewhat detailed and thorough coverage in the press, and here the length of the stories was probably due to the large numbers of people executed together as to the notability of the gender. When Ella Moore was hanged with four Black men as part of the punishment of the "Eastman rioters" in 1882, for example, the *Atlanta Constitution* filled four dense columns.[46] Likewise, with a quadruple hanging in South Carolina (two pairs of people hanged on the same gallows for two different crimes), the *Charleston News and Courier* covered the case with five columns of print, constructing the scene at the gallows (behind walls, so this coverage gave readers special access) and reviewing the crimes.[47]

This was more coverage than usual in column-inches, but in tone these stories were not out of keeping with the coverage of the executions of men. The chief way the coverage of Black women diverged from the "norm" in terms of executions of men is that there was a higher proportion of cases in which the question was asked: does this crime deserve the penalty of death? It was not overtly stated in most of these cases, and the executions of men could likewise raise this issue in rare moments. But when a woman claimed innocence, or when men were involved in the crime and a woman was an accessory to their actions, there was more of a tendency either to ask the question or, alternatively, to pointedly answer it by stating that all thought she was guilty and deserving her fate.[48] Both responses speak to an ideological challenge the public faced in terms of the executions of women.

That was especially true if the accused was a white woman, though interestingly, this was not a problem with all white women. The two white women executed in the South in this period received very different coverage from one another. Mary Snodgrass was about as marginal as a white woman could be, and her record in newspapers differs little from the coverage of Black women. Like African American women, lower-class white women, particularly if known to have a "bad character," found no protections from southern ideals of the purity of white womanhood.[49] A "lewd woman" run out of a Kentucky town, Snodgrass ended up mothering a child with a Black man and ultimately was caught holding the month-old infant in her fireplace, burning him to ashes.[50] The story of this murder and hanging was (clearly) extremely graphic, but it was not long and it hardly mentioned the scene at the gallows, expending its ink instead on the horror of the crime and how there were many people in the community so affected by the brutality of this killing as to want her lynched. This was a woman not just behaving in an unwomanly way but even betraying the most fundamental, perhaps even sacred, duty she has: protecting and nurturing her child. That it was a child of a mixed-race encounter opened up another avenue for horror for many whites at the time.

That marginalized coverage is quite in contrast to that of the other white woman hanged. She was characterized as an accomplice to the crimes of a man, which raised questions in the minds of many about the appropriateness of the noose as punishment for her. In the story told of this crime and execution, the press reveals the difficulty of reconciling the murder with its view of her as powerless and vulnerable. This treatment of her execution ("Miss Eberhart Hanged") was thorough: a dense five-column story with eight separate headlines.[51] This was, by far, the most compassionate coverage of the female condemned in the era: a "poor girl" at the center of the "saddest scene" of this "tragic drama" that "moved many to tears." Here the vulnerability of the condemned was emphasized, placing it in the context of a controlling man who was seen as the more active evil drawing her into crime. It was a public execution, with heavy rains limiting the crowds to perhaps 700, half of whom, according to the *Constitution*, were African Americans; the paper pointedly noted the twelve white women in attendance. The pattern of the event and the coverage was like others for the most part: a prayer, Bible readings, she spoke to the crowd, announced that she was ready, followed by the drop. What made this story more exceptional was how the paper elaborated upon her back story: columns about her life and the crime.

The length of the article speaks chiefly to the curiosity and discomfort fostered by a white woman being executed, but there was more that made this moment distinctive from reports of executions of men. Twice the report outlined her looks and what she was wearing, and not just at the hanging but also the day before when reporters interviewed her: her black hair "neatly arranged in plain style, being plaited into two very long braids," for instance. While newspapers might remark on a condemned man's suit for a hanging, this attention was not common. Note the words used: long hair, neat, plain. These are not words signaling her sinful nature, but rather her womanly value or perhaps even "she is like us."

More than such a superficial focus on her looks, the report in the *Constitution* overtly discussed how disturbing it was to the local community to kill a white woman:

> It was a most heartrending spectacle—a distressing and horrifying sight to see *a woman hanged*; and especially was it unpleasant to the people of this community who had, almost *en masse*, petitioned the Governor to commute her punishment to imprisonment in the penitentiary for life, but he refused. The grand jury, who proffered the indictment against her, to a man, and every one of the jury who convicted her (except two, who could not be found,) and a large number of the best men and women of Webster and Sumter counties, signed this petition, asking the commutation of the sentence on the ground that she was young, ignorant, did what she did by the great influence Spann [the murderer Eberhart abetted] had over her, and was all her life a good, kind-hearted girl, never having done anything wrong or improper, except being implicated in this crime.[52]

The coverage of Susan Eberhart's execution was almost tortured as it condemned her while also being appalled by the tragedy of a woman's death in the ignominious noose: "The best men and women," "good, kind-hearted," but "influenced." Of those who voiced an opinion about Eberhart, "very few can be found who believed she ought to have been hanged."[53] This outpouring of print about Eberhart might point to an explanation for why there were so few white women executed. Prevailing gender norms pulled the wider public toward seeing a white woman, even if she murdered or was complicit in murdering someone, not as evil or a lost cause but rather within the frame of a weak innocent who had fallen from grace, led astray by men.[54] In 1916, a white woman in North Carolina was convicted of aiding her lover in killing her husband. Despite the conviction, she was not executed; the governor commuted her sentence to twenty years in prison, saying "the killing of this woman would send a shiver through North Carolina."[55] White women don't do this sort of thing; to explain such horrors, look elsewhere to assign blame, these examples seem to be saying. This is one more circumstance that demonstrates the power of white womanhood in the minds of southern whites. Even more starkly, it demonstrates how African American women, along with thoroughly marginalized lower-class white women, were denied even a measure of that power.

The last execution of a woman in the South in this era was also exceptional: the first electrocution of a woman in the region. In 1912, Virginia Christian fought with her employer, Ida Belote. Those working on Christian's behalf characterized Belote as a very difficult employer and as the one who started the violence, throwing things at Christian and accusing her of theft until Christian retaliated by smashing her on the forehead with a broom handle. She ultimately gave this fight a grisly end by shoving a cloth down Belote's throat.[56] That Christian was defending herself from Belote was certainly the line of defense Christian wanted to provide in court. Her own attorneys kept Christian from testifying, however, concerned that her coarse ways of talking would alienate the jury more than her testimony would help.[57] Christian was a sixteen-year-old, uneducated African American girl working as a domestic. She was tried and convicted (the jury took all of twenty-three minutes) and scheduled to die in the chair just five months later.

But there the story shifts from the norm. As with criminal cases later in the century (like the Scottsboro Boys in the 1930s or any number of cases in the civil rights era), several outside groups became interested in her case and attempted to intervene. Mary Church Terrell (an African American writer and activist) submitted to Virginia's governor hundreds of signatures from members of the National Association of Colored Women asking him to reduce the punishment for Christian to a term in prison. The National Association for the Advancement of Colored People, formed just three years earlier, sent a representative to Hampton, sought lawyers to continue to press the case that her sentence should be commuted, and published their protest—"Christian Virginia vs. Virginia Christian"—in *The Crisis*.[58] Her young age, possible mental disability (she was called "dull" by many reports), and the evidence that this was not a planned murder but rather a scuffle that turned deadly (perhaps even a fight started by Belote) were all factors these activists focused on.[59] The NAACP called her "a sacrifice to society," for white Virginia "made this girl what she was and then brutally killed her for it."[60]

More locally, one of the most vocal African Americans in Richmond, John Mitchell, editor of the *Richmond Planet*, was more circumspect. The *Planet* had no coverage of either the crime or the trial, with the first reference to the case appearing when an appeal to the Virginia Supreme Court was filed.[61] This raised the possibility of an African American woman being heard in

Virginia's system of justice, which would be quite an unusual story for his readership. The paper's first front page coverage announced her appeal to the governor.[62] Two more front-page stories appeared at the time of her electrocution, both exceedingly brief.[63]

The only really substantive engagement with the issues of capital punishment, her case, and her gender in Mitchell's *Planet* arose in a brief report of the governor refusing to commute, accompanied by an equally brief editorial.[64] Here Mitchell describes the "diabolical" crime of Christian against the "aged, frail" Belote, and voices how the choice over commutation was a "knotty question" facing the governor, and how Mitchell was "prepared to accept" the governor's decision in this particular case. In Mitchell's opinion, however, "in the case of a woman . . . we esteem it to be different" how one balances punishment and mercy than with men, making him conclude that mercy for Christian would have been the best path. The tone is so very accepting that it is hard to discern, even, that Mitchell believed another decision than death would be more just. The graphic nature of the crime made this a very difficult case for local African Americans to champion.

This condemned woman earned extensive attention from the local and national sources, and from the perspective of these activists, this was a case for mercy.[65] No. The governor refused anything but a two-week stay of execution to allow for any new evidence to surface. As no evidence was forthcoming that might mitigate the case against her, he allowed the execution to proceed. Virginia Christian was electrocuted on 16 August 1912. She was the first woman in sixteen years to be executed in the South; she was also the first Black woman condemned to death in the South to receive extraordinary support from organized groups inside and outside the region in her defense, something that would become more commonplace in the coming generations.

But in this era, this was an exception. Almost all executions of women were of Black women, and they were not offered much protection due to their gender.

Execution Days When the Condemned Was White

That contrasts with one of the two executions of white women, treated so kindly by the press and with many working to save her. If the execution of white men rarely had such commentary—most were poor whites who were offered little respect from the law or in the press—they did earn more coverage, and that press coverage differed in some ways. White convicts were somewhat more likely than Black ones to diverge from the common story of religious redemption, either being silent on the gallows or lashing out at authorities and at the crowd assembled. But the record of executions of whites is similar in every other respect, including the likelihood of being executed publicly, to African American executions described in the last chapter. Except with more attention given to them. And that matters.

This similarity in terms of the public versus private nature of executions is particularly telling and is one piece of evidence (along with how religion at the gallows shifts our understanding of what these events meant for the crowds who assembled) that points to how we've misunderstood the nature and meaning of public executions in the history of the South. Capital punishment of whites was just as likely to be in public as were executions of African Americans. No racial divergence in the tendency for an execution to be in the open or behind walls occurs until the twentieth century, and by then executions in public were rare enough that any racial divergence held little relevance. Many more Blacks than whites were given the death penalty in the South, and in that, there is clear evidence of racism, but not so in the public nature of those executions. In fact, in tabulating all public and private executions (that I could identify) in the South in five-year increments between 1876 and 1905 (the period in which most states were transitioning to privacy), half of those five-year spans had African Americans executed more in public, and half had whites executed more in public.[66] After 1905, almost no whites were executed publicly, but very few Blacks were either.[67]

While the vast majority of the 3,181 individuals listed in the Espy file (plus additions from Hearn and Laska's lists for their six states) as executed in the South between 1866 and 1920 were African Americans, 537 of these condemned (or about 17 percent) were white.[68] The public execution days for white condemned were not distinctive. As with the public executions of African Americans, they tended to involve a religious ceremony and were popular events with mixed-race, mixed-gender audiences, and they were focused on the words of the condemned. "He will make his statement first," said a sheriff introducing the first of two white condemned on the scaffold, "and I want you all to give him your attention."[69] "Doc" Taylor spoke for an hour and a quarter to a crowd of 4,000, quoting from the Book of Revelation, singing a hymn, and saying that a friend had a few words to say. When ask who the friend might be, Taylor responded, "The Lord Jesus Christ" and began a Bible reading. More dramatic even than most of these events were, Taylor was dressed in white linen and promised that after three days, he would arise from the dead to preach to moonshiners and mountaineers.[70] Condemned for murder, Philip Nicholas received these words from his minister on the gallows: "Depart, Christian soul, out of this world, in the name of God, the Father Almighty, who created thee; in the name of Jesus Christ, the son of the living God, who suffered for thee; in the name of the Holy Ghost, who sanctified thee; in the name of all the angels and saints of God. May thy soul be this day in peace and thy abode in Holy Zion. Through Jesus Christ, our Lord. Amen."[71] When Charley Harris confessed the murder of his brother, the crowd of thousands sang with him "Sweet By-and-By," he expressed his hope to see them all in heaven, and the minister's fervent prayer for his soul affected many. "The crowd bowed respectfully and many groans of response went up in the course of the passionate appeal. . . . Just before the drop many shouted 'Good by [sic].'"[72]

More often than with African American condemned, white executions could diverge from this norm, and in more than one way. The condemned could vilify all present and the process that led him to the gallows. "With a curse on his lips, with eyes bloodshot and with the expressed wish that the people of Greenville perish in the fires of hell, Ashley Cocke died here today."[73] Or he could be silent, avoiding the religious elements so common to these moments and expediting the trap falling open. Or white condemned could show that they wanted to avoid the public nature of the events, asking for a private execution or even attempting suicide to keep from hanging.[74] None of these divergences from the norm were commonplace, nor were they unknown among the more numerous African American condemned. But proportionately, divergences from the religious norm for gallows services were more common among white condemned than Black.

In the newspaper reports of executions, the most obvious distinction in terms of the race of the condemned was that the press printed much, much more on white executions, on average something like twice the column inches for whites compared with the column inches for Blacks. In this, the press was expressing white interest in whites (and limited interest in African Americans) that pervaded every aspect of the South. Black executions were the norm, so while they were reported in the press, they seem to have been considered ordinary: Blacks were expected to commit crimes and their executions were therefore expected as well. White condemned were more "newsworthy" for being infrequent, and their coverage was more sensationalized.[75]

In fact, the most sensationalized stories of crime and of executions in the South were stories of whites committing capital crimes, particularly when the accused was of the upper class. When Thomas Cluverius was convicted in Richmond of killing his pregnant cousin, he was sentenced to death, and at his execution, the *Richmond Dispatch* filled its entire front page with the story on the day of the execution, and again on the day after, including images and a recap of the case, appeals, developments, and the publishing of his own story in book form to sell amid the crowds expected to be drawn to the jail downtown. And this two-day riot of print had followed in the wake of two weeks of front-page stories leading up to the day of execution.[76]

Stories like Cluverius's became public obsessions, for they confounded the public's expectations: a crime and criminal that "didn't fit" the common stereotypes. For whites in the South, no lower-class white or any-class African American condemned could confound them in this way, for whites expected criminality from this quarter. But when a white lawyer and Sunday-school teacher like Cluverius committed murder, many white southerners could not believe it, wondering if he really could have thrown his pregnant cousin into the city reservoir, killing her. Even if they believed he committed the heinous crime, they might further wonder whether his high-priced lawyers (Cluverius had three) would nevertheless succeed in saving him from the noose.[77] This resulted in a flood of print on the execution and how (and *if*!) it would occur: would the governor commute?

With such a sensationalized crime, the whole narrative of the case—discovery, arrest, preliminary trial, trial, appeal, punishment—earned rapt attention. But the end of these cases—the gallows—was particularly important in this sort of white-crime sensation. It was not only the moment when the story would be over but also the moment when, with nothing but God's judgment awaiting them, criminals might unburden themselves of the truth: would he confess? If the public were tortured by the questions raised by such cases-that-did-not-fit, a confession would serve as a sort of ideological balm, allowing them to understand how this disruptive occurrence might have happened, and thereby settle the troubled waters of their worldview.

Most executions of whites did not receive the extraordinarily intense coverage of Cluverius's execution, and that has to do with class. Most were of lower-class whites who, like African Americans, had a reputation for crime and disorder. For them, a death sentence would be more commonplace than confounding. But it was also rare for a story of the execution of a white criminal in the South in this period to be as brief as a paragraph, as many were for African Americans. It was more common to have an execution of a white condemned (of any class) covered in a multicolumned story, perhaps even complete with illustrative woodcuts or, later in the period, halftone photographs.[78] The white press of the South did not care about African American condemned in ways they cared about white condemned: treating them as individuals with particular stories worth telling. African American condemned were noticed, but rarely were their stories found worthy of investment.

BY LOOKING AT WOMEN CONDEMNED, this chapter emphasizes how capital punishment in the South was almost always of men, and when a Black woman (as well as a marginalized white woman) died on the gallows, little was different from the story told of the hanging of Black men, just as little was different for those Black men accused of burglary or attempted murder, or robbery. It is still more striking that the events on execution day when the condemned was accused of sexual crimes were so rarely different from executions for murder. It was only sometimes that whites were frenzied over rape, or, rather, that such frenzy carried over into actions on the day of execution, even if the rhetoric of the South was so often overwhelmed by the topic. Instead, evidence abounds of a southern legal system dealing with sexual crimes in normal ways and like other crimes: the average execution for a sexual crime in the South was much like any other.

White women *might be* treated differently in the story of death at the gallows, but their executions were so rare as to make any generalizations from that fact unwise. Whites were almost never executed for crimes other than murder and (much less often) rape, and when they were executed for murder or rape, they tended to engage in religion at the public gallows as Blacks did. Whites *did* receive more press for their executions, but they did not generally (unless they were upper-class whites fostering sensationalized coverage) receive a different *sort* of coverage. Executions of whites were no more likely, proportionately, to be public or private than those of Blacks.

So what does this heightened interest in white crime and punishment in the white press tell us? White, male editors created norms for southern journalism that mirrored their wider worldview, and these norms defined their coverage of crime, violence, and punishment, just as white prosecutors, juries, lawyers, and judges defined the results in courtrooms. "It is an unwritten law seemingly, that no white person is to be hung in this state, no matter what the crime may be," wrote the editor of the African American *Savannah Tribune*. A white man was scheduled to hang, but the day before the execution "he was allowed to escape and has not yet been apprehended," while "every technicality has been resorted to" to save the life of a white woman condemned for murder. "All of these things go to show that it is only the Negro who is to pay the penalty on the gallows," the editor concluded.[79] Not true, technically, but it remains that the overwhelming majority of executions were of Black men and for a whole range of crimes.

None of this quite makes sense without the white supremacist ideology that supported these views. Whites mattered to other whites in the South in fully human ways; white criminals were individuals to other whites, and as such, their individual stories mattered. Class mattered too, and there was a very noticeable difference in the coverage of poor as opposed to middle-class and upper-class white condemned. Newspapers sated that interest. African Americans were not quite, not fully, human beings to white editors or to their readers. This white (and male) perspective affected the received, public understandings not merely of criminals and their appropriate punishments but also of religion that was so prominent on execution days.

How did whites and Blacks see race, violence, punishment, and religion? Their positions were so far apart as to be infuriating to many Blacks trying to have rational and engaged conversations about these issues. W. E. B. Du Bois, responding to an insulting screed from the white Virginia novelist Thomas Nelson Page in 1907, wrote—and then crossed out—his angry response in a long essay he submitted (but failed to see reach print) to rebut Page's calumny: "Black men are in the world to stay. There is no danger of their dying out in America, much less Africa. They are probably the sturdiest and most persistent of the world's races. ~~They will never die out. Mr. Thomas Nelson Page's family will die with him, because he has no children, but my grandchildren will walk over his grave.~~ If this is so, whites and blacks must meet and by every token they must meet as human beings."[80] Even with these lines deleted, the northern, white journal that published Page's harangue would not touch Du Bois's response. What was it that so infuriated Du Bois? The next chapter takes us to the heart of the problem of racism residing in the minds of white southerners, a problem that had a dramatic framing effect on their ideas of religion as well as punishment, including the punishment of death.

CHAPTER THREE

Shoot the Sheep-Killing Dogs
Racism in Southern Punishment

> There are some things so well understood by those who know the negroes as to appear to them almost truisms. For example: . . .
>
> That negroes under subjection are, for the most part, docile, amiable, tractable, and pleasant to deal with.
>
> That negroes in power are, for the most part, arrogant, swaggering, dangerous, and intolerable . . .
>
> He exhibits for the most part just what a trained mind would expect him to exhibit: the deeply founded marks of an undeveloped race, which so far has never as a race wholly emerged from that primitive condition . . .
>
> The only barrier that stands between the whites of the North and the negro race . . . is the white race of the South. We of the South are in the battle line to-day; while the whites of the North are in the reserves. Let our battle lines be swept away, and they will have to face to-morrow what we face to-day.
>
> —THOMAS NELSON PAGE, "The Great American Question," 1907

> One of the greatest obstacles to the solution of the race problem to day is the attitude of some of the most intelligent and honest white men of the South. Altho they believe they study colored people rationally, estimate them justly and discuss them dispassionately, they seem mentally and spiritually incapacitated to do any of these things. . . .
>
> For the last twenty years the interest once manifested in the Negro by the North has been growing beautifully less . . . and if they are frank enough to state the reason, they will reply it is because of the Negro's brutal conduct toward the white women of the South. The slanders uttered by Mr. Page and other distinguished southern gentlemen, whose words, unfortunately, carry great weight in the North, have borne abundant and bitter fruit. . . . The rapidity with which the South has poisoned the mind of the North against the Negro has succeeded in withdrawing from him its sympathy . . . , while it resembled nothing so much as legerdemain.
>
> —MARY CHURCH TERRELL, 1907 response to Page, unpublished

Stories are how we understand our world. We weave narratives from the facts around us that we choose to attend to and to value. While built from the factual matter of the same recent past, the stories that whites and Blacks spun from those selectively chosen facts to explain race, religion, violence, and crime were, unsurprisingly, virtually incompatible.

For African Americans, justice was central to their framework for understanding the period and the punishment regime that was a part of it: we are a nation of laws and the Constitution, and an obvious, incontrovertible fact about the South and race was the violation of those protections by whites and the unfairness of a legal system betrayed. Everything else was secondary to those fundamental concerns, a common sense not too far removed from the common sense of our own era, looking back.

White southerners in the late nineteenth century combined their belief in the law with a complaisance with lynching and a panoply of inequities in the judicial system. These contradictions require us to do much more work to understand how they could likewise feel that they were in the right, that their perspective was in keeping with tradition, the law, wisdom, and civility. That they did believe that they were in keeping with these values is clear; that they were not insane seems a reasonable assumption to make of any large group of historical actors. They simply saw these issues from an entirely different vantage point than either African Americans of their day or (most of) us looking back on them from the distant future. Their common sense was a different common sense, one with an adamantine core of racism. We are all trapped within our own ideologies, after all: "a creature as well as a creator of his culture." There is no reason to think southern apologists at this time were *knowingly* misrepresenting the realities of race, violence, and the South, for they were all themselves caught within "a mythic evasion of reality."[1] In a sense, we all are: it is the human condition to be caught inside of the stories we tell about ourselves and the world.

It was not that white southerners had a radically different perspective on the laws or the Constitution or religion. Certainly, they had a more circumscribed concept of federal as opposed to state authority, but not significantly different ideas of crime or punishment, with the notable exception of the crime of Black-on-white rape. But even that was more a difference in their understanding of race than of rape: southern white men were conflicted, perhaps even complacent, about legal penalties for rape when the accused was a white man, at least when he was of standing and the woman was not.

The southern white understanding of the nature of African Americans is the important difference in ideology between our time and theirs: our mainstream view is much closer to the era's African American perspective. The implications of this upon the punishment regime of the South—as well as upon white ideas of Black religion—were profound. Crucially, these southern, white understandings of African American nature were broadly shared by whites outside the region as well, defining in many ways the *national* understanding of race relations.

The postbellum southern white view of Blacks will never make sense to most of us, but if we understand that the starting position for southern whites was that African Americans were not really human beings, not quite, we can begin to see the internal logic that frames both the ideas southern whites vocalized and the actions they took. Southern whites believed that Blacks were best likened to horses or dogs: "The North believes the Negro is a human being, . . . whereas the South believes the Negro to be a quasi beast of burden, belonging chiefly to the mule family."[2] They are useful parts of society, possibly earning the regard or even fondness of whites, but fundamentally requiring the guidance and control of whites to continue being a constituent (and dependent) part of civilized society. When a chicken stops laying or a cow stops producing, it becomes a burden rather than a boon to the community. And when a dog becomes rabid, or when a horse becomes a danger to those seeking to harness it, you put it down. On the farm, one might regret the necessity and even feel a pinch of pain for the loss of a good work animal, but this requires no hand-wringing or explanation: it is the only reasonable action to take.[3] And it is no sin; indeed, there isn't really any choice in the matter. You contain the crisis, take the dog or horse out back, and shoot it. One cannot become too sentimental about work animals; one has to think of the wider community. It is simply being responsible.

What is different, of course, from the common view today or from the view of African Americans at the time was that many if not most white southerners appear to put the entire African American race into something akin to the "work animal," subhuman category. Train African Americans sternly to get them to obey, with fences containing their field of action, with small rewards for good behavior and physical punishments to keep them from straying from their roles; curb when necessary. Give them enough provender to be as productive as they can be, shelter enough to ensure a long work life, training enough to maximize their productivity, but do not treat them better, coddling them, for that would spoil them for the work. Most of the actions of whites make a kind of (internal, horrific, God-forsaken) logic from this perspective, for the brutality is productive when work animals require training, as long as one does not respect them as being anything more than animals in the service of humans and meant to be exploited. Few whites in the South of the late nineteenth century seemed to value Black rights appreciably more than that, and white outlaws, at least, "thought no more of shooting a Negro who didn't jump to one side of the road quickly enough than they thought of shooting a sheep-killing dog."[4] Religion plays a role here: treating a *heathen* like a beast was much more acceptable than treating a devout Christian so. Accepting Blacks as true Christians would increase the difficulty of maintaining the myths at the heart of southern white supremacy. Crucially, few white northerners valued Black rights much, either.

Whites made the laws and practiced the punishments, and therefore much of this chapter is focused on discerning their views. In this study of racism, that is where the disease was manifest. African Americans used data, the law and Constitution, common sense, and outrage at white brutality to challenge the white supremacist view. But their story confronted rather than confirmed white assumptions, while the story white southerners told absolved whites of responsibility. In the two generations after the Civil War, whites north and south tended to choose absolution over any story that asked them to do the hard work of challenging and changing their views. This echoes, of course, across the generations. The storytelling outlined here helps to define the context for the changes in the justice system and in capital punishments explored in the second half of the book.

Black Religion as Disorderly Hysteria

Beast, barbarian, dog. Fueled by these fears about Black abilities and their deficits, whites increasingly interpreted the events at the gallows as examples of African American primitivism and the limits of their moral natures. Religion at the gallows when the minister was a white man was one thing: guiding the underclass in morality and the penalties of wrongdoing. But after the Civil War, when African Americans were worshipping in their own, separate churches, whites no longer controlled the nature, expression, or message of religion. And the minister given authority to speak to a huge mixed-race crowd? Now it was a Black man.

Black religion at the gallows was emotional, physical, communal, and centered most on the grace of God's forgiveness of the sins we all commit. Even though southern white evangelicals might share most of these values and styles of religious expression, whites tended to view Black spiritual practices with dismissive condescension. Consciously for some and implicitly for others, this dismissal reframed Black religious authority as absurd.

White correspondents and editors regularly demonstrated their confusion about how to interpret this boisterous religious fervor of African American crowds. Most often, white newspapers ignored them or merely mentioned that there was a religious ceremony when printing brief reports of executions. When giving more elaborate treatment, white papers at times described them as interesting eccentricities and at other times as a reflection on the low nature of Black social and emotional development. Occasionally, newspapers printed last speeches in dialect, almost in the style of minstrelsy.[5] At times, white papers gendered this condescension: Black women in the crowd were particularly noted for moaning, swaying, calling out, and speaking in tongues.[6] One article described a convict's religious ecstasy as "better than chloroform" for making him into a "driveling and maundering idiot" in the hours before he was hanged.[7]

Many whites seemed to see Black services less as religious expression and more as public disorder, something important to keep in mind when reading white commentary on execution scenes. Whites described Black religion as "scenes of frenzy, of human passion, of collapse, of catalepsy, of foaming at the mouth, of convulsion, of total loss of inhibition" and worse than the Indian ghost dance.[8] A rural Alabama lawyer went so far as to call the African American "a naked, snakeworshiping savage" and claimed that few of them had intellectual and moral qualities "superior to those of a monkey."[9] "Moved by hysterical mutterings" of the condemned on the scaffold, wrote the *Atlanta Constitution* in 1892, "the negroes drew near the gallows, and moaned sympathetically and chanted the weirdest of weird songs. Daniels [the condemned] was so wrought up that he acted like a man run mad. He swayed up and down in harmony with the strangely sad music, while a curious, half happy, half idiotic expression played about his features."[10]

Even more whites saw the emotional, physical, and noisy displays of Black religion as childlike, a set of beliefs and rituals that failed to achieve any deeper understanding of how religion should shape conduct and morality.[11] A "burst of religious enthusiasm" in African American camp meetings was merely a "temporary intellectual drunkenness" in which "strong religious feeling" trumps all else, leaving a "profound insensibility to every principle upon which religion rests."[12] "The colored people did not believe that religion had anything to do with conduct and resented any attempt to convince them of it." Instead, Black churches were filled with "shouting, praying, singing, all manner of excitement, hysterics, trances, loud calls upon God."[13] "Religion and practice are with them two separate matters," according to a member of the American Missionary Association. "One of them will make the loudest professions of religion and will yet be guilty of the most unblushing violations of the law."[14]

William Hannibal Thomas, a Black man considered a "traitor to his race" by many African Americans, offered in 1901 the very critique of Black character and religion that whites found most compelling. Whites then eagerly promoted and amplified his views, for a Black man saying what whites wanted to hear was very useful. He argued that Black religion was an amalgam of Christian superficialities covering a persistence of savage "fetich" (or voodoo) worship. "The most heinous crimes are committed by those who read and write and are members of negro churches." "The negro is a moral pervert . . . ignorant of ethical distinctions." Thomas specifically called out the gallows moment, saying that one explanation for the criminal bent in the Black population in general "is to be found in the fact that negroes guilty of heinous crimes are taught by their religious teachers that God will pardon them, and that in becoming pardoned all sense of guilt is expunged; so rapists and murderers sing and shout on the gallows and claim to be regenerated men." Far from seeing benefit in this, Thomas frames it as actively promoting crime: "Such teaching is therefore an unconscious or deliberate crime-breeder, and crime flourishes and will continue to flourish among freedmen so long as the doctrine obtains that all evil is condonable, and every infraction of morality a matter of intercession and forgiveness."[15]

At times, the danger of African American religious enthusiasms were painted in stark terms, and not merely by reminding readers that antebellum insurrectionists pretended religion: Nat Turner preached (and, regarding his punishment, famously said "was not Christ crucified?") and Denmark Vesey founded a church.[16] In his Reconstruction novel *Red Rock*, Thomas Nelson Page painted a revival scene: "Moses was speaking at the moment, mounted on an impromptu platform, swaying his body back and forth and pouring forth a doctrine as voluble in words as it was violent in sound and gesture, whilst his audience surged around him, swaying and shouting, and exciting themselves into a sort of wild frenzy." Page goes on to hint at the revolutionary and violent potential of these moments: "'Don't de Book say, as we shall inherit the uth?' cried the speaker, and his audience moaned and swayed and shouted in assent." White observers, Page continued, knowing this had to be stopped, prompted a local official to take action, and when he ordered the crowd to disperse, "it did almost immediately, dissolving like magic." The official told the speaker to leave the village: "The trick-doctor cringed, and with a whine of acquiescence bowed himself off."[17] Here is a fictive lesson of threat and solution, offered by Page in a few paragraphs: strong action by white men is necessary to keep the frenzied Black men from moving from fetich trance to violence.

It is entirely plausible as well that further fictions were published as facts. One article in 1905 claimed that a Black bishop had written these words: "But through his death and resurrection we may commit sins of lying, stealing, Sabbath breaking, getting drunk, gambling, whoring, murdering, and every species of villainy, and then come to God through our resurrected Christ and enter heaven in the end."[18] If true, that would be a rather disturbing vision of religion, indeed; but it seems as likely to be a white fiction. More commonplace than extreme claims like these were for whites to see Black religion as heathen, its preachers as unequipped to lead, and its churches as sites of potential danger.[19] At an 1883 execution, "bohemian" entrepreneurs were selling around town a supposed confession, purporting that the man condemned for rape claimed "his people are going to the devil" and that "colored people go to the church to do their devilment."[20] The condemned denied from the scaffold that he said these things, and ten ministers signed a rebuttal to it. But this conflict might reveal what at least some whites *wanted* the story at the scaffold to be.

These perceived failures of Black religion were ascribed by some whites in the South to *im*morality, but others saw an even deeper problem: something more like *un*morality, the incapacity of those in the race to recognize the nature of (or existence of?) a moral code.[21] Do horses, do dogs recognize morality?, whites of this opinion might ask. Their religious emotions "are merely a physical drunkenness; a species of excitement, indeed, that resembles the effect of over-indulgence in liquor, the fumes of which, rising to the brain, produce an exaltation of feeling that is expressed in vehement movements of the body, ecstatic laughter, and boisterous singing." This is a "mania," a "sensual gratification," rather than "true religious feeling"; it is religion as a "code of belief and not a code of morals."[22] In this way, southern whites could perceive both education and religion as actively bad for African Americans; a southern Episcopal bishop vented his spleen over the nature of Black religion:

> They have colleges and newspapers, missionary societies and mammoth meetings-houses; they have baptized multitudes, and they maintain an unbroken revival; and yet confessedly the end of the commandment, the morality, the godlikeness which all religion is given to attain, is further away than at the beginning. Their religion is a superstition, their sacraments are fetiches, their worship is all wil[d] frenzy and their morality a sham. . . .

> Utterly ignorant men, gifted with a fatal fluency of speech, unable often to read the Bible in English, much less in its original tongues, became the blind guides of the blind followers; the result is that in some places within my personal knowledge a revival meeting has been going on every night since the surrender of Johnston's army. The orgies of their so-called worship are such as to cause any Christian man to blush for the caricature of our holy religion therein portrayed.[23]

This perspective of Black culture and systems of belief was not merely held by a racist extreme in the South; it was affirmed by the nascent field of anthropology. Anthropologists in this era were prone to thinking in evolutionist terms, and the "half-bacchanalian, half-devout" Black culture was problematic to position in those terms.[24] Some focused on Black "spirituals" in positive ways, crediting the influence of (white) Christians on African American spirituality. But others focused on "conjuration" or "fetich" religion, highlighting the persistence of a savage past. Evidence of continued belief in superstition, or "conjure," became proof of the limits of development for Blacks as well as the present threat of regression. Control of their passions was merely a veneer, easily cast off to reveal more savage ways: "a crater of primitive passion just underneath the crust of religious culture."[25]

This was no fringe white supremacist perspective, but the sort of argument that might be found in the pages of the *Journal of American Folk-Lore*.[26] Blacks were "almost certainly nearer to the anthropoid or pre-human ancestry of men than the other marked varieties of our species."[27] This racist phrase is made all the more disturbing by being not from Thomas Dixon's *The Clansman* or from a speech by South Carolina's "Pitchfork" Ben Tillman but rather by a Harvard scientist. Louis Agassiz, also a Harvard professor, popularized the idea of separate creations: just as there are zoological provinces for different species in the animal world, there were "natural ranges of distinct types of man."[28] Darwinism convinced some that "reversion to type" would mean the de-evolution of Blacks to the point that they were uncompetitive with other races; survival of the fittest must necessarily also mean "death of the unfit."[29] It was only natural. Such ideas circulated still more widely in popular forms: when *Tarzan of the Apes* was published in 1914, Chicago-born Edgar Rice Burroughs's view of Blacks as cannibals (not even the apes in his story ate their own) and Tarzan's independent discovery of how to fashion a noose and how to slip it over the head of an African who threatened Tarzan's (ape) mother were concepts not, in fact, outside of the norms conceived of by whites in this moment.[30] Instead, they represented that disturbing norm, north and south.

From this perspective of Black religion and Black moral incapacity in general, whites tended to dismiss African American religious expression at the scaffold as a mockery of the Christian humility demanded by the moment. As white North Carolina papers scoffed, the gallows services too often gave a "halo of renown" to condemned: "Soon, the scaffold will be considered quite the auxiliary to the church."[31] The *New York Times* elaborated on this theme:

> The colored preachers tickled his vanity by making him the central figure of a baptism in public and of an uproarious prayer-meeting; and they brought him to a state of wild excitement by their hymn-singing. Judged by the standard of the Southern colored preacher, Lee was a thoroughly religious man, for he sang hymns with fervor and flapped his arms as if they were wings, while expressing a determination to fly to heaven. There is nothing strange in the fact that the negro, whether a preacher or a mere "professor" can fancy himself sure of heaven, although daily violating half of the ten commandments. Lying, stealing, and adultery are not inconsistent with his religion, for he can sing hymns and flap his arms as vigorously after stealing his neighbor's chickens or committing some grave crime as he could the very hour when he "got religion."[32]

Perhaps it was even *necessary* for white southerners to dismiss Black religion. Denying African Americans the standing and respect of Christianity might be a precondition for white control of the South to be complete, or at least a particularly helpful step in that direction. "To whatever level of vice or crime they may fall," wrote one white observer of Blacks, "they still retain and disclose the same religious aspirations, untouched by the least taint of hypocrisy and unobscured by the smallest shadow of doubt. These aspirations are entirely disconnected from their own careers; being common to the murderers, ravishers, and thieves, as well as to those who, on the whole, are respectable men and reputable citizens."[33] If seen as nonhumans, or at least as humans outside of the ambit of Christian brotherhood, Black southerners might be treated in entirely distinct ways from white, Christian southerners. Heathens required a different response.

In fact, religion in the hands of people not believed to be capable of discerning its truths could be dangerous. Certainly under slavery, even if Black preachers were allowed to preach to enslaved peoples, they were under white authority, and often whites sought to use that authority to focus religious messages on control, particularly after 1831 with Nat Turner's rising.[34] Whites wanted control from Black religion, order. So when white papers described the scene at the gallows as "disorderly," what did they mean? For they often interpreted average African American religious services as something akin to frenzy, an orgy, a public disorder.

A White Supremacist Punishment Regime

Whites in the postbellum South believed that African Americans were little more than animals, that they were regressing, that they required the firm hand of whites to thrive as a race, and that they were incapable of moral judgment. Criminality, then, must be expected, for the norms of civilized society itself would be outside of their ken. And punishment? Punishment must be both firm and harsh, based less on what is fitting for punishing white crime than on what was needed for managing domestic animals. Whites in the postbellum South might have really preferred slavery to solve this problem, for in that time, so whites strained to continue to believe, the races were in their appropriate places and society functioned as it was meant to function.[35]

But in the absence of slavery and with post–Civil War constitutional amendments inhibiting the free flow of white power, what forms of control could they devise to punish criminal behavior of African Americans? After all, several punishments that white southerners had deployed for generations were gone: the whipping post, transportation out of state, and the use of the death penalty in de jure race-specific ways. This is in addition, of course, to the loss of the abundance of punishments that were available to each slaveholder over their enslaved: that was dramatically over in 1865, forced at gunpoint, and taking with it not just the worst sin in America's past but also a massive amount of the white South's wealth and power.[36]

White power remained pervasive—dominant—in the South after the Civil War. Owning almost all the land, the remaining wealth, and, with the spare exception of a few Reconstruction years (white "reconquest" came quickly), almost all of the political, legal, judicial, policing, and other official positions, southern whites retained startling surpluses of power of every sort. But objective data like this would convince few of those southern whites who lived the history. They acted on their own understandings and perspectives of what was happening and what it meant, and more apt than a discussion of the facts of southern social conditions is a discussion of how that reality was perceived by those living it. Those perceptions were based less on the realities around them that they (and we) could measure than on the stories, biases, and beliefs that they embraced to make sense of them. Particularly important was their starting position: what did they assume society *should* be? The reference point for many whites in the postbellum South—the position or understanding that they viewed as "natural" and that they employed as their common sense to compare and judge how different was the world around them—was the antebellum South's white monopoly on power and authority.[37]

Judged from that (extreme, skewed) reference point, almost everything in the late nineteenth century was moving in the wrong direction for southern whites wanting to maintain that monopoly.[38] Black literacy? Rising 10 percent each decade, offering increasing numbers of African Americans the simple protection of greater knowledge, particularly in regard to the contracts they were asked to sign.[39] Black home and farm ownership? Never challenging the massive advantages held by whites, they were nevertheless growing as fast as anything grew in the South over the next two generations. From near zero in 1870, the number of Black homeowners in the South grew sixty-fold by 1910; Black farm owners grew eleven-fold in those years.[40] Fundamental elements of personhood were now possibilities for African Americans: getting married and having a family, moving about the South, and quitting a job when conflict arose; these things African American southerners did in abundance.[41] Add to that the example of Black voting, of Republican judges, and even a growing number of examples of exceptionally talented African Americans and a (slowly) growing Black middle class, and the white South had to work much harder to maintain the fictions that white supremacy was based on.[42] Looming in the background was the incontrovertible fact, important in the South for generations before the late nineteenth century and for generations after, that the more populous North and West would dominate the federal government in perpetuity.

In the words of Mary Church Terrell, the white South engaged in "frantic, hysterical efforts to hold in perpetual subjection a heavily handicapped race and to coerce others into adopting their standards of conduct and accepting their views."[43] A Freedmen's Bureau agent phrased it more mildly when he reported that in his district, whites were "smarting under a lost sense of mastery."[44] Living more separately than ever before, Black and white southerners increasingly, in a particularly apt phrase from Edward Ayers, "feared each other with the fear of ignorance" as they "faced each other across an ever-widening chasm."[45]

In the wake of the Civil War, whites invented a crisis, merging their belief in the animalistic impulses and lack of self-control in Blacks with the power of a tale of women endangered, a combination that made the extremities of white reaction appear—at least to anyone capable or willing or eager to believe this tale they spun—to be defensive rather than brutal, in the service of civilization rather than racist murder.[46] The white view of the Black population as, in the words of Thomas Nelson Page, "a vast sluggish mass of uncooled lava . . . apparently harmless, but beneath its surface smolder fires which may at any time burst forth unexpectedly and spread desolation all around" has, of course, rather dramatic implications on policing, the criminal code, and the methods of appropriate punishment.[47] The degree to which African Americans were punished, whites came to believe, was due to the degree to which they showed themselves, when free of white authority, to be without any control at all.

Prompting particular fear were vagrants: African American strangers to a community, moving through with no known past and no whites to vouch for them. Post–Civil War mobility made this a possibility new to whites, and they, leery of any Blacks acting free, were particularly concerned by unknown Blacks in their midst. These transient African American men were disproportionately targeted for lynchings, and southern states fostered a series of vagrancy laws to try to control them. Local African Americans could find these vagrants of concern as well: loose cannons introduced into the midst of their own communities' sensitive race relations.[48]

Before Reconstruction, southern whites created punishments to suit not just the crime but also the race of the perpetrator. In this new, post–Fourteenth Amendment era of Blacks with citizenship rights, how does one punish a beast? The most extreme southern race-baiters had rather extraordinary things to say about the combination of Black savagery with white law, such as the following:

> He acts under the law of his phylogeny of millions of years, which is brutality and force, while living under a civilized government, by whose laws he must be tried and punished. Incapable from the limitation imposed upon him by his Creator to make a weapon better than a club, he here avails himself of the white man's inventions; refuses to accept the hoe and plow, and arms himself with razors, pistols and guns and prowls through the woods to murder the white man, to rape white women, burglarize dwellings, burn barns, and steal, knowing that he will be harbored and protected by his own race, and if caught, will be protected by military force and tried by the most humane laws.[49]

Most whites did not frame the case so horribly, perhaps, but for many, prison was not the solution for Black crime. In the antebellum era, prisons were for whites; Blacks were an economic commodity, and having them lie fallow in prison rather than earning for their owner made no sense. Slave punishment, then, tended to be physical (whipping, say) or extreme: death or, given the economics of the matter, sale and transportation out of the state.[50]

After the Civil War, it still made little sense to many whites to have Blacks sitting around being fed out of the public coffers, particularly when those coffers were barren in debt-ridden, postwar southern states. The convict lease system took care of the funding and the get-them-working elements of this problem, and for many crimes, this was the direction in which southern states moved. For major crimes, it was prison, or it was death. The laws no longer referenced race, but the legal system nevertheless did: "From the letter of our statutes, a stranger might justifiably infer that they applied to all persons within the state, without regard to race, color or previous condition of servitude, but nothing is farther from the truth. The judges, lawyers, and jurors all know that some of our laws are intended to be enforced against everybody, while others are to be enforced against the white people and others are to be enforced only against the negroes."[51]

Punishment was particularly important for Black miscreants, whites seemed to believe, because other impulses to restrain criminal instincts in African American communities were completely absent: they had no respect for the law. Look at how they shelter criminals rather than aiding in their arrests, they would say. This conveniently (for whites) shifted blame onto the Black community for any extremities that the police (or mobs) might need to engage in: "If a white man commits a crime, all whites do not conspire to shield him and aid him in escaping the penalties of the law. If a white man is arrested, all whites do not assail the arresting officers; he is left to the remedy of the law. If a white man has committed rape and murder and a mob catches and lynches him, all white men, however they deplore and denounce lawlessness, do not feel it necessary to declare the miscreant innocent and a martyr."[52] Making a comparison to a colonial experience under rebellion, one writer in 1899 emphasized how subversive this attitude was to the rule of law: "The white Caucasians of the Philippines regard a juramentado as a peculiarly fiendish criminal; many of the brown Malays regard him as a saint and emulate his deeds. The white Caucasians of Georgia regard Sam Hose as a peculiarly fiendish criminal; many of the black Africans, I fear, regard him as an innocent man and a martyr."[53]

White southern apologists tried to deploy data in service of their arguments, and some of the worst interpretations of statistics anywhere in the annals of American history can be found in the work of southern apologists defending their perspective with "facts" about Black crime. Most commonly, the statistics trotted out to "prove" the rising Black criminality in the late nineteenth century merely counted the number of prisoners by race: data showing the rise of Black incarceration since the Civil War. To give one example among dozens, according to an article in a professional journal, Black prisoners in the South numbered 6,031 in 1870; only twenty years later, the figure had more than tripled, to 19,244.[54] This was a part of a trend in the nation of deploying data to deal more scientifically with issues, and in terms of race, this was often accompanied by ties between African Americans and some inherent proclivity to crime.[55]

Some white apologists even lined up these rising Black prison populations with rising literacy rates in the late nineteenth century to argue that education was spoiling African Americans. In 1904, Thomas Nelson Page transitioned to his discussion of crime in his book on African Americans with "what have the thousands of churches and schools and colleges, maintained at the cost of more than a hundred and fifty million dollars, produced? . . . What fruits have they brought forth, of moral stamina; of character; of purity of life; of loftiness or even correctness of ideals?"[56] And from there, crime. Another stressed that an African American with education will not stay on the plantation; he hoped that they would leave the region entirely: "idle negroes soon become criminals."[57] "It is the negro who has been born since the war—the negro with the pencil behind his ear and a school-book in his hand—who has reverted to barbarism, and is guilty of this savagery" of rape.[58] Other white supremacists found it helpful to note the high rates of crime and imprisonment among Blacks in the North, where they received the most freedom and the least oversight by whites.[59] That's what freedom brings, they argued.

Why were such bad statistics so prominent in the work of white apologists? They did not need to be good.[60] Whites *wanted* to believe that the problem was not with racism or social conditions (very difficult things to deal with and elements that might implicate *them*) but rather with the Blacks themselves. These data merely needed to provide window dressing for arguments like these: "Unfortunately for the race, this depressing view [William Hannibal Thomas's horrific portrait of African American character] is borne out by the increase of crime among them; by the increase of superstition, with its Black trail of unnamable immorality and vice; by the homicides and murders, and by the outbreak and growth of the brutal crime" of rape.[61]

African American writers fought back, emphasizing that if "in the courts they do not receive justice," then any statistics of convictions or incarcerations merely measure that injustice, not criminality. "There can be no accurate measurement of criminality without a fair dispensation of justice."[62] Further, both Black and some white commentators noted how the foreign-born-white share of prison populations in the North were even higher than that of Blacks in the South, another bit of simplistic data that undercuts the simplistic racism being deployed in these figures.[63] The fact that Blacks earn longer sentences in prison than whites for the same offenses means that their portion of the population in any state's prisons is amplified further than if one measured individual crimes committed.[64] And of rape? "Statistics show that, out of every hundred negroes who are lynched, from seventy-five to eighty-five are not even accused of this crime, and many who are accused of it are innocent," wrote Mary Church Terrell, in the only Black response to Page's 1904 series of articles that saw print in a national journal.[65] She continued by making her own observations of crime north and south, showing that in 1902, a higher rate of Chicago white men were accused of rape than were southern Black men.[66] The idea that crime and education were linked was easily countered by comparing the actual literacy rates of prisoners with the general population's, showing that prisoners were *less* literate than the overall population, not more.[67]

In addition, racism itself fosters crime. Any lawlessness among Blacks can be easily accounted for, wrote another African American observer: "With the injustice, the malice, hatred, and contempt because of color confronting him at every turn, all that is bad in the race is constantly being roused to assert itself."[68] Another presented a list of thirteen white men in Virginia convicted of rape, none of whom were given the death penalty; "just so long as the courts make such discrimination in favor of white criminals who never suffer the extreme penalty of the law, but punish with death all Negroes who are fortunate enough to escape the mob and to fall into the hands of the law, just so long will the Negro doubt the justice of courts."[69] Whites pathologized a Black man who simply stood up for himself as a man: "The qualities which in a white man would win the applause of the world," wrote Charles Chesnutt, "in a negro would be taken as the markers of savagery."[70] A Louisiana African American paper wrote that the courts of Mississippi might as well be abolished altogether: "Innocent and guilty Negroes would continue to be lynched, as usual, and white miscreants would escape as heretofore."[71]

"Nothing is easier in the United States," remarked W. E. B. Du Bois in a line that has remained true from generation to generation, "than to accuse a black man of crime."[72] Another Black editor wrote that "the concurrence of two reasons was sufficient to justify the hanging of negroes by mobs in the South; the first was that a crime had been committed, and the second that a Negro was seen in the neighborhood."[73] Editor John Mitchell could be as frank in his assessment of the situation as any southern Black man in this period. And when Thomas Nelson Page claimed in 1904 that free Blacks were now reverting to barbarism, Mitchell pulled no punches when he charged Page with throwing "history to the wind": "White men have become barbarians. Human beings have been roasted while they lived and red-hot irons forced into the quivering flesh while the mob danced to the 'music' of the howls and wails of the victims. . . . If the white man reverts to barbarism on such short notice, what should be expected of the Negro?"[74] Yet in the South after Reconstruction, these African American perspectives of race, justice, and punishment were heard only in Black communities. Blacks were speaking out, over and over. But who was listening?

For most of the region and most of this era, legislators were writing laws and juries were assigning penalties informed only by the white perceptions of race and punishment. They conformed to the constitutional requirements of race neutral phrasings of laws, but that does not imply equity. Whites, considered to be fully human by white juries, required one kind of punishment regime; Blacks, still not quite considered to be human, required a more physical form of punishment to suit their supposed brutal natures.[75] It is the penalty of death, both when legally imposed and when imposed through the horror-crime of lynching, that speaks most clearly to this issue of race and physical punishments. And regularly at the gallows, the differing stories of punishment and justice and religion, a white view and a Black one, were laid bare: "Among the people of both races the excitement was intense—the whites being gratified that the law was vindicated, and the blood of a valued and esteemed citizen avenged; while the negroes were infuriated that so many of their brethren should be thus summarily ushered into eternity for the murder of just one white man."[76]

Who Is Listening?

Storytelling is important, and it matters at least as much as the "facts" to consider who can hear those stories and who chooses to listen to them. Southerners were not merely trying to tell themselves tales, calling out to their allies in their respective white and Black echo chambers. If white southerners and Black southerners believed in different realities in terms of crime, race, and Black religion, another constituency for these arguments was important to both of them.

At the very least, the North held the potential to be a counterbalance to the overwhelming power of southern whites, and southerners of both races were very concerned about what the North would or would not do. After all, it had changed the nature of the South, radically, in the last generation and would continue to dominate the national government going forward. Both Black and white southerners tried to sway northern whites to their way of thinking on race. This was not a fair contest: white editors in the North were eager to hear from southern whites but reticent to publish anything that might disturb their predominantly white, national readership by challenging their views on race. In fiction, essays, and speeches, white southerners built connections to white readerships nationwide, pitching themselves as experts and acting as though they were social scientists. African Americans strove mightily to affect this story line in the white, mainstream press, for it was essential to the future of the race to have the nation understand what the white South was doing. As Charles Chesnutt wrote to W. E. B. Du Bois, the "thinking whites" "are after all the arbiters of our destiny."[77]

Particularly important to white southerners' success in winning over the white North were moderate voices, or, better, voices perceived to be moderate in this immoderate era. These include Virginia writer Thomas Nelson Page, author of fiction, essays, and *The Negro: The Southerner's Problem* (1904). The danger of his "moderate" views was not lost on African Americans in this era: his "pretense of fairness" and "sugared sophistries" "give him standing among liberal people, and put him in a position to do Negroes deadly harm, where [South Carolina's Ben] Tillman could not get a hearing," making Page "the most dangerous person in America to Negro rights."[78] African American editor John Mitchell thought that fire-breathing racists like Tillman or Governor Vardaman "can do us little harm," for they cause white allies to come to the defense of African Americans. "But the cool, calm, apparently fair, but still incipient attacks upon our vital political rights by men of Mr. Thomas Nelson Page's stripe tend to carry conviction to the phlegmatic northerner unless the fallacies of their argument are plainly exposed."[79] His arguments, then, are particularly telling, because to us, looking back, there is nothing at all moderate or fair in Page's arguments.

Among Page's lectures to whites across the nation in 1904: that the problem started when "the Negroes had been worked on by the ignorant or designing class" of carpetbaggers during Reconstruction, an era that was worse for the South than was the war. The Freedmen's Bureau's "enthusiasts honestly believed that they were right in always taking the side of the down-trodden Negro." The crowning error, a "national blunder," was suffrage, "infusing into the body politic a whole race just emerging from slavery." Blacks were taught by northern "doctrinaires" to aspire beyond their abilities, "and here lynching had its evil origin." "One fact, I think, cannot be soundly controverted—that the estrangement of the negro from the white race in the South is the greatest misfortune that has befallen the former in his history, not excepting his ravishment from his native land."[80] To Page, the solution to the problem was for Blacks to keep to their place; it was natural for them to do so. They had no family values (having tribal rather than family associations), and "the negro does not generally believe in the virtue of women. It is beyond his experience." Left to themselves, their situation would "closely resembl[e] a reversion to barbarism."[81]

The important element here is not that a southern apologist would write such things but how, north as well as south, whites in 1904 approved of Page's perspective, which resonated with what they apparently wanted to believe. The *New York Times* thought that Page had "wise things to say" about lynching, and, overall, the book was "a survey of the problem which interested persons (every man and woman in the South and most good Americans outside of that distressful country) should certainly find helpful."[82] *The Nation* called it "honest, kindly, and, barring a few extravagances, moderate."[83] *The Outlook* said it was a "sincere, broad-minded expression of a Southern view . . . and a hopeful interpretation of the future which Southerners face."[84] Academic reviews were likewise glowing: the *American Journal of Sociology* reviewer thought it was written with "a sanity of spirit and a painstaking thoroughness" and that the author displayed to a "remarkable degree that openness of mind and impartiality of judgment which make up so largely the scientific attitude."[85] Another academic reviewer agreed, calling the book "considerate, conservative, yet hopeful . . . probably the most sympathetic book yet written by a Southern man on this subject."[86] Page's ideas on race resonated.

Throughout this era, African Americans responded forcefully to racist arguments like these, but few white readers ever saw those responses. In African American newspapers and journals, Black writers wrote that Page was wrong: wrong about Blacks wanting "social equality" (a "demagogue's phrase"); they asked for civil and legal equality, as the Constitution requires.[87] Wrong that lynching was for rape: less than one-quarter of lynching victims were even charged with that crime, something clear from Page's own figures.[88] Wrong that respectable Blacks failed to condemn rapists and other criminals, but rather, they *also* condemned a prejudicial justice system. If we protest a case, they would say, it is due to reasonable doubt of guilt: an attempt to "uphold the sacred majesty of the law."[89] Page was "pretending to be fair and impartial" while slandering African Americans, particularly educated ones.[90]

Page, they claimed, ignored the fact that southern whites exploited race feeling for political ends for generations, deepening suspicion and distrust between the races: a fundamental part of the problem. Page also impugns the progress of the race in the last generation; instead, suffrage was one of the "wisest measures" ever instituted.[91] Page was no expert at all, for he was most familiar with the slaves of his childhood's plantation; African Americans of 1904 were strangers to him.[92] In sum, "Page owes the American public an apology" for his presumptuous, unchristian, pestiferous, and wrong "argumentum ad populum" that African Americans are unchangeably inferior. "No man is sharp enough to outwit the plain truth."[93]

Whites rarely saw any of these arguments. At least some African Americans would have seen both the arguments of whites and the responses of Blacks. Some might read the white, national periodicals, but also many of the African American responses included a reiteration of Page's arguments in order to refute them. Within the African American community, this surely served an important function of building a common sense about the racism facing them in this desperate era, as well as reinforcing the logic and strength of the arguments against that racism. "They may not have set the terms of the initial discourse" on race, wrote Khalil Gibran Muhammad on African American writers like Du Bois in this era, "but they most certainly altered it over time in unanticipated ways."[94] This was a part of a much larger effort in what Kidada Williams calls the "counter public sphere" of the Black press to offer its own narrative of race and racism. Du Bois's *Souls of Black Folk* was only the most famous example of a much larger current of cultural work in this moment circulating within Black communities.[95]

But whites, reading the white periodical press, rarely went out of their way to know the nature of (or even the existence of) African American critiques. Their understanding was shaped instead by the variety of white writers being published. Compared with Thomas Dixon or Ben Tillman, Page sounded moderate. The universe of racial commentary visible to most whites in the North as well as the South—including virtually no Black voices and yet including a wide range of extremely racist white ones—was almost entirely askew from the more inclusive universe of opinions shared with African American audiences. The common sense of each race was built out of thoroughly different contexts.

They were so different because white, northern editors made them different: African Americans tried—demanded—to be heard in the national press but were rejected, except for one 1904 essay by Mary Church Terrell. Amid a flurry of essays by Page in 1904, the magazine *McClure's* agreed to publish Terrell's response: "Lynching from a Negro Point of View." In this singular moment, a national audience had a Black perspective before them, making some of the arguments outlined above. The more common story, experienced by Terrell for the rest of her career and by other notable African American voices like W. E. B. Du Bois and Charles Chesnutt, was to have their submissions rejected by northern editors.[96]

Page published his torrent of essays in national journals with large circulations among whites both north and south: one in the *North American Review* (estimated circulation of 30,000), two in *Scribner's* (175,000), and three in *McClure's* (369,677).[97] Then the essays recirculated as a book, published prominently by Scribner's. The editors of these journals were white, and they presided over a "journalism of white experts writing for an overwhelmingly white audience."[98] They had been publishing racist and stereotypical works for generations without qualms; what gave them pause was discomfiting their white national audience with the challenging perspective from the African American point of view: "for the sake of effect we must keep the interest and friendliness of Southern readers," an editor once told Ray Stannard Baker.[99] After decades of rejection that followed her one searing article in the national press, Terrell lashed out: "Editors will accept anything which makes colored people appear ridiculous, criminal, or undesirable, but they will reject anything which shows the obstacles against which they are obliged to contend, [t]he thousand and one humiliations to which they are subjected every minute in the day and the injustices of which they are the victims at the white man's hand. . . . Anything showing that up is taboo with a vengeance."[100] In this, Page would probably tend to agree, but he would surely celebrate the fact that "the great monthly magazines . . . were not only open as never before to Southern contributors, but welcomed them as a new and valuable acquisition."[101] . . . As long as the southerners were white.

A particularly revealing moment occurred in 1907 in the wake of yet another Page essay on race in *McClure's*, a portion of which began this chapter. W. E. B. Du Bois wrote to ask for equal time, criticizing Page's "Negro propaganda" and suggesting that even the "demand from your southern circulation" did not call for such a one-sided argument. "Will you not permit the other side to be heard?" he asked bluntly. S. S. McClure eventually assented to see an article from Du Bois, who submitted "Black Social Equals" in early 1908, but *McClure's* declined to publish it, writing, "The fact is, we consider it a rather unwise thing to print."[102] What did they find from Page that was apparently "wise" to print? The "mongrelization" of America with the "specter that stands ever at the door" of rising numbers of Blacks, a "debased" and "undeveloped race," kept in check only by southern whites' "absolute belief in the superiority of the great white race" and willingness to ensure that "this superiority should be maintained by every means in our power." "Are we ready to make of the American people a negroid nation? This is the aspiration of the negro."[103]

Northern white editors denied African American authors access to their audiences, turning much of the national print media into an echo chamber for the white, southern view of race as well as for northern voices agreeing with them.[104] In an era when Ida Tarbell and others shocked Americans repeatedly with stories of the underside of Progressive America, even the editors of muckraking publications rarely critiqued the South on its racial regime.[105]

The arguments of Thomas Nelson Page and others increasingly resonated with northern editors and their white readership for many reasons. If some in the white North had compassion during and just after the Civil War for the plight of Southern Blacks, that was quickly replaced by what Nina Silber has termed "the culture of reconciliation" with its "policy of forgetfulness."[106] Northern whites had increasingly disturbing interactions with "others" in their own midst: rising numbers of rural, illiterate, and non-Protestant immigrants from southern and eastern Europe as well as, after 1898, the inhabitants of new territories to manage in the Caribbean and the Pacific. For many northern whites, keeping the sections together and healing the (white) nation was worth sacrificing African Americans.

For that matter, few northern whites were ever very interested in racial equity to begin with. With the exceptions of Quakers and Abolitionists, northern whites before the Civil War were typically uncomfortable with African Americans, thought Blackface Minstrelsy was hilarious, were fine with limits on African American rights to vote or even to move to their states, and embraced the Republican Party in part for its insistence that slavery (and therefore Blacks) would not move any farther west into territory where free men like themselves might want to move.[107] Even racial liberals in the North tended to see Blacks as culturally inferior, and most in the North were not racial liberals.[108] In various phrases from the at-least-tentatively allied-to-Blacks Freedmen's Bureau and Radical Republicans: their goal was to allow "their native character" to "determine their place in society. Their specific gravity will fix their true level." If after a fair trial the Negro "proves himself an unworthy savage and brutal wretch, condemn him, but not until then." "Give the colored man equality, not of social condition, but equality before the law, and if he proves himself the superior of the Anglo-Saxon, who can hinder him? If he falls below him, who can help it?"[109] To northern whites in the wake of the Civil War, simply granting citizenship rights to Blacks was less some sort of moral imperative than it was an experiment. It was not just southern states, after all, that were required to change their laws to be race neutral in light of the post–Civil War constitutional amendments.

Page and others provided northern whites with a compelling story that exonerated them and blamed others: despite all of the efforts of whites, and despite being given freedom, schools, and federal protection, ran this line of thinking, African Americans themselves were sinking of their own weight, finding their level in our democracy, and it was a low level.[110] This story of African Americans themselves being the cause of the "problem" resonated for many whites, for it solved an issue that had rankled. It was not a solution to any problem in race relations or any problem facing African Americans, but rather a solution to the white problem of how to justify ignoring the plight of African Americans. This was an era, after all, when the Republican Party in the South became "lily-white," when a Republican president condemned Black soldiers in Brownsville, Texas, in what one African American leader at the time called an "executive lynching," when Springfield, Illinois (Lincoln's home town), had its own race riot, and when the national Republican Party (in 1912) declined for the first time to include a plank on African American rights in its platform.[111]

Far from being supporters, northern whites were more like skeptical and distant observers of this social experiment in the South, and as the nation moved on from the Civil War, they did not become less skeptical; they did, however, become much more distant. In 1896, Frederick Hoffman, who pitched himself as a foreigner and therefore particularly objective on the issue of race in America, published *Race Traits and Tendencies of the American Negro*. Focused on the urban North, this was the first statistical portrait of African Americans since the Civil War. His conclusions surely pleased Page and other southern apologists: "In the statistics of crime and the data of illegitimacy the proof is furnished that neither religion nor education has influenced to an appreciable degree the moral progress of the race. Whatever benefit the individual colored man may have gained from the extension of religious worship and educational processes, the race as a whole has gone backwards rather than forwards."[112] The actual realities and complexities in the history of race in the South were inconvenient; in contrast, Thomas Nelson Page and other white southerners (abetted by northerners like Hoffman) were eager to provide precisely this simpler story that so many whites throughout the nation longed to hear: we tried, and they simply are not at our level.

Because whites did not want to hear even their most reasoned and well-supported arguments and because white editors in the North shut them out, African Americans trying to affect this narrative and the rhetoric of race in America largely failed, a cultural defeat in the "nadir" littered with defeats. But African Americans were persistent (and successful) in building their own counter public sphere, challenging white power within their own publications at every turn. And year by year, decade by decade, they built foundations that other generations would stand upon when the national press chose to begin to listen.

In an undated manuscript of a talk given by Mary Church Terrell long after her response to Page was published, she urged, among many other things, that no one in the race "resort to violence" but rather to "insist on justice." "I wish to urge no member of the race to play the role of Don Quixote and try to charge the fierce giant of prejudice and well entrenched power with a paper sword."[113] In this generation, in the South, such metaphors of powerlessness shot through with idealism ring true.

IT IS SURELY TRUE THAT no generation in American history has faced more changes and at a quicker pace than white and Black Southerners in the generation after 1860. Whites experienced that change as loss and as terrifying, unsure of where it would stop. The traditional understanding among whites in the South about the effect of the loss of white control was simply disaster. This was amplified by the stories they told themselves about freedom and African Americans, relating tales of Haiti devolving into child-sacrifice and cannibalism: "within fifty years the negroes had become savages."[114] As Thomas Jefferson wrote in imagining a post-slavery South: "Deep rooted prejudices entertained by the whites; ten thousand recollections, by the blacks, of the injuries they have sustained; new provocations; the real distinctions which nature has made; and many other circumstances, will divide us into parties, and produce convulsions which will probably never end but in the extermination of the one or the other race."[115] Elsewhere he wrote even more famously that slavery was like holding a "wolf by the ear and we can neither hold him, nor safely let him go. Justice is in one scale, and self-preservation in the other."[116]

With the Civil War, the North forced the white South to let go. History would now test Jefferson's theses, right here and right now in ____ County, and whites were horrified by what the culmination of this vast social, cultural, economic, and political experiment might be. The fall of the revered antebellum social structures smacked of apocalypse. Believing the antebellum way of life both natural and perhaps even ordained by God, the shifting postbellum realities were imbued with a sort of sacred panic for many.[117] In the history of the South for the next century, these core, white fears were never far from the surface, and each marginal advance of the Black race added its weight to the worry whites carried: where will this path take us?

These fears began to ebb in another generation, as white southerners rebuilt a racial system and reinforced their racial ideology in ways that won over whites in the North. In 1908, a historian from Richmond College, Samuel C. Mitchell, took something of a victory lap in the pages of the *South Atlantic Quarterly*. Titling his brief essay "The Nationalization of Southern Sentiment," he wrote that northern whites had so shifted their opinions that "the leading periodicals of the North abound in instances of a kindlier outlook upon Southern conditions," so that now "the South appears to have been placed merely at the 'bloody angle' of the far-flung battle line of racial adjustment."[118] Ray Stannard Baker agreed that the color line was moving North, where so many were tired of the effort, apparently feeling, "We have helped the Negro to liberty; we have helped to educate him; we have encouraged him to stand on his own feet. Now let's see what he can do for himself. After all he must survive or perish by his own efforts."[119]

According to Samuel Mitchell, this changing view in the North was due, in part, to its own "frictional experience" with immigrants and racial others in this era of mass immigration and empire: "It is to some the pleasing, though to others startling, fact that the Republican party, in its work of imposing the sovereignty of the United States upon eight millions of Asiatics, has changed its view in regard to the political relation of the races, and has at last virtually accepted the ideas of the South upon that subject." This was coupled with a "saner acquaintance" with southern conditions, including "the frank acknowledgement upon the part of the North of the blunder-crime of Reconstruction."[120] Less than a decade later, and in the wake of the opening of *Birth of a Nation*, the Baltimore *Afro-American* came to a similar conclusion about the North, titling an article "Southern Propagandists Are Now in the Saddle."[121]

If southern whites found solace in this story, Frederick Douglass, were he still alive in 1908 to respond to Professor Mitchell, would surely have called this sentiment out for being another example of "this old trick of misnaming things, so often displayed by Southern politicians."[122] And it was working still. But bound up with the changes Professor Mitchell triumphed over were other changes he does not choose to report: the expansion of segregation, the scourge of lynching, and the burdens of debt peonage and the convict lease system. These changes African Americans noticed, discussed, and made a part of the story they told; they are also central to the stories we tell of the South a century later.

Yet persisting in this era of Jim Crow were the voices of African Americans, in crowds of whites and Blacks, men and women, claiming the authority of God's word, and defying white notions of Black religion and criminality. The attention and authority Blacks earned at the public gallows—presided over by Black ministers from now-independent Black churches—increasingly stood out as an exception to the ways African Americans were segregated and silenced in the late nineteenth and early twentieth centuries. And these moments were regular events in the life of the South, for the region punished with the death penalty more than any other part of the nation.

How does the white southern view of Black crime and religion, echoed and promoted so effectively in the North, deal with the authority of Black religion at the gallows? The second half of the book centers on how this ideology of racism was translated into changes in punishment, and that evaluation starts with the sweeping trends in the use of capital punishment in this era.

CHAPTER FOUR

Counting the South's Legal Executions

> The negro is much more criminal as a free man than when he was a slave. . . . The negro is increasing in criminality with fearful rapidity, being one-third more criminal in 1890 than in 1880. . . . The negro is nearly three times as criminal in the Northeast, where he has not been a slave for a hundred years. . . . More than seven-tenths of the negro criminals are under thirty.
> —JAMES VARDAMAN, *Leslie's Weekly*, 1904

We count those things in the past that are countable, and that includes crimes and punishments. As above, historical actors can use such numbers ("twist" them might be more apt in this case) to prop up a weak argument. Historians likewise use numbers, and must use them cautiously, not only to avoid such prejudices and because historical data are inevitably incomplete but also because quantitative data speak eloquently only to some questions we might want to pose.

Legal executions were much more common in some eras and some parts of the nation than in others, creating trends in their numbers, but ones that have been much less often studied in terms of the South than have lynching's numbers. To date, scholarly works on the South concerning capital punishment have tended to focus their attention on the era after 1908 when southern states began to have executions under state authority; before that, every execution was under "local" (county sheriff) authority. The data are much more dependable after 1908, but this framing misses many of the trends in the history of capital punishment in the South, including its late nineteenth-century high point and how different were the punishment regimes in different areas.[1] Despite statistical study discrediting it, perhaps the most common argument in the historical literature about capital punishment in the South remains the contention that lynching was replaced by legal executions in the early twentieth century.[2] Instead, capital punishment fell after the 1890s even as lynching numbers likewise declined. This draws our attention to earlier decades, and recent additions (from Daniel Hearn and Lewis Laska) to our lists of executions exaggerate still further the importance of this earlier, nineteenth-century high point in capital punishment in the South.

Today, the South is known for its willingness to execute convicts; it is home to ten of the top fourteen states to use the death penalty since 1976.[3] In the last several generations, a majority (it has often been a vast majority) of American executions took place in the South: Texas alone had many more executions (573) from 1976 through 2021 than did all of the states outside the South together. But even without Texas, the remaining eleven states of the South likewise outpaced by a significant margin the thirty-eight states outside the region in executions since 1976. In 2020, all but one state execution in the nation were in the South; in 2021, all but three were.[4]

This is not a new phenomenon, and neither is the fact that American executions are skewed toward people of color. Racism has always been bound up in discussions of southern justice, just as it remains entwined with the discussion on the national scene to this day.[5] Four out of every five people executed in the South in the generations after the Civil War were African Americans; that is almost the proportion scholars find of African Americans among the victims of southern lynching.[6] This was no sideshow in the South's police state tasked with managing lawlessness and the underclass in the era of Jim Crow. It was a key element of that machinery of control.

This book is not a quantitative history of capital punishment in the South, but rather a study of execution days and the shift from public to private executions, and that focus pulls away from rather than toward capital punishment's numbers. Yet this chapter reveals trends that are novel and meaningful, trends that can guide our attention as we consider the qualitative evidence at the heart of this study. In particular, it reveals that our view of the South has generally misplaced capital punishment within the history of the Jim Crow police state. This chapter lays out the quantitative data of southern capital punishment as well as the flaws in those data, yielding correlations and trends that might be worth pursuing. Others may wish to take quantification further.

That may be particularly true because there are meaningful patterns here. These data point not only to the South's high volume of executions but also to the extraordinarily high number of executions of African Americans as the key element of that high volume, to how the whole nation, not just the South, had that racial skew, and to how capital punishment was most prominent early in the postwar period, slowly diminishing in the early twentieth century, just as lynching was diminishing as well. If religion at the gallows shows us how we need to reinterpret the place of executions in the South's history, this chapter explores how we need to adjust our ideas of just when and just where capital punishment was most often deployed.

The Geography of Capital Punishment in the South

The South's very high execution numbers stand out against the punishment regimes of states outside the region. But this comparison is quite complex. Several northern states—each of which, notably, had few non-white citizens—had ended capital punishment altogether by the late nineteenth century, and clearly that marks a different path in terms of punishment.[7] Others, particularly in the West, had rates of execution as high as those in the South.

Even without figuring in the South's smaller population size and even using the original Espy file data which, as we will see, dramatically undercount the region's executions, the South stands out as the most important region of the country in terms of the history of capital punishment. In the 1840s and 1850s, according to the Espy file, the South accounted for over 60 percent of all of the nation's executions despite having less than one-third of the U.S. population.[8] Philip Schwarz found evidence of 628 hangings of slaves between 1785 and 1865 in Virginia alone.[9] Even without adding in executions of whites and free Blacks, this number—more than seven executions each year—shows just how central capital punishment could be to the slave regime that precedes the period under study here (compare with table 4.3 for the postwar period).

In the 1880s and 1890s, the South executed approximately three times more convicts (relative to the region's population) than did states outside the South.[10] Overall, for the period between 1866 and 1920, executions in the twelve states of the South under consideration here, according to the original, undercounting Espy file, totaled 2,740 (table 4.1).[11] This number of executions is exceptionally high. Only seven states outside the South—all of them among the ten most populous states in the 1920 census (larger populations necessarily entail larger numbers of most things, including crimes, some of which would be capital crimes)—had more executions in this period than did Florida, the smallest southern state in terms of both population and execution numbers.[12]

A variety of forces influenced this prominent use of the death penalty in the South, including the fact that many states in the region applied capital punishment to more crimes than did states outside it, and no southern state ever abolished the death penalty—until Virginia did so in 2021.[13] Perhaps more important was the level of southern violence in general: the region had many times more murders (the crime most often earning the death penalty) than did states outside the region.[14] A contemporary study claimed that Texas

TABLE 4.1 Number of legal executions, 1866–1920, by state

State	No. of Executions		State	No. of Executions	
	Espy	+H/L		Espy	+H/L
Georgia	424	+149	North Carolina	214	+92
Texas	335	—	Arkansas	200	—
Virginia	269	+76	Kentucky	155	+9
Louisiana	260	—	Mississippi	155	—
Alabama	260	—	Tennessee	144	+25
South Carolina	228	+109	Florida	96	—

Note: The net additions from the work of Daniel Hearn and Lewis Laska (460 in total) for the six southern states they have studied are included for comparison. Espy file; Hearn and Laska.

had more murders in 1878 than did ten northern states together and that Massachusetts averaged twenty homicides a year in the 1870s, while South Carolina, with half the population, averaged five times that number.[15] If crime rates were high in this era, it follows that rates of every sort of punishment, including capital punishment, would be high as well.[16]

This trend in violent crime can go a long way to explaining the South's patterns in capital punishment use.[17] Whether one positions this violence in relationship to southern notions of honor, or in regard to racial repression, or to the prominence of Scots-Irish traditions, or to other factors, it is clear that violence in general yielded extraordinary levels of violent crime and therefore capital punishment. Bertram Wyatt-Brown reported that one observer was surprised by how *low* capital punishment rates were in the South given the widespread violence witnessed.[18] This tradition of violence found ideal circumstances to flower in the post–Civil War period: chaos and fear washing through a population that in the wake of the war had not only disrupted communities but also a superabundance of guns. Before the war, only 38 percent of murders by whites and 7 percent by Blacks were with guns; after the war, those figures were 80 percent and 57 percent, respectively.[19] With guns all around them and hundreds of thousands of young men having been trained in their use, the postwar period in the South had all the raw materials for a bloodbath.

All of this adds up to the fact that most discussions of capital punishment are discussions largely of southern history, and race plays a massive role in that fact. Whites were executed more often in the South than in other regions of the country, demonstrating that more than race was involved in this high use of the death penalty.[20] But what substantially inflates the overall execution numbers and rates for the South is the fact that a third of the South's population was African American, and African Americans were executed on an entirely different scale than whites. That was true nationwide, but as almost all African Americans lived in the South, this racially skewed use of the death penalty was, in substance, a largely southern phenomenon.

Comparing trends from different places and eras is useful, but which data should we compare? Are counts the best measure of the prominence of capital punishment? Counts are intuitive, for they are straightforward and on a human scale; that has virtue. But populations vary tremendously both over time and for different regions and states. Counts of crimes or of punishments, then, will tell us more about the size of the population and less about crime or punishment. In that way, it is helpful to compare these counts with the relative populations of these eras and regions to give a *rate* of execution, here rendered in the standardized formula of: count ÷ number of years in the period ÷ population × 100,000.[21] This rate is then comparable to other rates for different periods or states or regions. But once a formula like this is involved, the result is a number that, in itself, means nothing intuitively. The rate of 0.566 for Georgia during Reconstruction means nothing—intrinsically or commonsensically—just as an index of wages, say, that amounted to 0.566 for a given year. But an index can nicely show trends in how wages change over the course of years, eliminating inflation's impact, even if the resulting numbers are not tied to the real world. So can standardized rates like these: it is not the decimal point that is essential here, it is the ability to make fair comparisons between different places and eras.

All of the counts in this chapter, and the rates built from them, should be considered tentative, particularly those depending on the Espy file. Quantitative data need to be treated with great care in the best of circumstances, even without such dramatic undercounts as are in the Espy file. Quantitative historians are precise in their claims and careful in their assumptions; the rest of us need to follow their lead. That care and precision work against the inherent tendencies of our brains to accept "close enough" as being meaningful, as well as the very human drive to impose stories upon data to make them sensible. We need to be trained away from our instincts, for we are using brains that are "machines for jumping to conclusions."[22] Trends built from lists of executions like the Espy file are "hard data"; they are also statistics, which are as bad, according to inherited lore, as "damned lies."[23] Where we can find them in the historical record, or, more accurately, *build* them from the historical record, they yield something quite valuable: an actual measure of something in the past that can be compared with other measurable somethings.[24] We have left the anecdote behind to stand on the firmer ground of objective data. Or at least that is what it can feel like.

The picture of the numbers of southern capital punishment below is the best picture I have been able to put together given the evidence in the historical record, but there are meaningful reasons to raise cautions in terms of interpreting these data. "Given the evidence in the historical record" comes with caveats far beyond the general ones above. In their study of the Espy file, Paul Blackman and Vance McLaughlin cite every kind of error. In particular, they point to dramatic problems with the data set before the twentieth century and in terms of at least minor errors: as many as half of all entries in the file might have at least errors of spelling or with the condemned's age. It is only in terms of the most basic information (numbers of executions in states and the race of the condemned) that they believe the Espy file and supplement can be a sound basis for analysis back to the Civil War, and even such fundamental data are not assured for entries that are before then.[25] That I stumbled upon forty-two executions not in the Espy file, as well as four others listed in the file when newspapers show that the condemned was granted a respite, gives further support to the caution offered in their subtitle: "user beware."[26]

Overall, states outside the region used capital punishment less than the South, with only the West comparable to southern states (table 4.2). As newer and more complete execution lists displace the original Espy file, these comparisons might shift, but it is likely to shift in the direction of emphasizing still more how prominent capital punishment was in the South. The reason for this is that the dependability of the original Espy file has a trend itself: it includes almost all executions after the centralization of legal executions, the moment when a state eliminated hangings scattered under local (county) authority and moved executions to centralized locations under state authority.[27] Before that change (in other words, most of the era under investigation here), the Espy file can be useful, but it should be used with a great deal of caution. The shift to executing under state authority happened at different moments in different states, from the mid-nineteenth century well into the twentieth. Because the South was late in making this change compared with the North (Virginia in 1908 was the first southern state to centralize), southern executions will surely be overrepresented among executions yet to be found: the South retained local (harder to find) executions longer. Many northern and midwestern states centralized earlier and therefore will have fewer future additions.[28] In their critique of the Espy file,

Counting the South's Legal Executions 87

TABLE 4.2 Executions in regions outside the South in the 1890s

Regions	No. States	% Black Pop.	1889–99 All Executions		1889–99 African American Executions	
			No. of Exec.	No./Year/100,000	No. of Black Exec. (Black % of all)	Black No./Year/100,000
N. Eng.	6	1.0	22	0.040	0 (0)	0.000
North	3	1.9	150	0.101	27 (18)	0.961
Midwest	7	1.4	84	0.043	15 (18)	0.574
West	8	0.7	107	0.301	9 (8)	3.442
Totals	24	1.4	363	0.084	51 (14)	0.819
South	12	37	625	0.305	479 (77)	0.649

Notes: These regions are New England (ME, NH, VT, MA, RI, and CT), North (NY, PA, and NJ), Midwest (OH, IN, IL, IA, WI, MN, and MI), and trans-Mississippi, non-South, non-Territories West (CA, OR, WA, NV, MT, CO, ND, and SD). Along with fifty-one African American condemned, the Espy file lists sixty-three condemned in these states as either race "unknown" or Hispanic, Asian, or Native American. The first column is the count of executions overall and for African American condemned; the second is an annualized, per capita rate (Exec./Years/100,000 in population). For the execution of African Americans, the African American population was used. All populations are estimated for the era's midpoint (1893). Note that this figure leaves out any state formed after 1889 as well as border states to the South (DE, KS, MD, MO, and WV). Source: Espy file; Carter, *Historical Statistics*, 1:180–359.

Blackman and McLaughlin noticed this fact—they have a bar graph showing how massive were the missing executions in the South as revealed by a supplement to the Espy file—but they do not focus on the region in their analysis.[29]

New evidence only exaggerates the prominence of the South in the history of capital punishment. In particular, the recent work of Daniel Allen Hearn and Lewis Laska, who have compiled new lists of executions for a number of states, demonstrates how the problem of missing executions is not a small one.[30] As of this writing, they have listed legal executions in six southern states, and those lists vary from the Espy file substantially and irregularly (table 4.3). A startling finding is that the newly discovered executions are dramatically skewed toward African Americans, far above the "normal" skew of race in capital punishment.[31] Papers printed much more on white executions, making them much easier to find in the historical record. That prejudice clearly affected the sources: the missing execution

TABLE 4.3 Comparison of Espy and Hearn/Laska executions in counts, 1866–1920

	1866–76 Executions/Year		1877–88 Executions/Year		1889–99 Executions/Year		1900–1920 Executions/Year	
	Espy	H/L	Espy	H/L	Espy	H/L	Espy	H/L
Hearn/Laska States								
Georgia	3.82	7.00	6.5	7.5	**9.9**	**13.64**	9.29	12.19
Kentucky	1.18	1.82	3.08	3.00	**3.82**	**4.09**	3.00	3.00
N. Carolina	1.27	6.55	5.33	6.08	3.27	4.73	4.76	5.19
S. Carolina	1.73	4.54	6.00	7.17	4.73	**7.64**	4.05	5.57
Tennessee	1.73	2.45	2.66	2.92	**3.00**	**4.09**	2.86	2.95
Virginia	2.36	4.27	3.00	3.33	3.27	6.27	**8.14**	**9.00**
6 State Totals	12.09	26.64	26.58	30	28	**40.45**	32.10	37.90
Other Espy States								
Alabama	1.45	—	3.58	—	**6.73**	—	6.05	—
Arkansas	0.82	—	**5.00**	—	3.27	—	4.52	—
Florida	0.82	—	0.83	—	1.09	—	**3.10**	—
Louisiana	0.82	—	**6.08**	—	5.00	—	5.86	—
Mississippi	0.27	—	3.08	—	**4.00**	—	3.38	—
Texas	2.73	—	7.17	—	**8.73**	—	5.86	—
All 12 States	19.00		52.33		56.82		**60.86**	

Note: The high point of each state's executions is in **bold**, and low point is in underline. Espy file; Hearn and Laska.

reports in the Espy file tend to be for Black condemned. The Hearn and Laska data also offered more thorough data for executions: correcting errors in the Espy file in terms of the race of the condemned, and adding data on race where the Espy file has "unknown." The undercount of the South is, in and of itself, probably the largest source of missing information in the original Espy file, and its undercount of African American condemned is the overwhelming share of that missing information.[32] If users should beware in using the Espy file in general, these may be the two most important things to be wary of, and both involve the South.

If the previous chapter showed how the South was not alone in considering African Americans to be particularly dangerous, these data show that the

South was likewise not peculiar in targeting more African Americans for executions. The region was quite peculiar, however, in that almost all African Americans lived there. Compare the rates for executing Blacks outside the South (table 4.2) with those for southern states (table 4.6). The Midwest rates are a little lower than most southern states, but rates in the North are comparable to southern states that executed African Americans the most, and rates in the West are about three times higher than any southern state in the 1890s. But other comparisons are as important: among these twenty-four states outside the South, fully half had zero executions of African Americans at all between 1889 and 1899.[33] The other half? They had rates above the average in the South.[34]

Racism was not restricted to the South, but it is also true that communities outside the South in this era had very few African Americans, and most of them of recent migration; that might also have consequences. The statewide population figures for African Americans in the 1890s outside the South ranged from merely in the hundreds for some New England and western states to approaching or surpassing 100,000 in the largest urbanized states of the North and Midwest. These smaller communities, in many cases, were of recent migrants from the South. In such situations, it makes sense to consider how imperiled such migrants would have been, lacking not just the support of a large African American community but also white allies who might vouch for any Black man accused of crime. A larger percentage of Blacks in the North or West than in the South would be considered "outsiders," and the more marginalized a person was in a community, the more likely that person was to receive a stiff punishment. This is a dynamic true for immigrant communities (foreign-born whites were punished in numbers comparable to African Americans in the North) as well as for racial "outsiders." Most northern Blacks were as marginalized a population as the North had.[35] This was surely the experience of many African Americans throughout the nation who got into trouble in this era, for it would be trouble in a very white world, one that increasingly agreed with southern racist attitudes.

Southern states varied broadly, and that in itself is essential to keep in mind. Some have twice (or more) the rates of execution as others for a given period (table 4.4); a single state can have twice (or more) the rate in one period compared with another period. There are many ways to read these lists of rates for southern states, and it is difficult to discern what might be a meaningful correlation, if any. The states we have the best data for (the Hearn and Laska states) are disproportionately settled (the colonial states) and the northern tier of the South. The South's frontier in the late nineteenth century was Florida and the trans-Mississippi states for the most part; none of them

TABLE 4.4 Comparison of Espy and Hearn/Laska executions in rates, 1866–1920

	1866–76		1877–88		1889–99		1900–1920	
	Exec./Year/100,000		Exec./Year/100,000		Exec./Year/100,000		Exec./Year/100,000	
	Espy	H/L	Espy	H/L	Espy	H/L	Espy	H/L
Hearn/Laska States								
Georgia	0.313	0.574	0.406	0.468	**0.508**	**0.699**	0.356	0.467
Kentucky	0.087	0.134	0.182	0.177	**0.196**	**0.210**	0.131	0.131
N. Carolina	0.115	**0.593**	**0.370**	0.421	0.192	0.278	0.216	0.235
S. Carolina	0.235	0.619	**0.584**	**0.698**	0.391	0.632	0.267	0.368
Tennessee	0.134	0.191	**0.168**	0.184	0.163	**0.222**	0.131	0.135
Virginia	0.189	0.341	0.195	0.216	0.191	0.366	**0.393**	**0.437**
6 State Totals	0.173	0.381	**0.299**	0.337	0.270	**0.390**	0.249	0.295
% Change	—	—	+73%	−11%	−10%	+16%	−8%	−24%
Other Espy States								
Alabama	0.142	—	0.273	—	**0.418**	—	0.283	—
Arkansas	0.158	—	**0.576**	—	0.277	—	0.287	—
Florida	**0.418**	—	0.284	—	0.252	—	0.411	—
Louisiana	0.109	—	**0.624**	—	**0.418**	—	0.354	—
Mississippi	0.032	—	0.265	—	**0.292**	—	0.188	—
Texas	0.304	—	**0.417**	—	0.352	—	0.150	—
All 12 States	0.170	—	**0.344**	—	0.305	—	0.246	—
% Change	—	—	+102%	—	−11%	—	−19%	—

Notes: The high point of each state's executions is in **bold**, and low point is in underline. These are annualized, per capita rates (Exec./Year/100,000) using the estimated population for the midpoint of each period (1871, 1882, 1893, 1910). Espy file; Hearn and Laska; Carter, *Historical Statistics*, 1:180–359.

TABLE 4.5 Overall and African American counts and rates of 1890s executions in Virginia and Georgia

Virginia	% of Pop. African American	Hearn Data			
		Total (Black)	Rate (Black)	New (Black)	% of Additions
SW Mountain	13	13 (7)	0.35 (1.48)	6 (4)	86
Shenandoah	16	3 (3)	0.17 (1.13)	1 (1)	33
Piedmont	42	10 (10)	0.30 (0.74)	4 (4)	67
Southside	50	20 (17)	0.46 (0.81)	10 (9)	100
Tidewater	50	24 (22)	0.41 (0.76)	14 (14)	140
Total VA	38	70 (59)	0.37 (0.83)	35 (32)	100

Georgia	% of Pop. African American	Hearn Data			
		Total (Black)	Rate (Black)	New (Black)	% of Additions
Mountain	9	7 (4)	0.43 (2.65)	1 (0)	17
Upr. Piedmont	29	20 (13)	0.39 (0.88)	3 (3)	18
Cotton Belt	62	64 (58)	0.66 (0.97)	22 (21)	52
South Georgia	43	43 (42)	1.08 (2.43)	12 (12)	39
Coastal	62	16 (16)	1.35 (2.20)	3 (3)	23
Total GA	47	150 (133)	0.70 (1.33)	41 (39)	38

Notes: This table gives a sense of how diverse each state was in terms of capital punishment. The column "new (Black)" refers to those executions in Hearn's registries that were not in Espy; "% of Additions" shows how much these additional (Hearn) executions shift the Espy file's numbers. Espy file; Hearn, *Georgia*; Hearn, *Virginia*; Twelfth U.S. Census, 1900, 1:533–34, 561–62.

have the more complete data that Hearn and Laska offer. Less settled areas tend to have a different relationship to law and order and punishment, so this could prove very important as we get better lists for these areas, particularly since the Espy file's (incomplete) numbers for those states yield high rates of execution already.[36]

Using the intrastate regions Fitzhugh Brundage introduced in his study of lynching for Virginia and Georgia, executions in the 1890s occurred throughout each state, but chiefly in areas with larger populations and particularly higher populations of African Americans (table 4.5). The mountain regions of both states had only 23 of the 220 executions Daniel Hearn found from 1889–99 in those two states. But those regions had execution *rates* for African Americans (which consider their much smaller populations in these areas) as high or higher than any others in these states: perhaps analogous to the rates in northern states being so high with few executions and such small populations. Notable in the other direction are the lower rates of execution for Blacks in Georgia's Cotton Belt and Virginia's Tidewater and Southside regions, where African American populations were much larger.[37]

How exceptional was the South in terms of its punishment regime and African Americans? In terms of legal execution, the whole nation in the late nineteenth century tended to execute Blacks at an entirely different scale than whites.[38] It seems particularly important to note that this was true in *every way*: within each intrastate region in Georgia and Virginia, within each state in the South, and within each region of the nation (save New England), African Americans were executed at a much higher rate than whites.[39] This points to a shared heritage in the racism of punishment that was not just expressed in an ideology shared broadly by whites across the nation but also put into practice in actual hangings.

But the distinctions between the regions are still more notable. The *overall* rates of the South were so much higher (table 4.4) than those in the other regions of the nation in large part because the proportion of African Americans in those overall populations (those earning the death penalty at a radically different scale) was low in the North, Midwest, and West (14 percent of those executed, enough to nudge the overall execution rate up a bit) and high in the South (77 percent of those executed, enough to shape that overall rate).[40] The disproportionate use of the noose for African Americans is *evident* in the numbers from throughout the nation, but it *defines* the numbers for the South.

If the whole nation had a racial skew in executions, the simple fact is that almost all African Americans to die legally from the noose did so in the South. The fifty-one executions of African Americans in the 1890s that the Espy file lists collectively for the twenty-four states outside the South are fewer than the executions of Blacks in Georgia or Texas or Alabama alone in that decade. There are *counties* in the South with more executions of Blacks in the 1890s (e.g., Savannah's Chatham County, with eleven) than most northern or western *states*.[41] That is illuminating too. Perhaps the best way to consider this is that the North had a punishment regime constructed with white criminals in mind and with racism skewing the experience of Black culprits within that system. In contrast, the South had a punishment regime designed with African Americans in mind.

Southern Capital Punishment over Time

Fifty-five years is a long span of time, and it is helpful to break out these numbers into different periods for comparison. The periodization used in this study has been shaped to capture two eras of extraordinary violence: Reconstruction and the 1890s.[42] In counts (table 4.3), the twelve states of the South, as represented in the Espy file, have rising numbers of executions in each period: more than doubling from a low point in Reconstruction to the era of reconquest (1877–88), and rising slowly thereafter in the violent 1890s and in the early twentieth century.

The additions to the Espy file from Hearn and Laska change this pattern.[43] There are relatively fewer additions in these new lists for the twentieth century, but a tremendous number in two nineteenth-century periods (and 460 new executions overall in these six states), including a more than doubling of the number of executions over the Espy file's Reconstruction tally. These additions are important in their sheer scale but also in how they shift our understanding of the pattern of capital punishment over time, particularly when solving for population by devising rates (table 4.4). Instead of a rise before a steady, long-term decline, as with the older Espy data, the trend in Hearn and Laska's lists is of consistent use of capital punishment throughout the last half of the nineteenth century, then falling sharply in the twentieth century, a fall even more steep than in the Espy file.

The most striking element of these charts (and least surprising) is how the rates of execution for African Americans are so much higher than the overall rates (table 4.6). This racial skew in the death penalty grew over time, it appears, but barely; it was already very high. In Reconstruction, 82 percent of those legally executed in the South were African Americans, according to Hearn and Laska; by the 1900s, that proportion rose slightly to 86 percent. The African American share of the additions and corrections to the Espy file from Hearn and Laska are absurdly high for all four periods: 89 percent of the net additions to the Reconstruction era, 112 percent in reconquest, 97 percent in the 1890s, and 103 percent in the early twentieth century.[44] In this period, the population of the South more than doubled, African Americans were increasingly leaving the region, and therefore the percentage of Blacks in the South's population fell with every census: just under 40 percent of the population of the South in 1860, African Americans accounted for just

	1866–76 Black Exec./ Year/100,000		1877–88 Black Exec./ Year/100,000		1889–99 Black Exec./ Year/100,000		1900–1920 Black Exec./ Year/100,000	
	Espy	H/L	Espy	H/L	Espy	H/L	Espy	H/L
Hearn/Laska States								
Georgia	0.549	1.082	0.621	0.871	**0.927**	**1.326**	0.674	0.912
Kentucky	0.320	0.440	0.585	0.638	**0.799**	**0.832**	0.746	0.764
N. Carolina	0.157	**1.233**	**0.822**	1.083	0.360	0.611	0.539	0.628
S. Carolina	0.335	0.920	**0.858**	**1.127**	0.583	1.014	0.444	0.627
Tennessee	0.165	0.358	0.408	0.512	0.428	**0.633**	**0.433**	0.443
Virginia	0.329	0.710	0.329	0.403	0.396	0.834	**1.022**	**1.164**
6 State Totals	0.329	0.844	0.613	0.732	0.598	**0.934**	**0.638**	0.784
% Change	—	—	+86%	−13%	−2%	+28%	+7%	−16%
Other Espy States								
Alabama	0.261	—	0.501	—	**0.842**	—	0.587	—
Arkansas	0.347	—	**1.339**	—	0.641	—	0.731	—
Florida	0.573	—	0.619	—	0.539	—	**0.802**	—
Louisiana	0.145	—	**1.069**	—	0.682	—	0.560	—
Mississippi	0.039	—	0.399	—	0.402	—	0.259	—
Texas	0.408	—	0.990	—	**1.102**	—	0.587	—
All 12 States	0.285	—	**0.672**	—	0.649	—	0.586	—
% Change	—	—	+136%	—	−3%	—	−10%	—

Notes: The high point of each state is in **bold**, and low point is in underline. These are annualized, per capita rates (Exec./Year/100,000) using the count of Black condemned and the estimated Black population for the midpoint of each period (1871, 1882, 1893, 1910). Espy file; Hearn and Laska; Carter, *Historical Statistics*, 1:180–359.

over 30 percent of the region's population by 1920.⁴⁵ A declining share of all demographic statistics might be expected to follow this steady downward trend, including crime and punishment statistics; instead, there was a slight growth in their share of those condemned to the legal gallows.

That is a growth in the Black share of executions despite their rate of execution falling; this is explained by the even steeper fall of executions for whites in this era (table 4.7). By the 1900s, the white rate of execution in the South in Hearn and Laska states was almost half that in the reconquest era. In every column, African Americans were executed more, but the amount differed: the Black rate was roughly eight times the white rate in Reconstruction and in the 1890s; six times the white rate in reconquest; and twelve times the white rate in the early twentieth century. In the Reconstruction era, the Carolinas had executions rates for whites more than twice that of Kentucky; it may be important that the former had Republican reconstruction regimes and the latter did not.

After the Civil War and despite all of the changes wrought in the laws of Southern states in the wake of the war, the rates of capital punishment returned to something like the rates the South had in the 1850s.⁴⁶ This trend was not just in executions overall: as table 4.6 shows, executions of African Americans likewise remained high throughout this period. In a parallel development, this era witnessed a transformation in other means of punishment to expand the tools of control over the underclass even as slavery's punishments were eradicated. This included the transformation of prisons from mostly white punishing institutions before the war to mostly African American ones after, as well as the invention and elaboration of the convict lease system in states throughout the South along with the new vagrancy laws that fed that system.⁴⁷

These patterns in the tables over time are worth some consideration. The reconquest era is considered a low point (or at least a lo*wer* point) in terms of racial violence like lynching when compared with the chaotic and pervasive violence of Reconstruction or to the lynchings of the 1890s. One might expect a low point in capital punishment in that era as well, particularly considering the fact that crime tends to rise during economic downturns, and the nation was in a severe depression in the 1870s and again in the 1890s. In fact, these two decades of depression were the high points of violent crime in the era and the two periods with the most new executions found by Hearn and Laska.⁴⁸ Despite these dramatic improvements in the execution lists, Reconstruction will continue to be the era most likely to continue to have missing information on hangings. With so much violence and disorder in

	1866–76 White Exec./ Year/100,000		1877–88 White Exec./ Year/100,000		1889–99 White Exec./ Year/100,000		1900–1920 White Exec./ Year/100,000	
	Espy	H/L	Espy	H/L	Espy	H/L	Espy	H/L
Hearn/Laska States								
Georgia	0.127	0.127	0.171	0.203	0.088	0.149	0.083	0.103
Kentucky	0.044	0.067	0.096	0.109	0.087	**0.109**	0.047	0.049
N. Carolina	0.048	0.191	0.070	0.090	0.065	0.106	0.057	0.057
S. Carolina	0.056	0.167	0.179	0.157	0.093	0.093	0.049	0.049
Tennessee	**0.078**	0.087	0.054	**0.093**	0.046	0.091	0.048	0.050
Virginia	0.046	0.069	0.100	0.120	0.076	0.085	0.092	0.085
6 State Totals	0.065	0.106	0.101	0.122	0.074	0.106	0.062	0.065
% Change	—	—	+55	+15%	−27%	−13%	−16	−39%
Other Espy States								
Alabama	0.016	—	0.052	—	**0.072**	—	0.054	—
Arkansas	0.022	—	0.071	—	0.032	—	**0.089**	—
Florida	**0.248**	—	0	—	0	—	0.124	—
Louisiana	0.067	—	**0.134**	—	0.149	—	0.098	—
Mississippi	0	—	0.074	—	0.063	—	**0.088**	—
Texas	0.093	—	0.111	—	**0.145**	—	0.028	—
All 12 States	0.061	—	**0.095**	—	0.084	—	0.062	—
% Change	—	—	+56%	—	−12%	—	−26%	—

Notes: The high point of each state is in **bold**, and low point is in underline. These are annualized, per capita rates (Exec./Year/100,000) using the count of white condemned and the estimated white population for the midpoint of each period (1871, 1882, 1893, 1910). Espy file; Hearn and Laska; Carter, *Historical Statistics*, 1:180–359.

general in Reconstruction, one can imagine not only that a large number of capital crimes would be committed but that the institutions of justice and punishment themselves were under considerable strain. On top of that, reliable data are more difficult to find in such an era of disorder. This was a region and era in which it was possible to have two competing police forces mobilized by two mayors claiming they were rightfully in office and engaging in running shoot-outs with each other: Richmond in the spring of 1870.[49] It was not an era conducive to the smooth operation of any judicial process, including capital ones, nor an era conducive to researchers finding easy answers.

More than one thing appears to be happening with these trends. Reconstruction and the 1890s were extraordinary moments of violence, dislocation, economic downturn, and political challenge for the South, and yet the capital punishment rates were barely higher in those decades than in the 1880s.[50] I would argue that while the rates of execution were relatively stable throughout the late nineteenth century, that fact obscures significant changes in punishment in the South. In the reconquest era, the economy had improved and rates of violent crime fell abruptly (in some parts of the South falling by one-third to one-half), both dynamics that might lower crime and therefore the use of capital punishment.[51] But many other things were changing in terms of crime and punishment in the region at just this moment. White Democrats were now again in control of the South in every meaningful way, and they expanded the reach of the death penalty, among other things. Murder was the crime that earned the most executions, and it was a capital crime throughout the period in all southern states (save Tennessee's five-year experiment with ending capital punishment for murder in the 1910s). But in some southern states, rape was not a capital offense during Reconstruction, but within two years of taking these states back, southern Democrats made it a crime earning the death penalty; some states added attempted rape to their capital crimes as well in the coming years.

At least as important, juries, judges, and prosecutors changed their nature in the South with reconquest. Juries regularly included African Americans in Reconstruction, but after 1880, that occurrence was rare enough to earn comment. In that year, the U.S. Supreme Court affirmed that the Fourteenth Amendment to the Constitution and other federal legislation outlawed official state action to discriminate against Blacks in selecting jury pools and juries, but only if it could be proven that Blacks were *intentionally* excluded; otherwise, the assumption would be that it was a fair selection.[52] The court decided that an all-white jury, grand jury, or even the wider jury pool did not, in itself, constitute evidence of discrimination.[53] If the set of decisions handed down in 1880 prohibited statutory discrimination, their chief effect was to give ample room for racial prejudice to flourish more informally in the practice of selecting juries.[54]

Judges and prosecutors in Reconstruction would have been appointed by Republicans, but with reconquest, it was rare for African American defendants to have allies overseeing trials. This was part of a wholesale set of shifts in southern justice: many infractions would be tried in courts without juries at all, the already rare circumstance of Blacks being on a police force was ended, and the phrasings chosen for constitutionally mandated color-blind legal wordings, "with due regard being had to the nature and circumstances of the offense," for instance, allowed for a continuation of punishment based on who the accused was rather than the evidence of that person's offense.[55]

Regaining white conservative control over every lever of power in the South seems to have also have influenced more whites to refrain from mob action, allowing more accused criminals to wend their way through a justice system that was now clearly again under the control of white Democrats rather than wresting them from the Republican-controlled judicial process via lynching.[56] It is unclear just how prejudiced against whites any court or Republican judge might have been during Reconstruction, but the historical record is clear that white Democrats made injustice against whites one of the charges against Republican governments throughout the South.[57] With reconquest, the whole judicial process was back in the hands of white conservatives.

As with any correlations, none of these contexts can be verified to have affected southern execution rates, but the many layers of changes in the use of legal, lethal force in this era are surely important to consider. It makes sense that if Reconstruction's chaos, coupled with the economic panic of the 1870s, created one set of circumstances to promote more violent crime and therefore more capital cases, in the period when those dynamics subsided precipitously, the South had another series of dynamics that kept capital punishment rates as high as they remained. For that reconquest period, those dynamics were removing Blacks from juries, removing Republican allies from judgeships and other positions of authority, fewer extralegal hangings taking accused criminals out of the system, and revised laws to increase the number of capital crimes.

Our best data (Hearn and Laksa) demonstrate a rise in the execution rate for the 1890s: for their six states, at least, the rate rose 16 percent over that of the reconquest era (tables 4.4 and 4.6). The 1890s were complex, with political challenges of populism, the deepest depression in American history to this point, and a tremendous number of lynchings in the South. It also appears to include the vigorous use of the legal death penalty as well. If the Hearn and Laska data hold for the rest of the South, this would be the high point of executions at least in the postwar history of the region.

Note in particular the capital punishment rate for African Americans (table 4.6) in Virginia in reconquest and in 1890s North Carolina: both are the lowest rate for each respective state. These states had innovative biracial challenges to white Democratic rule in those decades: the Readjuster movement in Virginia in the early 1880s and the fusion ticket in North Carolina in the 1890s. These might be the most successful political challenges to conservative Democrats in all of the South in the generations after the Civil War, and each resulted in regimes putting allies of African Americans into judgeships as well as being in control of who was prosecuted and with what charges. That each of these moments was also a low point in these states in the use of capital punishment against African Americans (and, also striking, *not* the low point for whites: table 4.7 shows higher rates for whites in these periods, in fact) at least seems an intriguing correlation worthy of more study.[58]

MUCH OF THE STORY of capital punishment in the South in this era is apart from its numbers, but several conclusions can be drawn here. The most important is the very large volume of executions in the South, and that we are in the midst of a transformation of our understanding of that scale. Blackman and McLaughlin wrote that the Espy file could be depended on in the last 150 years at least for some of its data on executions. But the new data from Hearn and Laska show how essential it will be to expand, revise, and correct the Espy file for the South, especially for the era before the twentieth century. Until executions were performed under state authority, the Espy file should be understood to contain perhaps two-thirds of the South's capital punishment.

The only trend from the Espy numbers that appears safe in terms of our new execution lists is the twentieth-century decline. In both Espy data and the new lists, the first two decades of the twentieth century witnessed a significant drop in the rate of executions, an era in which lynching rates (and counts) were likewise declining.[59] The new numbers from Hearn and Laska show rates of execution falling 24 percent overall from the 1890s to the first decades of the twentieth century.

These new data pull our attention back into the nineteenth century in terms of the southern history of the death penalty, the period when executions were local and public and religious; the period when states were most active in trying to change those things. The region's startling amount of violence overall is key to this era, but so too are a range of shifts in the nature and use of capital punishment during and after Reconstruction as the South amended its laws in the wake of the changes the war wrought. In this, the period of reconquest between eras of tremendous violence is as interesting as any other period.

Note how any semblance of protection for African Americans appears to have mattered. Virginia in the 1880s with the Readjuster Party in power, North Carolina in the 1890s with its fusion coalition in power, and most areas of Georgia and Virginia with larger populations of African Americans: in all three cases, the rates of capital punishment were lower than in other times and other places. The more marginal the proportion of the African American populations (within the regions of states in the South and also outside the South), the higher the rates.

Perhaps the most fundamental question about numbers in this sort of historical inquiry is, what are we looking for? The execution of a man *means* what, in and of itself? Or, better, the range of possible meanings of each execution is huge: broad enough to draw into question any particular generalization about the nature of these events. An execution, for example, could function within a community as just or as unjust, and it could be seen in religious terms (and as teaching more than one religious lesson), as punishment well deserved, as the act of a prejudiced, white-controlled state, or as a crime itself: a state-sponsored murder. It could be public or behind walls, on a local courthouse lawn or involving an electric dynamo in the bowels of a distant state prison. Another execution, in another moment and in another community, might be different in every one of these ways. These individual moments are not interchangeable. They are not merely "one execution" that can be easily and simply added to or compared with another "one execution," at least in terms of their cultural meanings. That poses quite a fundamental problem for quantification.

More, the impact of any particular execution could be quite distinct on different individuals and populations, each of which might be important to understand. We might want to know what *effect* a (lynching or) legal execution of an African American man, say, had upon the local Black population. Or we might want to know about its effect on the *white* population: did the (lynching or) execution sate the desire within the white community to address whites' fears through violence, "teaching a lesson"? Or was this particular execution unsatisfying in those terms, leaving whites feeling the need to, more forcefully, reinscribe the violent boundaries of white supremacy in this community? These are all, of course, very distinct questions, yet all are important to considering how an execution (or a lynching) acted within southern society, its function, its effect. None of these questions are particularly aided by counting, nor are they revealed by the resulting trends.

Yet numbers are essential. The specific numbers are not as important to this particular study of execution events as are how they differed over time and space, how they might be incomplete, and how they can foster further questions to consider. I am confident that almost every number presented in this book is imprecise, in fact (as are most historical numbers). But that in no way means they are irrelevant or unhelpful: the best numbers we can find at any given moment can point us toward further issues to investigate. Here, they point to the high point of executions being in the late nineteenth century, centering our attention on that era, and on the wide diversity of intensity in its use: in terms of race, in terms of states and regions within them, in terms of different eras over time. The South did not have one static punishment regime; in different places and eras, the rate of execution could be several times that of other places and other eras. In particular, the numbers of executions likewise draw our attention to distinctions between settled and frontier areas: the West in terms of the nation, and the high rates that even the (surely incomplete) Espy file numbers suggest for Florida, Texas, and other trans-Mississippi states. These are important ways the quantitative study of capital punishment can orient us toward issues and areas to investigate, and they are issues this study keeps in play. Other historians with more experience with (and faith in) quantitative methods will take this discussion of numbers further. I look forward to their work.

This huge number of executions—the most in the nation, the most in the postwar history of the region—meant that more than once a week (on average) for generations, someone was legally executed in the South: a steady, constant exercise of state power. These moments were not just scenes with a noose and the punishing hand of a southern sheriff; they were also scenes of sanctification. Except, on rare occasions, when the scenes at the scaffold were uncivil, an exception to the norms and trends for the region. It is important to take up those uncivil and exceptional moments, for they too have lessons to teach.

CHAPTER FIVE

Uncivil Executions

> It was all the soldiers could do to keep back the crowd of people and get room enough for the officers to execute the prisoner. . . . When the prisoner admitted it and confessed his guilt [to rape] the people began to clamor for his blood and life. Nothing but the prompt action of Judge Bugg and his assurance to the people that there would be no delay in the law prevented the prisoner's lynching.
>
> —*Louisville Courier-Journal*, 1 August 1906

No one in the South ever said of the uncivil executions explored in this chapter the words so common to the religious exercises at the scaffold: "as usual" or "of course." These were the legal executions out of keeping, the ones betraying the norms.

Yet if these executions were in no way representative, they remain illuminating, just in a different way, for these disruptive or violent executions held an outsized place in the culture of their moment as well as leaving a larger trail through the historical record than did more typical execution exercises. They tended to be the legal executions referenced later in memoirs or made note of by local historians, and they made much more of a splash in the press at the time; they were also most likely to earn national rather than just local attention. In a few cases, they inspired legislators to change the laws of capital punishment, and this chapter begins the work of showing how southern executions changed over time. Because of this prominence in the historical record, these uncivil executions hold a similarly prominent place in the historical scholarship: the ones we have most noticed. Some, in truth, were little short of legal niceties framing what was essentially a lynching, given sanction by a justice system rushing culprits through a parody of a judicial process, as in the above example. Others seem almost like a skirmish in a simmering race war. These were executions and crowds that disturbed.

It is with these reports of executions that the problem of evidence is the most acute. All told, this chapter investigates several dozen cases that have left evidence of some sort that the experience was more dominated by white crowds and that they were in some way behaving more like a mob and less like a congregation. But unlike numerical data, where we need only know that an execution occurred to be able to count it, these instances require a depth of description of the crowd and their actions that extant sources only sometimes offer. Few official records would speak to what a crowd said and did, and so it is the choices of newspaper writers and editors that define what we know in these cases.

Newspaper coverage is a very imperfect vehicle for this analysis, for many if not most executions simply were not reported with the level of detail that could reveal the mood and the action of the crowds. That in itself might be considered evidence that it was rare for anything too uncivil to occur on execution days, for newspapers lived for sensation, devoting more print to any newsworthy, readership-fostering occasion of public disorder. But it also means that this study surely misses instances when crowds behaved in a violent, disruptive, or even lynching-like manner: if a paper devoted five sentences to the execution, how much can we know about it?

If newspaper evidence might miss some executions with violent or disruptive crowds, a second flaw in the sources might cut in the other direction: that the impulse of editors to focus on sensation might, in fact, exaggerate the spirit of the crowd, giving readers an exciting story to attract them. In particular, whites interpreted the emotional religious style of African Americans as being disorderly and could therefore tar the religious elements of execution days by characterizing this style of spirituality as being an uncivil disruption of public order itself. Care is clearly required here.

This chapter offers all of the evidence I could find that goes in the opposite direction from the book's theme: it is full of examples of rough crowds and disturbing echoes to lynching. History is complex and layered, and if the most important theme in the history of public executions in the South is the civil and religious service at the scaffold, it remains true that out of the thousands of executions in more than a thousand counties of the South over two generations, other sorts of events occurred at the scaffold as well. To give context to these disorderly executions, the chapter begins with lynching, outlining trends in the nature of those events. In particular moments, execution crowds were very much like legal lynchings witnessed by mobs. As important, however, is the fact that those particular moments were few.

The Sacred and the Profane: Lynching in Comparison

This was an era of mobs. In the late nineteenth century, at the high point of capital punishment in the history of the South—the same generation when most southern states also turned away from public execution—white southerners lynched in tremendous numbers. The South witnessed more violence, in fact, than in any other region of the nation; the post–Civil War generation of southerners witnessed more violence than any other era in the South's history. African Americans of the South reaped the whirlwind as whites fought to the death (of Blacks, usually) to preserve their privilege.

Lynching stands out in this effort and has received meaningful and illuminating attention in the last thirty years from scholars of the South (and, increasingly, of the West and beyond).[1] Lynchings were akin to the brutal whippings (which could similarly end in death) of enslaved Americans by overseers and owners. Each was designed to cow not just an intransigent member of the underclass but also, by example, the whole local underclass population. Under slavery, when Black lives held cash value to local white men, this "correction" typically fell short of death, but lynchings were not unknown in that era, and capital punishment was very prominent in the South then as well as later. After emancipation, whites could, without any white man losing cash value, take this "lesson" further, even as nonlethal physical punishments like whippings became illegal.

The extralegal violent punishment of African Americans after the Civil War surely signifies weakness rather than strength in the white supremacist regime, for a strong and assured social order would not require such a chaotic form of barbarity as lynching. In frontier communities, in Reconstruction, in communities under political or economic duress, or whenever and wherever whites faced what they perceived to be a less deferential generation of "New Issue Negroes," lynching was a tool for whites to attempt to hold on to their artificially privileged position.[2] Lynching never was a thread of southern history unique to one period (or unique to the South), but rather it was a part of a wider set of racial violence tools woven into the warp and woof of a South built upon an array of legal and extralegal repressive measures from the 1600s through to the twentieth century.

Lynchings and public executions happened concurrently, but their trends do not line up in any clear or obvious way. It is even a challenge to discern the trends, for, if it is difficult to find all of the legal executions in the historical record before they were centralized under state authority, it is even more of a challenge to create a definitive list of extralegal killings. They share with legal executions all of the difficulties of finding sources, but lynchings also require the historical record to offer the information to distinguish them from simple murder. Given these challenges, it is proving difficult to determine just how many lynchings there were.[3]

At present, the best lynching lists we have start around 1880 and chart a rise to a peak in the early 1890s and a slow decline thereafter. There were more lynchings (2,672, and that number does not include Texas) than executions in that time frame, with a rate of 0.48/year/100,000 from 1882 to 1888, rising to a rate of 0.63 during the peak of the 1890s (1889–99), and thereafter falling steadily (to below 0.30) in the first two decades of the twentieth century.[4] Lynchings were slightly more skewed toward victimizing African Americans than was legal capital punishment: 88 percent of southern lynchings between 1882 and 1920 were of African Americans, according to Stewart Tolnay and E. M. Beck.[5] Of three studies exploring lynching trends all the way back to the Civil War (for small parts of the South), each found a high number of lynchings in that earlier era, higher in fact than each found in the 1890s.[6] This raises an intriguing possibility that the high point of a "lynching era" might best be located in Reconstruction rather than the 1890s, where most scholars place it.[7] Espy file numbers imply that our quantitative data on legal executions are more questionable for earlier decades, and scholars of lynching say similar things about their lists. William Carrigan observed that "lynching inventories do not become anything close to reliable until the last decade of the nineteenth century."[8]

Yet, just as in executions, a focus on counting misses much of what was important to historians in terms of mob violence. A single lynching might terrorize a Black community an order of magnitude more than another lynching (if fear were somehow quantifiable) or less than other forms of intimidation that do not leave such numbers in the historical record for us to count. The particular numbers available to us (of lynchings, of executions, or of population sizes, say) were only some of the elements of a community's experience. Other factors often fostered the terror or failed to do so: how much publicity a lynching received, how gory it was, how clearly guilty of a crime (or clearly not guilty) the victim of the lynching was, and whether the victim was an outsider to the community or one of their own. The evidence we have of Black participation in some lynch mobs is convincing that lynchings had vastly divergent impacts on the African American community: they were nothing close to equivalent experiences.[9]

In terms of this qualitative experience, mass lynchings and public executions shared an assumption that the public theater of hangings could be beneficial, albeit beneficial in different regards.[10] Both lynching and public executions could attract crowds to witness retribution against (supposed) criminals, most of whom (but not all) were African Americans. Both could be theatrical, with speeches, prayers, confessions, and audience participation.

In the aftermaths of each, spectators might clamor for relics and mementos: twigs from the tree, a bit of the rope, a view of the body. Supporters of each would claim law and order was being upheld, strengthening the community and policing the boundaries of civil society. Detractors of each would claim the event celebrated gore and disorder or even that it was criminal itself.

Lynching and public execution occurred in the South concurrently. Sam Hose was lynched in 1899, one of the most notorious lynchings in Georgia's history. Just seven years before, Georgians might have been in the crowd of six thousand that congregated to see the public hanging of Charles Johnston for murder, an execution considered orderly and legal. In fact, despite its being illegal in Georgia after 1893, public executions of three different African American men occurred within two years of the 1899 Hose lynching.[11]

If the parallels between public execution and mass lynching were many, the two differed in ways far beyond the fact that one was legal and one was not. Lynching crowds were characteristically white; public execution crowds were characteristically mixed-race, and when the condemned was African American, Blacks outnumbered whites as often as not. Sheriffs and crowds generally treated African Americans humanely in public executions; mass lynching crowds tended to dehumanize the victim, even turning them into tortured masses of flesh and bone.[12] Public execution began to be phased out in the 1880s and 1890s in favor of executions behind barriers; lynching rates seem to peak in just those years.

Most importantly, lynchings and public executions were opposites in terms of how people understood them. For African Americans, lynching was simply brutal murder, the terrifying action of bloodthirsty beasts who ushered a man to his maker not just without the protections of the law but also spiritually unprepared. At the gallows, a South Carolina man thanked the community for the trial: "giving me time to prepare for death."[13] In a religion-centered culture, this was a meaningful issue, for the state of the soul was perhaps the most important element of a devout Christian's life, and a lynching would deny him the chance to make right with God. "I might have been carried away unprepared," said one man at the (legal) gallows, "without a moment's warning. The thought makes me shudder. How grateful then I must be to Almighty God. . . . He has furnished me with the opportunity of preparing myself to appear before a higher tribunal which cannot be deceived. The many sins of my past life have been washed away."[14] In this way, a public execution could be seen as the condemned forfeiting his life—justly or unjustly, as so many early church martyrs forfeited theirs—with the hope of redemption and a new and better life in the hereafter. A lynching was among the worst sins and horrors of the age; a public execution often resembled a religious rite, complete with women and men together singing and praying for a saving grace granted this sinner before them.

For many whites, lynchings and public executions could be inversions of each other in an entirely different way. Public execution failed as an effective instrument of legal punishment, control, and racial terror. In some cases, festive or violent disorder marred the solemnity many whites believed was necessary for any lessons to be learned. More commonly, whites decried the display of what they interpreted as an African American charade of false Christian values coupled with the mock-heroism of the condemned on the public scaffold. In his 1905 article on lynching, Ray Stannard Baker reported that he "heard intelligent citizens argue that a tough negro criminal, in order to be a hero in the eyes of his people, does not mind being hanged. He is allowed to make a speech, the ministers pray over him, he confesses dramatically, and he and all his negro friends are sure that he is going straight to Paradise."[15] An editor put it this way:

> The reason why southern mobs of white men prefer to visit summary punishment on black criminals is this: the Negro with his superstitions and his weird notions of religion looks upon a legal execution as something of a social event, much as the ancient Irish are reputed to have regarded a wake. To his mind the ebony-hued murderer or rapist, black cap in place and Negro minister exhorting loudly by his side, is a creature entirely out of the ordinary—one who has achieved prominence in the public eye ordinarily denied members of the race and worthy of no little envy. But this method conveys no warning and teaches no lesson to the untutored minds of other Negroes.[16]

Lynching, in contrast, was a more effective lesson-teacher, and it was even more firmly under white control. As this white editor continued, "With a lynching it is different. The legal execution is cold-blooded and business-like; the lynching is anarchistic and the passions of men are unrestrained. The spectacle of a body swinging from a limb by the roadway carries with it a grewsomeness [sic] which Negroes for fifty miles around do not forget for a generation."[17]

This was not the only time such sentiments were expressed. "It may be necessary to impress" Blacks of the seriousness of crime, wrote another southern white editor about the failures of legal capital punishment, "through the outrage expressed in a lynching than in an orderly hanging, where, from blackened hillsides around, the man is lead [sic] to the scaffold in the midst of lamentations of hysterical negresses and the viciously sympathetic shouts of men."[18] Terror and awe were the goal, and some whites complained that even some lynchings failed to provide them: "For a time, a speedy execution by hanging was the only mode of retribution resorted to by the lynchers; then, when this failed of its purpose, a more savage method was essayed, born of a savage fury at the failure of the first, and a stern resolve to strike a deeper terror into those whom the other method had failed to awe."[19]

If religious ceremony anointed legal public executions with an element of the sacred, lynching was a profane perversion of the practice. Yet that is not how many southern whites saw it. At least when legitimized by community support and the proper decorum, a lynching could even be considered by the white community as a sacred obligation to purge society of sin. As Donald Mathews showed us, a white man in Georgia in 1899 did not see the dissonance between his yell of "Glory be to God!" and the corpse of Sam Hose, burned alive before him. For some whites, at least, lynching was a more Godly practice than was a public execution, one in keeping with white Christian ideas of the purification of the race and region.[20] In rare moments, something like that spirit infected legal executions, giving an entirely different cast to the execution experiences.

Disruptive or Violent Legal Executions

Public executions are disturbing to the modern sensibility, but many elements that might be jarring to us are signs less of incivility at the gallows than they are signs of a different sort of civility in the nineteenth century. We should be especially cautious in investing any particular significance to reports of crowds calling out and being vocally disorderly, at least if that is the only evidence of boisterous behavior. Newspapers rarely gave definition to *how* crowds were calling out, and the tendency was for the crowd to be vocal in a religious way, and for those crowds (and those vocal in the crowds) to be African Americans rather than whites: "The larger portion of the assembly was negroes. . . . When the drop went down many screams were heard from all sections of the crowd."[21] As a religious ceremony, executions that include calling out would be quite different from any sort of disorderly lynching-like behavior; almost the opposite, in fact. Since the vast majority of public executions had mixed-race crowds and religious elements, it seems most commonsensical to assume that, barring other evidence (such as referring to the calls as "cheers" or describing the calls as from whites in the crowd), references to crowds calling out would most often represent enthusiasms of a religious character.

It is likewise complicated to interpret the meaning of members of a gallows crowd gathering relics or souvenirs—a bit of the noose, a scrap of the hood—at a public hanging. Anyone who has read about racial violence in the South has a visceral response to the reports of souvenirs gathered at lynchings, and perhaps there are few reading these words who have not already read of the butchering of Sam Hose in Georgia in 1899, followed by the display in an Atlanta store of a jar containing his knuckles.[22] This grotesque element of bloodthirsty barbarism colors our understanding of any reference to souvenir-seeking. Understandably. African Americans at the time likewise saw relics of lynchings as an element of "the white savage yelling and howling in fiendish delight around a human holocaust."[23]

Yet it is unclear this is the appropriate context for interpreting the evidence we have of people desiring the relics occasionally sought in the *legal* executions of criminals, although one reference to members of a crowd clipping the fingernails of the deceased surely warrants that comparison![24] I have found a dozen instances between 1866 and 1920 of this desire on the part of at least some in a crowd; this surely misses many other such moments, for papers do not frame this sort of activity as peculiar. It is not clear how commonplace this taking mementoes was: certainly, some ropes were used many times in hangings rather than being cut up and distributed. There seems to have been an understanding that some were "good ropes" for a hanging; others broke or stretched in ways that marred the proceedings.[25] But it was common enough for crowds to want souvenirs (even if this desire was not always fulfilled) that papers reported the fact casually. Most of the reports simply mention that the noose or the hood worn by the convict—each of which might sometimes be cut into pieces to share around among the crowd—was a desired memento of this moment that was important in some way to some in the crowd. In the execution of a man condemned for murder where the crowd was as Black as it was white, "the rope that hung the negro was cut in small pieces and distributed out among the crowd, the Atlanta boys each getting a small piece."[26] The bodies of the executed could be the focus of this interest in seeing and perhaps bearing witness: some reports speak of funeral homes inundated with crowds eager to view the body after an execution.[27]

There is no pattern in the historical record in terms of which executions yielded relic seeking, and the executions of whites were as likely to include this sort of desire for mementos as the executions of Blacks. When a white lawyer in Richmond was executed in 1887 for murder, a judge had to bar a local man from displaying and selling pieces of the silken, multicolored rope used at the hanging.²⁸ "As soon as the rope was cut," reported another paper on the execution of a white man in Texas, "the crowd rushed to cut it up and save as relics."²⁹ In the execution of a white man for rape and murder, the rope "was seized upon by relic hunters who divided it into small bits, each appropriating a part."³⁰

Some executions simply seemed to invest power or meaning to the physical world around them: they were important in some way, and so the physical objects associated with them became important as well. One man, asked about his taking a piece of the rope in the hanging of a man condemned for rape, said it was for "barn protection," that he would nail it up above the barn door to discourage thieves.³¹ Another noose was taken by the son of the woman the condemned man had been accused of raping and murdering.³² Those seem rather pointed instances of relic-seeking, but in general the taking of relics was reported in a more matter-of-fact manner. In fact, in an execution of two Black brothers for murder in Tennessee in 1882, after religious services ("Do what you please with our bodies, thank God, Jesus will take care of our souls" and the hymn "I'm Going to Ride the Evening Train") and the subsequent drop, the African American minister "announced that people could purchase part of the noose, giving a contribution" to the condemned's widow and children.³³

There might be multiple explanations for why, in different circumstances, different people wanted a relic from a hanging. The simplest explanation seems to be that this desire speaks to how important these events felt to those in the crowds. Being a part of a massive crowd can itself be a powerful experience, and these public executions could be among the largest crowds ever assembled in a community. That they are imbued with religious authority and that they involve witnessing a man's death might give them still more depth or resonance for some.³⁴ Donald Mathews reflects on this kind of moment taking people out of the ordinary, a timelessness that sparks a "thrill of quasi-participation," mixing "transgression, sacrifice, punishment, death, and popular democracy."³⁵ Perhaps it was the one time in a given generation and a given county that this occurred. What seems clear is that there is little evidence from the historical record requiring us to see instances of souvenir-seeking as related to the butchery of lynching victims by impassioned mobs.

IF NEITHER CALLING OUT nor saving relics were, as a rule, very convincing evidence of disorder at the gallows, other executions clearly served as lightning rods for real or feared violence. The sheriff and other local law officers would attend all executions, but some reports emphasized the presence of extra guards, an indication of a perception, at least, of the potential for disorder or violence. Yet even here these dangerous executions came in two quite divergent types: some were in fear of white mobs; others were in fear of Black rescue. Those were very different things; interestingly, they largely happened in different eras and in different places, too.

Never was a condemned African American man on the day of execution actually rescued in this era in the South; there was apparently never even an attempt made by African Americans on the day of execution.[36] But there was a great deal of resentment in the Black community over issues of justice, and at times, authorities grew concerned that an execution might serve as a focal point for those resentments, perhaps even with an attempted rescue and violence. This could be interpreted as evidence of Black militancy; it could also be read as evidence of white fear in this era, the threat of insurrection realized.

In at least thirteen instances, state or local militia were mobilized to guard an execution from the (perceived) anger and possible reprisals of the African American community.[37] Some of the reports of these executions merely mention that a rescue was feared: "The anticipated interference with the execution on the part of a mob did not materialize," despite reports that "the negroes of Southampton and some from North Carolina would make an organized effort to stay the execution."[38] Another such report simply described the arrangement of the guards, saying "to prevent a rescue should it be attempted."[39]

In other cases, newspapers reported a tense racial situation that could sound like a standoff, or a feud, or even, as some reports called it, a race war. "The Troops Called Out to Suppress a Negro Rising" was the headline of a 1884 article on the Georgia execution of a man condemned for rape. The Albany Guards and the Jackson Light Artillery were mobilized because local Blacks "had threatened that they would rescue him if they had to kill every citizen in the city and burn the town of Dawson."[40] Similar fears of a disturbance led North Carolina's governor to send the Granville Grays to an execution in Oxford of an accused rapist/burglar.[41] In this case, the condemned's brother was in jail for having tried to torch the town three months before when he thought the condemned would be lynched. Likewise, a posse from Richmond, Arkansas, advised authorities that the condemned should not be brought to the town before the day of execution because "trouble with the Negroes was expected."[42] Even after an execution, some sheriffs took action to avoid more disorder. In Florida, a sheriff refused to send the body of an executed murderer back to his home town on the train: "This was done in order to avert any clash that might be precipitated when the bodies would be unloaded and taken out from Archer tonight."[43]

In at least a couple of cases, it was both the Black *and* the white populations that were stirred. Extra guards attended a 1907 Kentucky execution for fear of rescue, but they were at the condemned's trial for fear a white mob might take him. "Afterward there was a race war in the section, Bevier and Central City, in which the crime was committed."[44] A report of a 1907 Louisiana execution describes both a rescue fear and a mostly white crowd tearing down the enclosure at the execution that occurred just twelve days after the crime was committed, one of the executions that might be called a judicial lynching. Resentment of the death penalty given this man condemned for attempted rape boiled over into death threats sent to the judge and to the husband of the woman supposedly assaulted by the condemned. "For this reason the attendance of negroes at the execution to-day was discouraged and negro gatherings in all parts of Covington were broken up by the officers."[45]

It is worth looking at the citations for these last few paragraphs: most of these moments of feared Black rescue occurred in Reconstruction or in the early years of reconquest; only five were after 1887. In that way, this seems connected to an African American militancy possible in early postwar years, a stance that became more difficult to maintain after white supremacy consolidated its gains toward the end of the century. Even more probable, these newspaper reports measure the intensity of white fear in those early postwar decades compared with later ones, when white control was more secure. "Extreme white anxiety over sexual liaisons between white women and black men was linked to fears of black men's political and economic independence," Martha Hodes found.[46] In eras of flux in the wake of the war and in counties with Black majorities, these fears were most acute. In nine of the thirteen cases I found, the execution took place in a county with a majority Black population, a proportion of African Americans much higher than the South's average. In fact, in only two cases of feared Black rescue was the Black population in the counties below the South's average.[47]

The potential for violence at the gallows in these cases was quite unlike the sort of violence white mobs would exact upon Black victims. Instead, it was more like an anti-lynching: violence in the service of freeing a Black man from (perceived) persecution. This would be one of the deepest fears of white southerners: organized action by Blacks to confront white authority with violence, an insurrection. Such stories of Black disorder, as they have throughout the history of the South, had utility for those wanting to deploy them to political ends. Having the media emphasize this threat, then, is something we should be very cautious about interpreting: here is a place where the white press might overstate the prevalence of this problem. The timing issue seems particularly suggestive in this way: Black crowds were most often cited as of concern in early postwar decades and in counties where African Americans were disproportionately prominent, where and when they might have a greater share of power. It is essential, of course, to keep in mind that despite the white fears and the guards and the stories in newspapers, these moments of insurrection or rescue did not, in fact, occur. They were simply feared.

Actual disruptions at the gallows were reserved for white mobs. These are the ones that made the biggest splash in the media of the time and that have therefore been the most common examples of public executions in the historical literature. These were the executions gone wrong, and they tended to be for crimes that fostered absolute outrage among whites in a community. Condemned who were not lynched by mobs of frenzied whites could still face execution before large crowds, and at times those crowds behaved in ways not very far removed from the mobs at lynchings, including overwhelmingly or exclusively white crowds who were calling for blood, surging toward the gallows, or cheering when the trap was sprung.

Extra guards were often present because of a previous attempt by a mob to wrest the condemned from jail. Three companies were deployed in a Thomasville, Georgia, execution due to an attempt to lynch the condemned that ended with four men treated for bayonet wounds.[48] In one case, the march to the gallows sounded like a military maneuver: soldiers with fixed bayonets in three different groups, and "as a precautionary measure wings scouted to the left and the right of the moving flank, and 500 paces in the rear a squad of four men . . . formed the rear guard."[49] But most lynch-like behavior in the judicial system occurred not on the day of the execution—what the sources centering this study would readily reveal—but in the days and weeks before that: at the time of arrest, during incarceration awaiting trial or execution, and in the courtroom when arraigned. The Atlanta Riot of 1906, for instance, was sparked by a supposed assault on a white woman; yet, when the man condemned for this rape went to the gallows the following year, he was hanged without incident.[50] Clearly, the South had something akin to "legal lynchings," and it will be studies of courtrooms and policing that will illuminate the ways the justice system of the South could resemble mob rule much more than will the events on these execution days.

But on the execution day itself, a moment controlled quite firmly by a sheriff, guards, and often a supplementary array of troops, it was very rare to find evidence of behavior that shaded over in the direction of mobs. At least thirteen executions between 1866 and 1920 appear to have these sorts of behavior, although I suspect there were more. Importantly, every one of them was at an execution of men accused of sexual crimes, showing just how much the obsession of white southerners with this issue had the potential (in particular circumstances) to fuel a mob mentality.

Years after public executions were banned in Georgia, a Marietta hanging was before a huge crowd. At the foot of a long hill, the placement of the enclosure was designed for viewing, and the troops in place gathered to one side with their guns on the ground. On that side the wall of the enclosure was connected only by ropes to the rest of the structure, and after a call of "Look out," the ropes were cut, and the wall fell away: a prearranged plan to make the execution a public spectacle. African Americans, who lined the roads leading to the execution site, nevertheless largely stayed away from the hanging itself. The victim of the condemned man's supposed rape, however, attended, as did her family. The condemned read a psalm, confessed his crime, and as the trap fell, a man in the crowd yelled, "'Hurrah! Three cheers for Cobb County!' and a great cheer from 100 throats rent the air."[51] Other enclosures were likewise torn, if not in such an organized manner.[52]

For a handful of cases, in fact, it is even more difficult to differentiate an execution from a lynching. "It was just fifty minutes from the time the jury took the oath until the trap door fell and the negro was pronounced dead," in the execution of a man condemned for rape in Mayfield, Kentucky, in 1906, wrote the *Louisville Courier-Journal* in the article that provides this chapter's opening quotation. Two different scuffles between crowds and soldiers protecting the trial occurred that day. Some of the estimated 10,000 people in Mayfield tore down two sides of the enclosure before the prisoner ever arrived.[53] This isn't just behavior that seems lynching-*like*; it is indistinguishable from a lynching in any meaningful way.

Rarely was the speed to execution that startling, but in a number of instances, the trial was held within a week or two of the crime being committed, and the execution took place a few days later. Generally, that speed was praised rather than censured: "swift justice" or something similar adorning a headline; one was titled more explicitly in contrast to lynching: "Much Better This Way."[54] The crime was committed "on Monday last," read the headline for the execution of one accused rapist still so wounded from his capture he was carried to the gallows.[55] Another man accused of the rape and murder of

Uncivil Executions

a fifteen-year-old girl was arrested within hours of the crime in Shreveport, and twelve days later was on the gallows. In this case, it appears that the execution had several elements of lynching—this speed, plus soldiers and a crowd outside the enclosure sending up a cheer for "fully a minute" until stopped by the sheriff—*and* elements of fearing African American retaliation. The condemned's body was not allowed to go to his brother for fear "a big funeral would follow and might bring on renewed excitement and possibly a riot." In addition, masked men patrolled "negro districts of Shreveport" warning that "white men are organized, with law and order their object."[56]

This behavior was not just in the executions of African Americans: white mobs venting their anger at white condemned could be just as much like lynchings.[57] Crowds pulled at the planks of the enclosure at the conclusion of the hanging of a white man condemned for murder, forcing the guards present to commence "hammering into the crowd with the muzzles of their guns" to drive them back.[58] If in an enclosure, papers wrote of the frenzy of the crowd to be in the jail yard when whites were to be executed just as when the condemned was Black.[59] "The curtains were drawn around the condemned man and then pandemonium broke loose among the crowds in the streets. They closed in on the high board fence surrounding the scaffold until it seemed it would be wrecked. Deputy sheriffs found it necessary to draw their revolvers to force the people back. After the crowds were beaten back by the officers the execution proceeded without mishap."[60]

Other times, the guards failed to keep crowds from tearing down the enclosures: "The cry went up to tear down the fence . . . a rush was made on the enclosure and in less than a minute, the large plank fence . . . was razed to the ground, the fifty special deputies who had been sworn in being overpowered."[61] The flimsier screens (some were made of canvas) were particularly in jeopardy from the crowds. And public elements could persist after the hanging, with bodies of white condemned, as with Black, on exhibition at the courthouse (or an undertaker's establishment) after a hanging.[62] As in private executions of African Americans, buildings around a jail yard were commonly overflowing with people on roofs, in windows, and climbing walls to see the death of white condemned.[63]

Whatever the race of the condemned, when white mobs dominated the execution-day events as in these cases, the religious ceremonies tended to be foreshortened or eliminated, demonstrating how these religious ceremonies were becoming seen as conflicting with white ideals of punishment. "He made no plea for religious advice. . . . There was no indication of that religious fervor which usually buoys up a condemned negro. No half gasped exclamations of 'I am going to glory—I hope to see you all in heaven,' etc."⁶⁴ Not seeing friends in the audience, the condemned more rarely spoke up at all and when he did, spoke more briefly.

These instances of relics and calling out, of feared Black rescue and white mobs, are eye-catching: they are full of action, fear, and behavior outside of what we think of as the norms. The chief finding here is just that: these cases were both few and well outside the norm, rare instances of feared African American rescue (that did not materialize), or of white mob disorder (that did). Yet they reveal much: the stark fears of whites in the immediate postwar period, especially sensitive to the threat of Black insurrection; the importance of these moments in the lives of those who witnessed them, seeking mementos and totems; and the only unequivocal disorder, that of white mobs disrupting the proceedings, turning these crowds that so often were congregations into something more like mobs.

The Shifting Nature of Executions for Sexual Crimes

Note the dates of these instances of lynching-like execution days in the citations for the last few pages: it is striking that most of the executions that have these violent and disruptive white mobs were in the first decade of the 1900s. If fears of Black rescue tended to be in counties with large African American populations and to be early in the post–Civil War period, white mobs at the legal gallows tended to be in the early twentieth century, and they were rarely in majority-Black counties: only three of the thirteen executions I have found with lynching-like behavior at the legal gallows were in counties with more than 50 percent of the population African American.

This early twentieth-century record of white mobs at legal executions might be, at least in part, measuring a growth in the *reports* of such mobs as much as any change in the actual behavior at the gallows, for the nature of the press and reporting had shifted substantially from the norms of the previous generation. Newspapers had a four-page, print-dominated format in 1870; by 1910, many papers had doubled or tripled in size, included images, and elaborated on sensational stories over the course of days and weeks.⁶⁵ To what extent do these changes in the press reframe the coverage of execution days, following up on sides of cases that they, a generation before, would have ignored? This could include mob behaviors that more extensive coverage could more fully include.

Note how these mobs (if few in number) were increasing over time, even in the face of falling execution rates overall after the 1890s. Similarly, executions of those condemned for sexual crimes—which were the target of every one of those white mobs—were likewise rising rather than falling in this period. Evaluating a *subset* of executions—in this case, those for condemned for sexual crimes—presents an additional challenge compared with executions overall. Dealing with smaller sample sizes (roughly one-third of lynchings and one-tenth of the legal executions were for sexual crimes) makes interpretation that much more challenging and any resulting trends that much more tentative. The additional layer of information to define the subset under study can also be challenging to discover. With the lists we have of lynchings, motives are sometimes stated, sometimes a man is in jail awaiting trial for a crime, but sometimes not. And in legal executions, more rarely, some of the newspaper articles were so brief or so focused on the scene at the gallows that the crime might not be mentioned at all.[66] In addition, the charge of rape can be one of the ways that lynching "was always entangled in lies,"[67] justifying a lynching as protecting white womanhood whether or not it really was. Legal charges of rape have the same potential for falsity.[68]

With these caveats and challenges in mind, here are a few patterns at least worth further thought and study. Sexual crimes (rape and attempted rape) were the second and third most common crimes to earn the death penalty, behind murder. But some states had a peculiarly high percentage of those condemned to the death penalty who were convicted of sexual crimes. In North Carolina (23 percent), Virginia (20 percent), Kentucky (17 percent), and Texas (17 percent), a disproportionately high number of legally executed men were condemned for these crimes, while Mississippi (3 percent) was peculiarly low, followed by Alabama (8 percent). These suggest somewhat different punishment regimes in terms of sexual crimes, with some using legal execution more commonly, and some states tending to wrest these criminals out of the justice system instead.[69]

Or to incarcerate them, which was the most common penalty for men convicted of sexual crimes in the South as it was in the rest of the nation. In the 1880s, the South overall averaged approximately five legal executions each year for sexual crimes and six per year in the 1890s; the South lynched an average of twenty-two annually in the 1880s and thirty-three per year in the 1890s for sexual crimes. But Diane Sommerville found that North Carolina *alone* had almost as many African American men (an average of thirteen per year) entering the penitentiary for sexual crimes each year between 1885 and 1889, a figure that rose to fourteen per year from 1895 to 1899.[70] It is possible that something like three times more men were incarcerated in the South

TABLE 5.1 Executions and lynchings of African American men for sexual infractions in counts and rates in the 1890s

State	Executions 1889–1899 of African American Men in Counts (and Rates)	Lynchings 1889–1899 of African American Men in Counts (and Rates)
Texas	14 (0.24)	n/a
Virginia	12 (0.17)	16 (0.22)
Kentucky	4 (0.13)	24 (0.80)
Alabama	8 (0.10)	47 (0.59)
Florida	2 (0.07)	30 (1.07)
Arkansas	2 (0.06)	15 (0.42)
North Carolina	3 (0.05)	8 (0.13)
South Carolina	3 (0.04)	19 (0.24)
Tennessee	2 (0.04)	34 (0.69)
Georgia	2 (0.02)	69 (0.69)
Mississippi	2 (0.02)	65 (0.74)
Louisiana	1 (0.02)	23 (0.35)
Total for South	55 (0.07)	350 (0.47)

Notes: These are annualized, per capita rates (Exec./Years/100,000) using the estimated Black population for the midpoint for the period (1893). Texas is not included in either of these data sets on lynching. Espy file; Project HAL; Brundage, *Lynching in the New South*, 270–80; Carter, *Historical Statistics*, 1:180–359.

for sexual crimes than were — combined — legally executed and lynched for them.[71] Lisa Dorr found something similar in twentieth-century Virginia. In her study of sixty counties in that state from 1900 to 1960, she found that of 288 African American men brought to trial on the charges of rape or attempted rape, seventeen were lynched, fifty were executed legally, and 181 received prison sentences, with a majority of those sentences being less than the maximum allowed; thirty-five men had their cases dismissed or were acquitted.[72] As much as white southerners used rape as a justification for lynching, prison appears to have been the most common punishment for this crime in the South.

As death for sexual crimes was a punishment generally reserved for African Americans, it is important to figure in the populations of African Americans with these figures to better get a sense of where and when legal executions and extralegal lynchings were most prominent (table 5.1).

Kentucky stands out in particular in this regard. With a comparatively small Black population, it had extremely high rates of lynchings and legally executed: only behind Florida in lynchings, and only behind Texas and Virginia in legal executions. Florida's high rate of lynching for sexual crimes likewise stands out. Note that in 182 execution reports that stipulate the race of the rape victim from 1866 to 1920, an overwhelming 89 percent of them were white women. The death penalty was not only used chiefly against African American men in terms of sexual crimes; it was also deployed chiefly to protect white women.[73]

Although legal executions trend downward in the twentieth century overall, capital punishment for sexual crimes, instead, rises.[74] In the first two decades of the twentieth century, executions for sexual crimes in the South grew considerably over the pace of the nineteenth century, according to both the Espy file and Hearn and Laska's lists (table 5.2). In per capita terms, both lists reveal something like a 50 percent increase in executions for these crimes. But this was not consistent throughout the South: Georgia, Louisiana, North Carolina, South Carolina, Texas, and Virginia account for most of the South's executions for sexual crimes in the early twentieth century; the other six states of the South, combined, averaged only 2.4 executions per year.

For a number of states, this pattern of deploying legal executions for rape more over time might indicate a growing willingness to leave such cases to legal remedies: the high point of lynching for rape in Arkansas, for instance, was the 1880s and 1890s, dwindling thereafter as legal executions for rape rose in the early twentieth century.[75] Mississippi almost never legally executed for the crime of rape, but all of its four legal executions were after 1897. For the South as a whole, the 1890s witnessed more than twice as many lynchings for sexual infractions as did the 1910s; in executions, it was the 1910s with twice the numbers of the 1880s.[76]

How to explain the ways these executions differ from the trends overall? There are several moving parts here. Law enforcement was shifting, unevenly, in terms of how it confronted mobs. In different moments in different states, sheriffs and state militia began to guard prisoners more effectively, and states moved prisoners out of localities where passions were high in order to keep them safe awaiting trial. In this way, crimes that might have ended in a lynching in 1890 might have resulted in a legal execution in 1910 due to greater effort on the part of authorities to avoid mob law. That was not the overall pattern of the relationship between legal executions and lynchings, for statistical studies show that there was no significant substitution effect between the two.[77] But here we are considering a subset of the overall numbers: for the

TABLE 5.2 Comparison of Espy and Hearn/Laska executions for sexual crimes, 1866–1920

	1866–76 Exec./Year		1877–88 Exec./Year		1889–99 Exec./Year		1900–1920 Exec./Year	
	Espy	H/L	Espy	H/L	Espy	H/L	Espy	H/L
Hearn/Laska States								
Georgia	0.36	0.55	0.67	0.67	0.18	0.73	1.33	1.57
Kentucky	0.18	0.27	0.5	0.5	0.45	0.45	0.67	0.71
N. Carolina	0.09	1.45	1.33	1.42	0.36	1	1.48	1.57
S. Carolina	0	0	0.17	0.17	0.27	0.36	1.19	1.57
Tennessee	0	0.09	0.17	0.17	0.18	0.18	0.52	0.52
Virginia	0.27	0.64	0.17	0.42	1.09	1.73	1.81	2.05
6 State Totals	0.91	3	3	3.33	2.55	4.45	7	8
Rate	—	(0.043)	—	(0.037)	—	(0.043)	—	(0.062)
% Change in Rate				−14%		+16%		+44%
Other Espy States								
Alabama	0.09	—	0.33	—	0.73	—	0.33	—
Arkansas	0	—	0.42	—	0.18	—	0.57	—
Florida	0	—	0.17	—	0.18	—	0.29	—
Louisiana	0.09	—	0.25	—	0.18	—	1	—
Mississippi	0	—	0	—	0.18	—	0.09	—
Texas	0.18	—	1	—	1.64	—	1.14	—
All 12 States	1.27	—	5.17	—	5.64	—	10.43	—
Rate	(0.011)	—	(0.034)	—	(0.030)	—	(0.042)	—
% Change in Rate			+32%		−12%		+40%	

Note: These are counts/year for the four periods, along with annualized, per capita rates (Exec./Years/100,000) using the estimated total population (for Hearn/Laska's six states and for all twelve states of the South for the Espy data) for the midpoint of each period (1871, 1882, 1893, 1910). Espy file; Hearn and Laska; Carter, *Historical Statistics*, 1:180–359.

smaller number of lynchings and executions for sexual crimes, this dynamic might be important.

In addition to changes in law enforcement, there were also changes in the laws themselves. In three different ways, states expanded the use of death as a possible penalty for sexual crimes in this era: for rape, for attempted rape, and for statutory rape of a minor under a specified legal age of consent. Fueling these legal reforms were shifts in the public understandings of sexuality and of sexual crime during this period, particularly after the 1880s when a movement to better protect women brought the issue of violent sexual crime pointedly to public attention. If popular understandings of sexuality changed slowly over generations, one of those generations was in the late nineteenth century when women activists engaged in a moral crusade to change the minds of Americans (and to change their laws) to better protect women. In this way, the very conception of sexual violence was in flux, and men were forced to update their understanding of how rape was wrong.[78] If it is unclear that there was an increase in rape, making it more of a pressing issue in this moment, what is undeniable is that the South was *talking about* rape more as this era progressed.[79] The crime was perceived differently in 1870 than in 1910, just as lynching was perceived differently over the course of that span.

In the antebellum period, rape did not earn the death penalty in many states if the accused was a white man: Alabama, Georgia, Mississippi, Tennessee, Texas, and Virginia (and in Kentucky a white man could face the death penalty only if he raped a girl under the age of twelve).[80] Not so, southern enslaved or free Blacks. *Every* southern state before the war had the penalty of death for a Black man (whether enslaved or free) who was convicted of the rape (or attempted rape) of a *white* woman.[81] While such rapes did not occur often, according to the historical record, the white *fear* of this crime—and executions for it—have a history much longer than the white panic that has been more thoroughly documented around the turn of the twentieth century.[82]

In Reconstruction, when race-specific antebellum laws had to be rewritten to conform with new constitutional amendments, three states (Mississippi, South Carolina, and Tennessee) excluded death as a possible penalty for the crime of rape.[83] All three of them introduced death as a possible penalty for rape within two years of white conservatives reconquering their states from Republican regimes.[84] The other nine states of the South wrote their statutes to punish rape with death, or more often, with the jury choosing, at their discretion, prison terms or death for the crime of rape.[85] This is one of the most clear ways the region differed from the rest of the nation, and it is from the earliest moments after the Civil War that this distinction arose. The South chose prison (the typical antebellum penalty for whites accused of rape) *and* death (the penalty for Blacks), simply making the antebellum range of punishments conform to the required post–Civil War race-neutral language. Juries would have discretion in terms of assigning penalties, allowing the South to have a sort of continuity with its antebellum punishment regimes. This is, of course, in addition to the discretion that prosecutors have over whether to bring a charge and what charge to bring.

Virtually no states outside the South punished *attempted* rape with death, and that is almost as true of the South after the Civil War.[86] Most states punished attempted rape with terms in prison or fines rather than the noose: Arkansas, Florida, Georgia, Kentucky, Mississippi, North Carolina, and Texas never included death as a possible penalty for attempted rape.[87] In addition, Alabama and Tennessee had laws to punish with death only attempted rapes of young girls: under ten and twelve, respectively; no executions for attempted rape occurred in this period in Alabama, and only one occurred in Tennessee.[88] But not Virginia and South Carolina: 75 percent of the South's executions for the crime of attempted rape occurred in these two states, with each introducing laws to punish attempted rape with the possibility of death (in 1894 and 1909, respectively); they each deployed this penalty robustly thereafter.[89]

Particularly instructive is the 1894 Virginia law proposed by a representative from Roanoke. This bill changed the penalty for attempted rape, which had not been a capital crime in the commonwealth before that time, to read "Attempts to commit rape shall be punished with death, or in the discretion of the jury, by confinement in the penitentiary not less than three nor more than eighteen years."[90] Three months before, Roanoke suffered from one of the most gruesome lynchings in the state's history, when a supposed assault and robbery of a local woman ended in the supposed perpetrator, (mis?)identified only by his "slouch hat," being taken into custody, then handed over to a mob, who killed him and burned his body to char.[91] After this horror, subsequent Virginia governors responded more strongly (by sending troops and removing prisoners from the localities of the crimes committed) when the threat of lynching arose, making this a turning point in Virginia: few lynchings occurred in the state after 1893.

The other effect of this well-publicized butchery in Roanoke was also important and trends in a rather different direction: that more Black men were executed legally in Virginia after 1893 due to death becoming a possible penalty for attempted rape. From the passage of this law to 1920, no white man in Virginia was executed for attempted rape; twenty-seven Black men were.[92]

Laws in the South made death a possible punishment for rape and in some states attempted rape, but there was even more activity in legislatures throughout the region on the laws governing the age of consent. The Women's Christian Temperance Union (WCTU) and other women's groups made age of consent laws a focus of petitions to legislators year after year in the late nineteenth century.[93] For a girl above the age of consent, the charge of rape required proof of being forced, a notoriously difficult thing to prove, particularly in an era when simply being sexually active would so mar an unmarried woman's character that this fact could be used in court to defend an accused rapist. For any jury (of men, of course), the reputation of the woman making the charge of rape could be a key factor in their deliberations. "Chaste" was even written into many of the laws defining who could be considered to be raped.[94]

In addition, working-class and African American women were generally assumed to be "notorious" and unworthy of belief on the issue of whether they had consented, no matter whether or not they had been sexually active previously.[95] Gender roles and norms of the era assumed that men were the actors and initiators in sexual matters and women were (or should be) passive and defensive: men took what women permitted them to take in terms of sex. It was the responsibility of women to deny them, and if they failed in that attempt, it was not merely the fault of men, from this perspective. It was natural: the way sex worked.[96]

The work of the WCTU and other groups over the course of more than a generation eventually bore fruit. States around the country, including the South, raised the age a victim of a rape would have to prove she was forced.[97] English common law had considered ten the age of consent, and in all but one southern state, ten or twelve remained the age of consent into the 1890s.[98] In the next generation — Georgia was the last in 1918 — every southern state raised its age of consent to fourteen, fifteen, sixteen, eighteen, or even twenty-one.[99] This placed more men in legal jeopardy for sexual crimes in the very era when rape became a central part of the white supremacist campaign against Black men.

Age of consent laws usually stipulated fines or imprisonment for their violation rather than a penalty of death. This was a complex development, and every state varied its punishments. Arkansas and Kentucky never had the death penalty for sex with minors of any age; this crime earned a term in prison. Other states had a prison term for sex with a girl in her teens, but the possibility of the death penalty if the girl was below: ten (Florida and Georgia), twelve (Louisiana), ten raised during this period to twelve (Alabama, Mississippi, North Carolina, and Tennessee), or raised from ten to fourteen (South Carolina), or from twelve to fifteen (Virginia), or even from ten to eighteen (Texas).

The active efforts of the WCTU and other women's groups, year after year, to change these age of consent laws kept the issue of rape before the public eye for decades. Could the efforts to reform laws on sexual crime have had a consequence of fueling the white obsession with rape that led to lynchings and mobs at the legal gallows? It is difficult to position this public effort with the fact that these decades witnessed a growing prominence in extremist language about the threat of rape, increasingly whipping white crowds into a frenzy: this was not static, it was a growing trend. There was comparatively little talk of rape as a problem in the South in 1870; by 1900, this issue of sexual danger helped to define how white southerners thought about race overall, including, of course, how prosecutors, judges, and juries thought about it.[100] This growing focus on a sexually charged racial vision surely would have an impact on some execution days when the crime of the condemned was rape. When Tennessee briefly (1915–19) experimented with abolishing the death penalty for murder, it retained it (and used it five times) for rape.[101]

There is one more curiosity in the data on executions for sexual crimes in the South: executions for the crime of rape were (slightly) more often private than executions overall. I have found no clear evidence of executions out in the open for sexual crimes (between 1866 and 1920) in Alabama, Florida, or South Carolina and none in Virginia after 1870, Tennessee after 1881, or Louisiana after 1882. The other six states of the South (Arkansas, Georgia, Kentucky, Mississippi, North Carolina, and Texas) all had public executions for rape in the twentieth century, though even with these states, that was rare: in all of the South, only fifty-five executions for sexual crimes in the whole period had no enclosure limiting the audience, and most of those were in the 1870s and 1880s.

The numbers here are small, and the divergence from the overall data is not large. One explanation might be that this small sample size is simply diverging slightly from the norm, which is what small samples tend to do, and therefore, we should read little into it. A second explanation is that it speaks to fears of a gallows experience that would be out of control if the execution were allowed to be public, given the passions in the community that were more likely to be awakened by these crimes. Perhaps the sheriffs, concerned by either the threat of lynching by incensed whites or the threat of rescue by incensed Blacks, more often called out extra guards in executions for sexual crimes, asking for militia from other towns, and eliminating the public from view.

But the simplest explanation for somewhat more privacy in executions for sexual crimes compared with murder is merely that the numbers of condemned for this crime grow over time even as laws were passed to make executions in given states private rather than public. Southern executions for rape in the decade after Reconstruction's end would likely be public, given the norms of that era. But twice as many men were executed for sexual crimes in the early twentieth century, when more states performed capital punishment behind enclosures, than in the 1880s or before, when the norm throughout most of the region was public executions. From this perspective, executions for sexual crimes were like other executions, just tending to be disproportionately represented in the era when privacy was the norm.

The issue of rape and the law was a moving target in this period, one that witnessed a shift in the place of rape in the ideology of white supremacy at the same time that consent laws challenged male prerogatives to sexual force in new ways. The South moved from an antebellum standard of race-specific legislation generally reserving the death penalty to Blacks to, in the postbellum period, every state punishing with the possibility of the death penalty for sexual crimes, and in some states, laws punishing attempted rape with death as well.[102] This is a place where state boundaries matter considerably, for different states wrote their statutes differently in regard to sexual crimes, but also they seemed to have different cultures in terms of its punishment. Every state in the South executed for sexual crimes, however, and unlike most of the trends in this study, those numbers and rates go up over time, not down.

THE SCHOLARSHIP OF THE SOUTH has tended to draw parallels between executions and lynchings, and it has paid much closer attention to the exceptional moments of mobs at the legal gallows than to the thousands of executions when the crowds behaved more like a congregation. Bertram Wyatt-Brown saw little difference between public executions and lynchings, writing that lynchings carried on the nature of public executions for a half century after legal public executions were banned.[103] Fitzhugh Brundage called public execution a "surrogate ritual for lynching," and Amy Louise Wood agreed, emphasizing the white crowds at executions and the many ways lynchings shared much with public executions.[104] Michael Pfeifer positioned public executions as a manifestation of the "rough justice" that persisted in the South, drawing a connection between the impulses among white southerners to retain legal executions in public and the impulses of white mobs to lynch, stressing the "communal supervision and racial symbolism of retributive justice."[105] A number of examples of public execution published in the literature are of some of the most massive crowds in the history of southern executions, often with disorder, troops, and more, leaving the impression that these represent the norm for public executions as a whole.[106]

These uncivil executions were disturbing moments at the gallows, but they were not how executions in the South were in general. They were how an occasional, exceptional execution played out. In perspective, it is notable that on several occasions, particularly early in the postwar period, whites were concerned about what African Americans might do. It is as important that no rescue attempt occurred. It is likewise notable how on several occasions, especially after the turn of the twentieth century, white mobs turned legal capital punishment into something very close to lynchings. It is as important that almost all executions in the South in the two generations after the Civil War were *not* this.

The end of public executions in the South was as complex a story as the rest of the themes pursued in this book. In two cases, states changed their laws on public execution by pointing to the problematic behavior of Black crowds at recent executions; both, like the fears of Black rescue, were in the first fifteen years after the Civil War. In two other cases, white mobs forced the issue for state legislatures to return from centralized executions in the state penitentiary to local hangings for rapists; both, like most of the white mobs that caused uncivil executions, were after 1900. Chapter 6 discusses those specific moments as well as the wider set of changes in the way white southerners shifted their thinking about the utility of public executions and the religious ceremonies at the gallows.

In the late nineteenth and early twentieth centuries, every southern state legislature voted to change how executions took place in its state, demonstrating how whites moved from valuing the lessons of public execution—valuing even the validation of that lesson in the form of religious services at the gallows—to seeing the public elements of executions as subverting the very goals of punishment and order.

CHAPTER SIX

Make It a Secret Silent Monster
Executions in Private

> The appalling mystery of a private execution strikes terror to the turbulent classes. . . . This mode of execution is full of horror. It weighs like a nightmare upon the evildisposed, and each one of them goes to his quarters stunned and thoughtful with this idea of inexorable justice that has done its terrible work so noiselessly and so surely.
>
> —*Louisville Commercial*, 3 April 1880

Every state in the South transitioned from public to private hangings in the late nineteenth and early twentieth centuries, eventually shifting to electrocution as the mode of capital punishment, typically performed in the bowels of centralized state penitentiaries. In the process, local crowds, the condemned, ministers, and sheriffs lost this moment of public authority. This change pushed in a particular direction: execution observers became white and male, and executions became more clearly controlled by the state.

These shifts are especially telling due to the wider context of pervasive lethal violence in the South, particularly violence against African American men. In the very years that witnessed the revisions to each state's capital punishment laws, lynching was endemic, and these mobs were beginning to receive concerted and widespread attention, forcing white southerners to defend themselves. If prisons were no solution to Black crime, whites taught themselves to believe that they *had* to lynch due, in part, to the lack of other sufficiently horror-inspiring tools to deploy to keep African Americans in their place. This argument fed the disease of lynching in the South, coupling the white supremacist notion that terror was required with the perspective that legal punishments were failing to provide it.

Capital punishment was one of the legal tools that whites deemed insufficient. This was despite white control of the mechanisms of justice in the South and despite the fact that the period experienced the high point in the use of capital punishment in the history of the region. The problem whites found with capital punishment was less any challenge to its *use* but rather in the problematic *nature* of those events. Public executions failed to teach the worst offenders the costs of crime in lethal terms: whites in power increasingly saw the sanctifying rituals at the gallows as undercutting rather than amplifying the necessary punitive lesson. From within the white supremacist perspective, the failure of public execution to terrorize the underclass in regard to the crimes of murder and rape was one element promoting the utility of the horror of lynching and, as we shall see, also promoting the utility of privacy in execution. Punishment needed to be a horror, and perhaps the "appalling mystery" of private, state-sanctioned killings would be the means to achieve this solemn, awe-inspiring terror.

If punishment is always, in part, preventative—to teach the costs of wrongdoing to potential future criminals and "prevent a repetition of their offences," in the words of one nineteenth-century observer—whites in the South seemed particularly focused on this social-control aspect of the judicial system in this era after the Civil War.[1] For whites in the South in this moment, the ghastly nature of lynching, so obvious to us, was apparently obscured by their pervasive fear, which pulled focus for them. More: violent punishment had been the norm. What was new was not the violence of the punishment; what was new was that so many traditional punishments were now illegal.

Punishment plays a central role in combating this perceived erosion of white control. For many white southerners, punishment should demand "blood for blood": an "occasional hanging clears the atmosphere of crime as lightning purifies the summer sky."[2] While this could apply to combating disorder generally, the particular fear was of African Americans; said one planter, "When a nigger gets ideas, the best thing to do is to get him under ground as quick as possible."[3]

In this era, even the legal execution of a man condemned for murder or rape was not the clear lesson that authorities desired it to be, obscured as it was by the public, religious, African American–led revivals at the scaffold that were the norm in the South. The arguments put forward in favor of a shift from public to private execution, and then to centralizing the process with electrocution, reveal how race, gender, justice, religion, punishment, and lynching were woven together as the attitudes of whites shifted over the course of generations in regard to the efficacy of their punishment regime. Lynching was a horror no matter what context it is framed within, but it becomes a horror more legible when placed in the context of white supremacy's perceived need for control, coupled with ways that the legal means of curbing the underclass were perceived to be failing to achieve those ends.

The Long Transition to Private Execution

It was over the course of generations that this faith in the utility of public execution evolved in the minds of white southerners. The gradual nature of this change tells us how tenacious was the cultural role played by public executions; that the change took place tells us how important it was for whites to control the narrative of punishment. Privacy in executions would consolidate white power and authority as well as undercut public, meaningful roles that African Americans and that women played at the gallows.

States in the North moved away from public execution in the antebellum period (the development receiving the most scrutiny from scholars of capital punishment), and western states followed just after the Civil War.[4] But the South continued to see virtue in public executions. In the 1850s, most white southerners seemed to agree with a Richmond editor that the "instructive lessons" of public executions had "a beneficial influence upon the moral feelings [of the community], and a restraining tendency in regard to the commission of crime."[5] This traditional view was the basis of laws throughout the nation up to the 1830s; it was commonplace much longer in the South. The views popular among whites concerning the nature of African Americans and their criminal proclivities helped to frame the South's entire punishment regime, including capital punishment. A judge in Georgia sentenced a murderer to a public execution in 1891 with these comments:

> This crime was so growing in our community that a public example must be made, that the people would know by their own sight that men had paid the death penalty for their crimes. . . . I want it to be known that death is the penalty for murder . . . [and] to a certain extent they will heed it, especially amongst our colored fellow-citizens, who are credulous and superstitious to a greater or less extent. As to the masses of them, you have to act upon their sensibilities rather than upon their judgment or their ideas. You have to act upon senses to make them understand and know: they have to see and feel.[6]

These sentiments were not easily uprooted, even if southern states started, equivocally, to change their laws in the mid-nineteenth century. When southern states passed legislation limiting public executions before the 1880s, they tended to allow for a substantial amount of local discretion, such as Virginia's 1856 law promoting private execution "unless the court direct otherwise."[7] These were suggestions, not mandates, and public execution was both popular and a tradition in the South. This is a revealing era, for local officials allowed for public execution as often as not in this era when they had discretion over how public to make an execution. In Georgia, for instance, twice as many executions were public as were private in the decade (1884–93) before the state strictly prohibited public executions. In Virginia's last decade of discretion (1870–79), half of the state's executions were clearly public, and most of the rest were within walls, but with large crowds watching; only one was clearly what we would consider actually "private."[8] The trend in this era of discretion appears to have been pragmatic. Executions occurred in jail yards (often with huge crowds inside and outside them as well as perched upon the walls) in those places (such as larger communities like Savannah or Richmond) that already had a jail fitted with a suitable yard. Smaller communities like Waycross or Bainbridge or LaGrange, Georgia, having no yards, held their executions in the open as was traditional.[9]

It was the generation of white Democrats reconquering the South after Reconstruction who undertook the greatest activity in southern legislatures on this issue, with eight out of the twelve states of the South enacting legislation against public executions between 1877 and 1893. The common sense of white southerners was shifting fast. By the 1880s some southern states began to word their laws against public execution unequivocally: executions would be inside an enclosure.[10]

But this tells us less than we might presume, for public executions continued, and even those within an enclosure might not embody our commonsense idea of what "private" entailed. Even after states strictly mandated that executions cease being in the open, it is difficult to say precisely when the last public execution took place in any state. Georgia ended public execution by legislation in 1893, for example, yet in the next twenty years, at least thirteen executions were clearly public, with hundreds or thousands in attendance, viewing the spectacle out in the open.[11]

Until each state centralized its executions (Virginia became the first southern state to execute in its state penitentiary in 1908), each of the 1,200 counties in the South had control of its own executions, and official practice was erratic.[12] Many localities and sheriffs decided either to ignore private execution laws or to adhere to them in the most perfunctory fashion.

In this way, the timing of this shift to privacy in executions is more complex than finding a state statute and parsing its wording.[13] Even when newspaper reports called an execution "private," that meant only that a barrier was in some way involved in the process; it did not mean that a crowd was not watching the hanging. Sheriffs often allowed as many spectators to witness the event as could comfortably (or uncomfortably) fit within (and, often, upon) the walls. "The execution was in private," noted the *Atlanta Constitution* in 1891, the example that starts this book's introduction. This story continued: "and took place in the jail yard in the presence of several hundred witnesses. There was an immense throng of negroes on the outside."[14] In another formulation of public features in a "private" execution, some convicts spoke to the crowd before entering an enclosure: from a window of the jail, from atop the coffin in a wagon, or even from a grandstand erected expressly for that purpose.[15] One sheriff solved the problem of the public wanting to witness a private execution by swearing in the whole crowd as special deputies.[16] Another threw open the gates of the stockade "just as Sheriff Garner touched the trigger," allowing hundreds to pass "in review of the swaying form," missing only the instant of the drop itself.[17]

If public executions were the norm up to the 1880s, this sort of mixture of public and private was most typical for execution days in the South in the 1880s and 1890s. In more than one county, a gallows was "enclosed" merely by fixing tenting around its bottom half; all of the public ceremony on the top of the scaffold took place in the open as was traditional. Then when the trap was sprung, the prisoner dropped out of view, so that the hanging, technically, was in the privacy of a very small enclosure.[18] Similarly, speeches and a religious ceremony might take place from the scaffold, which "was then enclosed by canvas and the trap sprung."[19] Other "enclosures" were still fainter gestures to privacy, such as a wooden fence just six (or even four!) feet high, a barbed wire fence, or even a strand of rope cordoning off an area around the scaffold.[20]

Even when an execution was more clearly inside an effective enclosure, there could be crowds packed within the jail yard or overlooking the enclosure, defying the attempts at privacy. Others, denied a view, might be allowed to parade past the body as it was either on the scaffold or in its open casket afterward.[21] It was commonplace for the barricades to be low enough that people could see over them from trees, windows, and particularly the roofs of adjacent buildings.[22] In a Louisiana case, "men and boys were on neighboring housetops overlooking the walls, people were to be seen gathering on the roofs of the distant Hennen Building and the Hibernia Bank Building, [and] several dozen maintained a precarious vantage point on the ladder which runs up the big smokestack of the powerhouse in Union Street, squares away."[23]

As these examples demonstrate, a host of southern sheriffs were complicit in allowing the public to continue viewing executions in some fashion. In a telling phrase, one sheriff in 1897 told a newspaper, "We don't want it altogether public," as he devised a pseudo-private execution arrangement in an era when the law mandated barriers.[24] Local sheriffs were caught between their obligation to obey the law and the fact that their constituencies (the people of the county, both white and Black) typically wanted executions to remain public. Charting a course between these competing forces, sheriffs tended to obey the letter of the law much more than its spirit.[25] "Enclosure," after all, can mean many things. The crowds often forced the issue, pushing past police and making authorities decide how much force they wanted to exert on the local people demanding to view an execution.[26]

Even half-hearted barriers, however, changed the nature of execution crowds. They might reduce the size of a crowd viewing the spectacle, but at least as important, when a barrier was introduced, the composition of the crowd inside of it became defined by the choices of the white sheriff. No longer would it consist of anyone who showed up; even if hundreds were allowed inside a jail yard, authorities would control the choice about who would be admitted and who would not, or at least who would be relegated to the "balcony" seats so much farther away, overlooking the walls.

Judging from the dozens of reports mentioning Black crowds outside walls, even inept barriers tended to whiten the crowds witnessing executions, raising the question of whether these laws were meant to foster privacy or to foster segregation. "The Courthouse and jail were surrounded fifty yards deep with negroes eager to catch a glimpse over or through the high fence."[27] One report stressed that African Americans might question whether the execution (of a white man who had killed two Black men) had actually taken place now that the hanging was behind walls. In light of this, the judge "granted two intelligent members of the race permission to see the execution so they could testify" to it.[28] This inclusion, of course, simply emphasizes the unusual nature of African Americans being in a crowd to witness an execution once hangings were private.

Privacy shifted the gender dynamics at executions as much as it did the racial dynamics. While few women were condemned to hang or were on the scaffold as religious leaders, they were in the audiences. Newspapers regularly made note of them, often from the perspective that their presence was particularly questionable: it was unseemly for women to witness these things, particularly white women. That does not mean white women did not want to be a part of these crowds: "Among the crowd who got up on the high jailyard fence and viewed the execution were many white women."[29] But it was African American women, particularly when they were vocally involved in the religious ceremonies, who received the most attention from the press. "Wails and lamentations were heard from the colored people, the women crying and wringing their hands."[30]

Once sheriffs effectively controlled who witnessed executions, women seldom were there. In an exceptional circumstance, the victim of a sexual assault might be allowed to witness the execution, but that appears to have been rare.[31] Such moments speak less to women's place at executions and more to white society's concern with sexual assault of white women in this era: the assault victim's presence heightened the element of vengeance. Even in the quite unusual circumstance of a local woman being the sheriff who was tasked with an execution, she demurred, with a former police officer performing this duty.[32]

For many years after barriers were introduced, crowds would continue to gather outside them, and newspapers often reported many of the same sorts of stories about religion and crowds calling out, even if they were not in sight of the scaffold: "When the trap-door fell a shriek went up from the scores of colored women without."[33] In 1880, after Kentucky made executions behind walls, a Black woman was discovered outside the jail walls by a reporter. She had her arms outstretched, "pouring out supplications" for the two condemned who would die the following morning. The reporter approached her when she was done, and she told him, "I am a Christian woman, and the fate of human souls concerns me . . . and to-night the thoughts that two men were sleeping their last and that two souls were being lost kept rushing through my mind until I could not rest."[34] She would not be able to be at the execution, but she wanted to do her part to usher these souls to a better place.

The desire to attend executions was strong among both whites and Blacks, and it took a generation before southerners were willing to abandon the tradition. In 1880, the *Louisville Courier-Journal* interviewed locals who were unanimously against the new legislation in Kentucky making executions private. The (presumably white) interviewees argued that seeing a public execution was "every tax-paying citizen's right," that adding mystery to crime only made it more attractive, that it was undemocratic to allow only a few to witness an execution, and that the effect of public executions was to be "struck by the terrible spectacle" in a beneficial way. "The crime is public, the trial is public, and I don't believe in sparing the feelings of murderers, etc., by giving them a private execution." A few days later, at the first private Kentucky hanging, one man remarked that he had seen enough of them, but "d___d if I wouldn't like for the children to see it."[35] A later, private execution led one newspaperman to harken back to "those good old times of Democratic simplicity" when "all executions were public": "Red tape had not traveled this far from Washington. Gruesome tickets with heavy black borders were not demanded by an official at the jail-yard gate. As the people made the law, the people were expected to be present and see the law enforced."[36]

Public sentiment certainly was not all in favor of the shift to privacy. In some cases, this opposition was overtly tied to thoughts of race and proper punishment. One North Carolina paper reported that in one case of a Black man condemned for rape, "there seems to have been a sentiment here that the hanging should have been made public as an object lesson to the negroes." This author found solace in the fact that "from the way in which the execution has been made the common topic however, it would seem that the end desired has been obtained."[37]

The publicity the media gave executions was certainly another way that they could be seen as public, at least in a sense. This exploitation of the interest in the gallows received criticism even in the antebellum period, a trend that grew over time.[38] Privacy advanced in the South in just the same decades that saw a revolution in the nature of images in the press as well as a dramatic expansion in the size of newspapers and the volume of print: from four-page, type-filled papers in the 1860s, newspapers doubled or tripled in size in the new century. Filling those expanding pages were not just more type and perhaps engravings of the condemned in his cell but also diagrams, drawings, and (by the start of the twentieth century) halftone photographs of the gallows scene and later, of the (empty) electric chair.[39] Complaints about such graphic coverage certainly can be found in the period. "We hardly know whether this is wise," editorialized the *Nashville Banner* on Tennessee legislation that allowed the press to be among the witnesses at now-private executions: "Minute details of the sickening and repulsive scenes are almost, if not equally, as objectionable as public executions. The liberty of the press is great, but that gives it no excuse nor permission to debase public morals. It has become the fashion of journals to publish the picture and the life of the criminal, the history of the crime, however revolting, and the details of the hanging with every exciting incident that might draw the attention of the curious."[40]

Apparently with this sort of objection in mind, many of the statutes for privacy (particularly in terms of electrocution) also stipulated that newspapers could not describe the scene, limiting this sort of publicity as well.[41] Some newspapers objected to this; wrote the *Charleston News and Courier*: "No reason whatever was assigned for this extraordinary discrimination against the members of the press."[42] Papers certainly cashed in on the interest in the executions: "The *Constitution* will contain a full account of the crimes of both of these murderers, and will have a special reporter at the scene of each execution, who will telegraph the particulars of the executions. Both accounts, complete and thorough, will appear in Saturday's *Constitution*. Newsdealers should send in orders for extra copies at once."[43]

If privacy was an issue for many, so was the loss of *local* executions when a state chose to centralize capital punishment in a more distant state penitentiary. A Louisiana newspaper in 1941 looked back on the state's brief experiment (1910–18) with centralized executions: "Since capital punishment is practiced for its deterring effects, the state long ago repealed the law, in effect for a few years, requiring that executions take place at the state penitentiary where they were bound to be less noticed than if carried out in the locality of the crime."[44] Local control is a key theme in southern history overall, and it should not, therefore, be a surprise to find it here.

Public executions were popular enough with both Blacks and whites that some southern sheriffs had to use militia, bayonets, reinforced and heightened barriers, and/or tricks to keep spectators at bay. One sheriff executed a man in mid-morning, for example, despite having advertised the execution as taking place later, "owing to the fact that large crowds of negroes usually collect around the jail when such events are in progress."[45] Fearing a Black riot, another Georgia sheriff hanged two men at sunrise.[46] Scheduling early morning executions became popular with sheriffs attempting to avoid crowds in the 1890s and after; most executions in Kentucky after the mid-1880s were at dawn. Another sheriff confronted the expectations of the gallows moment by clearly articulating to the condemned that "no singing or campmeeting exercises of any kind would be permitted on the scaffold and that all such preparations would have to be attended to before leaving the jail."[47] Another sheriff affixed an additional wooden barrier atop his jail yard walls to prevent a view of the hanging from surrounding buildings— *and* executed the condemned in the early morning.[48]

The tradition of local, public execution was hard to dislodge in the South, and in two different states, threats of lynching in capital cases of rape led legislatures to reverse course on privacy in execution, if only for the crime of rape, and if only for a time. Each was a response to white mobs fostered by the particular situations of these cases. While not a wider trend, they are telling exceptions to the overall movement toward privacy.

In 1901 Arkansas, a mob was threatening to steal the condemned from the hands of the law if the sheriff tried to protect him and execute him in private, as state law demanded. A state representative from Arkadelphia, where the execution would take place, was concerned that "the barricades will be broken down in order that the hanging may be in full view of the public." He asked for this change in law as an immediate and pressing need to "avert possible bloodshed next Saturday."[49] In response, the legislature proposed and passed a law that the governor quickly signed (all in four days) to allow condemned rapists—but no one condemned for other crimes—again to be hanged in public, and a few days later, several thousand braved the rain in Arkadelphia to see the hanging.[50]

In the process, all the arguments for and against public execution were aired, with a number of state representatives against this bill seeing "no good in permitting the public to go to a hanging as if it were a picnic," and at least two major state newspapers editorializing in like fashion. "The effect" of public executions on the people, to one opponent in the legislature, "was to make them calloused." But others believed that it could be beneficial, and especially compelling was the argument that making executions public for the crime of rape could avoid trouble in this case: "There was an organized crowd of one hundred men who will assist in breaking down the barricades in Arkadelphia if this bill does not become a law next Saturday."[51]

When John Wesley was executed before 2,000 people in the rain that Saturday, the execution was very much like those public executions that came before it, if before a crowd more white than usual. The condemned asked for the opportunity to speak to the crowd and confessed to the sheriff not only the crime he was convicted of but two others; several hundred women and even more African Americans were in the crowd.[52] For the editor of the *Arkansas Democrat*, the lesson here only reinforced that of earlier public spectacles of death: "The fear and abhorrence of such scenes, the dread of a like punishment which the friends of the law making executions public claimed would be experienced by men of brutal propensities, are notably absent." Instead, "their extremely emotional natures are aroused and they experience a sympathy for the victim of the gallows, which generally resolves itself into a religious frenzy."[53]

This law making executions of rapists public remained in effect for only four years, and while at least three more public executions took place in that span, never again were the passions raised in the way they were for John Wesley.[54] The execution days simply resembled the tradition of the camp meetings at the gallows: mixtures of public and private elements, religion central, and African Americans prominent both on the stage of the gallows and in the audience. In 1905, the legislature voted overwhelmingly to end this exception to the ban on public executions in Arkansas.[55] The brevity of this return to public execution coupled with the ordinary nature of the reports of later executions under this law point to this change as having most to do with the specifics of the Arkadelphia community in 1901 rather than some broader return to a faith in public executions. In this one moment, the threat of mob action had a clear and definitive effect on Arkansas law, linking public executions and lynching in a way the historical record rarely otherwise supports.

Except for exactly that sort of connection in Kentucky in 1920. In that year, mob pressure forced the return of public executions, providing for the last legal, public executions in the South and nation. White lynchers attempted and failed to abduct Will Lockett from the Lexington courtroom during his trial, a riot that ended with five dead and more than a dozen injured as law enforcement, in a rare show of force, actually protected the accused. The jury convicted Will Lockett of rape and murder just thirty-six minutes after the trial commenced and amid "a fusillade of shots" from the mob surrounding the courthouse and from the hundreds of guards, armed not just with rifles but also with machine guns, who defended the courthouse.[56] Despite his being protected from lynching then and there, this is just the sort of "legal lynching" that can blur the distinction between legal and extralegal violence: the mob pressure ensured that there was little possibility of actual justice for Lockett in that courtroom, and the governor signed the death warrant the very day the jury met.[57]

The Kentucky legislature responded to this deadly chaos—white men wounded and even killed in a fight over the life of a Black man convicted of rape and murder—with legislation that would require rapists to again be hanged in the locality where their crime was committed.[58] Some argued that this was "yielding to a morbid sentimentality of blood lust," but the argument that seemed to carry the day was that "if it is a step backward to protect our women then let us step backward. Go back to savagery, if need be, to protect our women."[59] By statute, these executions were to remain behind enclosures. In practice, they became huge public events, for a sheriff could interpret "enclosure" broadly.

Will Lockett was executed in the electric chair shortly before this legislation passed. The only way his execution differed from the norm for private electrocutions in the bowels of a state penitentiary was that, in addition to the allowed doctors, law enforcement officers, and members of the press, the victim's family was allowed to attend.[60] On six occasions over the next sixteen years, executions of men convicted of rape in Kentucky were before crowds in the hundreds and thousands, one with a barrier only four feet tall, another with an eight-foot barrier but with the gallows towering above it, and two with barriers that were merely wire fences.[61]

The transition to private executions was difficult, slow, and later than statutes imply; it was also bound up with white, male ideas of what was proper in terms of race, gender, and punishment. In these ways, privacy in executions in the South meant something quite different from what it meant in the North. In Arkansas and Kentucky, links were close between a mob spirit and public execution, at least in very particular moments. In the other states of the South (and in Arkansas and Kentucky apart from those two moments), no such connections are clear. In fact, the trend in the evidence is that it was not public but private executions that were seen as fostering greater terror in the underclass; public executions were seen, increasingly, as not merely failing in that effort but as embodying an entirely different, disturbing spirit. One African American condemned in 1896 tried to extend this different spirit into his private hanging when he brought a large sign which he asked to be displayed outside the enclosure. It read, "Jesus hath redeemed; I have a building with God not made with hands, eternal in the heavens."[62]

Debating Public and Private

The twelve states of the South shifted away from local, mixed-race, mixed-gender public executions at different times, leaving a scattering of data in both newspapers and state legislative journals regarding the impulses of legislators in these moments. While various arguments were in play, of course, the tendency in these debates was to argue that public execution was failing to deter criminals, that the state needed stronger control of the events on execution days, and that this means of control should be private executions. In particular, public executions were seen as too civil, producing little terror and thereby failing to play their designed part in preventing future crime. Table 6.1 offers the sweep of votes changing the nature of capital punishment from public to private, as well as when the practice was centralized under state authority and when electrocution became the method of capital punishment.[63] The table also offers several particularly interesting wrinkles in the trends of those changes.[64]

Some of these votes were overwhelming and some were contentious, with the most interesting division over eliminating public execution being between the political parties. Votes for and against privacy appear to have been scattered throughout each state in ways that do not yield any geographical pattern I could discern.[65] Representatives and state senators from rural,

TABLE 6.1 Major state votes for changes in execution

		Privacy Vote			Centralization in Penitentiary Vote				Electrocution Vote	
	Year	House	Senate	Year	House	Senate	Year	House	Senate
Alabama	1878	74–20	Unanimous	1923	53–10	26–4		Same bill with centralize	
S. Carolina	1878	74–15	16–12	1912	Not found	NVR		Same bill with centralize	
Virginia	1879	NVR	NVR	1908	58–8	27–8		Same bill with centralize	
Kentucky	1880	(41–41), then 44–37	Not found	1910	64–3	24–3		Same bill with centralize	
Tennessee	1883	54–14	21–5	1909	54–35	23–8	1913	64–2	27–4
Louisiana	1884	62–18	19–4	1910	83–10	27–1	1940	Not found	Not found
Arkansas	1887	53–21	21–8	1913	66–24	26–2		Same bill with centralize	
Georgia	1893	Unanimous	Unanimous	1924	115–45	26–21		Same bill with centralize	
N. Carolina	1901	NVR	NVR		Same bill with privacy		1909	NVR	NVR

Mississippi	1916	81–37	21–7	Not centralized in era		
Florida	1923	43–15	21–9	Same bill with privacy	1940	104–18
Texas	1923	91–19	14–9	Same bill with privacy		30–9
				Same bill with privacy		

Additional Votes on Capital Punishment

	Year	House	Senate	Issue
Arkansas	1901	52–27	23–5	Return to public execution for the crime of rape
Arkansas	1905	81–10	26–1	Ending (again) public executions for rape
Kentucky	1920	68–16	(16–17), then 20–15	Return to (semi-)public hangings for crime of rape
Louisiana	1918	82–22	25–11	Return to local execution rather than centralized in state pen
Tennessee	1915	51–44	20–11	Abolished capital punishment for most crimes
Tennessee	1919	80–5	21–10	Reinstated capital punishment for a number of crimes

Note: All votes are in favor versus opposed to the issue (e.g., privacy, centralization, electrocution); "unanimous" means in favor; votes in parentheses are the issue not passing; "NVR" means no vote was recorded in the respective journal. Sources: see endnotes.

from urban, from coastal, from mountain, and from Cotton Belt counties voted for and voted against changes in the nature of capital punishment in their states.[66] For several of the state votes to make executions private, party affiliations are available for the legislators, revealing that Democrats more than Republicans sought privacy in executions in the South. Democrats tended to be overwhelmingly in favor of this change, often voting 80 percent or more for ending public executions: 40–6 in the 1883 Tennessee House, for example, and 52–12 in the 1884 Louisiana House.[67] Republicans, the minority party in all of these states at the time of these votes, were notably more divided over the issue, sometimes having a majority against private executions (3–4 in the South Carolina Senate in 1878, for example), and sometimes a majority voting for privacy, but with a larger number of their members in opposition: 6–4 in the Louisiana House in 1884, for instance.[68]

Especially in terms of the votes taken in the 1870s and 1880s, the Republican Party tended to be more conscious of how laws affected the African American population, so these votes seem particularly illuminating. Far from wanting to protect African Americans from some sort of perceived humiliation in terms of public execution, the Republican allies of African Americans were notably cooler toward the idea of privacy in capital punishment. It was conservative Democrats, taking back the reins of the government and passing a range of segregationist legislation, who saw executions behind barriers as fitting into their plans.[69]

At least as revealing as these differences between the parties were the points of view put forward in these legislative debates and in newspaper editorials at the time of passage. These were the moments when the problems of public execution were sifted through the white supremacist view of race, religion, and justice, yielding concrete decisions to change state punishment regimes. In southern debate over public and private execution in the late nineteenth century, proponents of private execution put forward some of the same arguments made by their northern and western counterparts: that it was more humane, civilized, and solemn to execute privately; that public executions coarsened those who watched them; and that they failed as an adequate check on crime.[70] At times, southern reformers targeted the dangerous behavior of the crowd. "A sort of frenzy for blood was set afloat" at a recent public execution, noted the *New Orleans Daily Picayune* in 1885, "and of the spectators on that day there were at least a dozen of them now prisoners in the Parish prison—several of them charged with taking life."[71] Public executions, editorialized the *Atlanta Constitution*, "never fail to draw a rough and disorderly crowd. Whisky always flows freely on these occasions, and feeds the passions. . . . The day generally closes with a series of fights and a general display of rowdyism."[72]

Even more than drunken disorder, public executions were criticized for being insufficiently solemn, with the crowd "laughing and carrying on as if witnessing a horse-race or a circus."[73] "It was, indeed, hard to decide whether the large concourse of people had not assembled at a picnic, fair, or political barbeque."[74] National press could take note of these moments, framing the region as a place of latent barbarity: "It is estimated that at least fifteen thousand persons, chiefly of the same race as the condemned men, had gathered to witness the should-be solemn act of the law's vengeance for the gravest crime known to it," wrote the *National Police Gazette*, "but the occasion of which was distorted into a barbaric holiday so incongruous with the spirit of the age and so revolting to the better instincts of humanity that it is difficult to realize that the weird scene we have depicted was enacted within two day's [sic] journey of one of the centers of the boasted enlightenment of our century." This article continues to chastise the "immense assemblage, composed of men, women, and children," ending with: "Fat beeves and sheep were cooked to feast the multitude, and an old-fashioned barbecue with its elements of semi-savage festivity was inaugurated."[75] Disorder—whether framed as drunken, violent, or improperly festive—could be found among both Blacks and whites at the gallows in some instances, and this disturbed many.

Only twice out of the many votes of southern state legislatures to make executions private, centralized, or via electrocution have I found that a particular execution or event spurred the change. For most votes, it appears that legislators shifted their perspectives about the utility of public executions more gradually. Even in these two instances, that is probably something of the case as well, but in Virginia in 1879 and in Kentucky in 1880, the discussion of the law clearly referenced executions that had just taken place, and in both cases, inappropriate behavior of Black crowds prompted the shift to private execution.

In 1879, some of the reports of a double execution in New Kent County, Virginia, included commentary that Blacks in the crowd behaved more like it was a picnic than a hanging, complete with a minstrel entertainment, patent medicine sales, and food providers and even ending with a ball that night.[76] This garnered unfavorable national attention for the execution of these two African American murderers.[77] Other reports, interestingly, were more measured, focusing on the executions going without a hitch, the religion manifested, the confessions given, and praising the sheriff for the good order that prevailed.[78] The Virginia legislature was then in session, and when it passed a bill prohibiting public executions in Virginia, the *Petersburg Index-Appeal* wrote that "this will put an end to all such gallows picnics and jollifications as was witnessed at New Kent Courthouse."[79] This was not Virginia's first bill for privacy; for twenty-three years, the state had a "soft" law that, in essence, suggested the use of an enclosure. Now privacy would be required. It worked: public executions in Virginia were very rare after this date.

Similarly, in Louisville in 1879, George Washington was executed publicly in a scene that disturbed many: the 15,000-person crowd, "the majority of them colored people," "became very boisterous, and surged in one living mass toward the jail." The "darkies" were "pouring in from all directions" and "with these people it was a gala day."[80] Washington had been convicted of raping an eleven-year-old German girl, and his accomplice in this crime, Charles Webster, was likewise condemned to be executed, though his execution had been delayed to the following year. When the legislature met in 1880, the "gala day" of the previous execution prompted a bill to end public execution in Kentucky. This bill provoked some of the most "vehement debate" in the South in terms of publicity and executions, with a newspaper reporting that discussions in the state house took hours, ending in a vote tied at 41–41; only after a minor amendment was added to the bill did it narrowly pass on a second vote.[81] Put forward by three state senators in order to spare their constituency in Louisville "the spectacle of next Friday" if Webster's scheduled execution were allowed to be public, the proponents were pushing for fast passage, while many senators remained convinced (as did many southerners overall in this era) that "public executions [were] wholesome and calculated to strike terror among malefactors. Mr. Owens [a state legislator] thought one public execution would do more good than all the sermons preached since the flood among that class of people whom the gospel sound seldom reached."[82]

The bill passed, the execution was private, and coverage of this first private execution (of two men, a white murderer as well as Webster) was intense. For days, papers printed updates on the legislation, and the *Courier-Journal* conducted man-on-the-street interviews about the change and reported their findings. They also wrote of the preparations for the event: all of this before the actual coverage of the execution on April 3. The coverage on that day was among the most intensive in print for any southern execution. Filling five of the *Louisville Courier-Journal*'s seven front-page columns, it included images of each of the two condemned men, a noose, a drawing of the scaffold, and a map of the jail yard noting the positions of the surrounding buildings and the scaffold.[83] In Virginia in 1879 and Kentucky in 1880, white legislators saw privacy in executions as a solution to a very specific problem of Black crowds and their behavior in public.

If disorder like that outlined in the above paragraphs were the only (or even the chief) complaint made by white reformers in the South, little would diverge from the story of public execution's end as told in the North or West: the South was late in ending public executions, but it did so for similar reasons as in those other regions. This is the traditional view scholars ascribe to this transition in the northern states as well as the progressive vision that southerners like to remember: inheriting a barbaric practice, we rose to greater civility and decorum.[84]

There are good reasons that scholars have considered public execution in terms of this civility argument. Michael Pfeifer, in particular, is convincing in making the connection between middle-class values (especially their concern for due process and the rule of law) and efforts to reform the older, more rural and lower-class ideal of retributive or rough justice.[85] More broadly, this fits a wider trend in the historical scholarship of this era emphasizing the middle-class insistence on civility, as well as Michel Foucault's description of the trajectory of punishment in the western world from public torture to pervasive, private, and internalized discipline.[86] Seth Kotch considers the role of lynching in influencing southerners to transition to a way of executing legally that might, at the same time, fulfill some of the goals of lynchers while being quite distinct from it: the new executions as a sort of mirror-image "anti-lynching."[87] In these ways, this public-to-private dynamic in the South seems of a piece with larger historical trends like these.

But the problem is that this explanation appears to fit this historical question only if one looks from a distance, or through the lens of this ideological shift, or with an eclectic set of data. The closer and more comprehensively one looks at executions in the South, the more this association between private execution and civility dissolves. Most importantly, the concern about civility was not the chief complaint of southern reformers of capital punishment. Yet, even if it had been their chief complaint, these contemporary critiques about "disorder" should be read with a great deal of caution, for, as we have seen, middle-class whites called "disorderly" a capacious range of lower-class and African American behaviors, including the Black religious enthusiasms that were so common at the public gallows. In particular, whites witnessing African American church services might use many of the same words as in the quotations about gallows disorder from the paragraphs above as they reported how aghast they were by the religious emotionalism that they interpreted as vestiges of barbarism. What Black southerners would describe as devotion and a celebration of salvation, whites might well describe as inappropriately festive, disorderly, rowdy, or frenzied, considering them entirely inappropriate to the experience of either the sanctity of church or the solemnity of capital punishment.

Even in the cases of 1879 Virginia and 1880 Kentucky, responding to particular Black crowds by ending public execution, it is less than clear just what white observers meant by "jollifications" and "boisterous" and "gala day." The most common word whites deployed to describe a "good" execution—"solemn"—was nearly the opposite of the exuberant, emotional African American religious practice. The very complaints of disorder, then, are best read with some nuance, not merely hearing in those words a call for civility but also paying attention to how those were the very sorts of words used to promote anti-Black arguments for segregation, reinforcing white authority. This is emphasized in the case of Virginia by how partisanship colored the newspaper coverage of this execution in a telling way. The papers that were horrified by the behavior of African Americans at New Kent in 1879 (the *Richmond Dispatch*, *Petersburg Index-Appeal*, and *Norfolk Appeal*) were all Democratic papers. In contrast, the paper that reported the events as being religious and well managed (the *Richmond Whig*) called itself a "liberal" paper and would, over the coming two years, support the biracial Readjuster movement that took over the Virginia state government.[88]

We should be particularly cautious in interpreting these arguments put forward by white observers about public execution's disorder because they appear alongside a critique of a different nature that was at least as prominent in the historical record: that public execution crowds valorized the criminal. The problem from this perspective was less the disorder of public execution crowds but rather the honor a criminal was earning on the scaffold before mixed-race crowds of thousands. In essence, public execution was *not nearly rough enough* to many reformers: it was not fostering sufficient terror and therefore not providing enough control.

Public executions, as we have seen, placed the convict in a disturbingly prominent role, and it was the ceremony—the Black religious revival at the scaffold—that was the problem with public executions, from this perspective, rather than the barbarity of allowing the public to gaze upon a killing or any fear of rowdyism in the crowd. "When murderers are executed as murderers, and not lionized by the people; when they are no longer allowed to pose as heroes on the awful death-trap, and to harangue the populace to their hearts' content, there will be fewer of them called upon to mount the gallows."[89] Thomas Nelson Page agreed: at first "the ordinary course of the law" was relied upon to combat Black rapists, "but it was found that, notwithstanding the inevitable infliction of the death penalty, several evils resulted therefrom." Not only did rapes continue, he says, but also "the criminal, under the ministrations of his preachers, usually professed to have 'gotten religion,' and from the shadow of the gallows called on his friends to follow him to glory. So that the punishment lost to these emotional people much of its deterrent force, especially where the real sympathy of the race was mainly with the criminal rather than with its victim."[90]

Timing might be crucial here: the opposition to public execution rose through the late nineteenth century, the early decades of the segregation of southern churches, an era when the South's racial regime was in flux. With the abrupt founding of thousands of African American Baptist and Methodist congregations throughout the South, whites lost what sense of control they thought they had over the religious life of their African American neighbors.[91] Instead of "tutoring" Blacks to morality, civility, and "true" Christianity, they now watched Black ministers leading their flocks in emotional release. Whites "no longer saw blacks worshiping the same Savior in song and prayer" and "never had relations with blacks that had any hint of biracial equality or common humanity."[92]

It was in just these decades that the religious revivals at the gallows—moments that made public and before white eyes and ears the demonstrative devotions of evangelical Black religion—came under scrutiny and under increasing criticism. "With freedom came a great subsidence into evil," wrote one white minister. "Negro churches sprang up everywhere, built largely by Northern money, in which there were shouting, praying, singing, all manner of excitement, hysterics, trances, loud calls upon God; but in which there was no religion, at least none of that kind which has its issue in a holy, humble and obedient walking before God."[93] The restraining influence of white ministers was gone, and "with freedom, the negro, *en masse*, relapsed promptly into the voodooism of Africa. . . . 'Moans,' 'shouts,' and 'trance meetings' could be heard for miles."[94]

What did whites propose as the alternative to these camp meetings on the scaffold? What was an ideal private execution in Louisiana? The convict "never once stating that he would 'go straight to Heaven and know everlasting glory.' . . . There was none of the 'Glory Hallelujah' sensational accompaniment."[95] Wrote the *Atlanta Constitution* in 1891, two years before the state moved to privacy in executions,

> Such spectacles . . . attract a few respectable people out of curiosity, but most of the lookers-on are always of the very lowest class. It is not conducive to public order to draw so many of these people together. Their worst passions are gratified and stimulated by the scene on the scaffold. . . . If the doomed man meets his fate with a show of courage, the crowd admires him, and among the vicious and ignorant there will be a secret ambition to rival his notoriety and go to glory in the presence of gaping thousands.
>
> Viewed from any standpoint, a public execution is a bad thing. It familiarizes people with bloodshed, and furnishes examples for imitation, and swells the volume of crime.[96]

Two years later, the editor of this paper continued his assault on public execution: "No good can result from these horrible holidays. They demoralize the labor element and encourage disorder. The murderers on the gallows generally tell the crowd that they have been converted and are on their way to heaven. Naturally, some of the ignorant negroes who listen to them go off under the impression that a murderer is a sort of hero, and that the rope line is a short route to glory."[97]

What was the solution to this problem of the public gallows, according to this editor? "It would be more of a terror if people were not so familiar with it. Make it a secret, silent monster, and the criminal rabble will dread it far more than when it is made the attraction of a holiday."[98] "Private executions save the public from scenes and incidents tending to promote disorder," again wrote the *Constitution*. How? "They prevent hardened murderers from posing on the gallows as heroes for the admiration of the young and weak-minded who take them for men of nerve and grit."[99] Black spectators at the execution of an African American man, according to the editor of the *Arkansas Democrat*, "are not generally impressed with the fear of death," and have more sympathy for the victim, perhaps even seeing him as a martyr.[100] To many whites in the South, the solution was to ban the crowds and increase the mystery of the state's deadly actions:

> A private execution is more impressive to the public, and more terrible to the criminal, than one in public. The "star chamber" understood the refinement of punishment, and it made its executions not only private but short. It tried its awful hand upon a victim, and he disappeared from the sight of men forever. The mystery that hung about its methods confirmed its dominion. Let us imitate in so far that our jail walls shall hide the operations of our law—let the public stand in

silent wonderment and know only when the dishonored coffin comes from the awful gates of the jail yard, that the law has avenged the wrongs of society.[101]

The crime of rape required something even more effective than lynching, argued the editor of the *Atlanta Georgian* in 1906: "some new and mysterious mode of punishment—the passing over a slender bridge into a dark chamber where in utter darkness and in utter mystery the assailant of woman's virtue would meet a fate which his friends would never know and which he himself would never come back to make them understand."[102]

When Kentucky voted for privacy in executions in 1880, the editor of the *Louisville Commercial* wrote that public executions "cast a glamour of false heroism around the victim of the scaffold" which "take[s] away from the death penalty its legitimate terrors."[103] This paper went on to celebrate the potential for private executions with the quotation that opens this chapter. "Instead of punishing our criminals we often pet and cajole them," thought the president of the Virginia Bar. "If we hang them we make heroes of them and waft them to Heaven with the tear and the triumph of the martyr. We let foolish women visit them in prison and weep over them and garland them with flowers."[104]

Many papers continued to celebrate and promote the effects of private executions after the passage of privacy laws in their states. A year after Louisiana made executions private, the *New Orleans Daily Picayune* wrote, "Old colored women met in Congo Square and discussed the coming event. Women and children on their way to Treme Market stopped with baskets and cast awed looks toward the windows of the chapel. There was something fearful in the knowledge that at such and such an hour two men were to be precipitated to death. The awe was increased by the fact that their death was to take place almost in secret."[105] In Charleston, three convicted murderers were hanged privately in 1878, "but for fully three hours and a half previous to the fatal moment were engaged giving vent to ravings about their hopes of salvation." What made this scene different from a public execution? The "vast crowd of negroes" attracted to the event ("probably more than three thousand") witnessed nothing: "under the recent law, however, the execution was private and the anxious throng had no opportunity to behold the dismal show."[106] After the passage of a privacy law in Georgia, the *Atlanta Constitution* continued on its offensive, lauding a law in Indiana requiring executions to take place in the dead of night:

> We can imagine nothing more depressing to the average criminal than a private midnight execution conducted in dead silence, with no

excited crowd of spectators to encourage him to pose as a martyr or hero.

The new Indiana fashion is infinitely better than the old way. Public executions are brutalizing and they increase crime. They cause thousands of people to quit work and congregate around the gallows to gratify their morbid curiosity. Among the spectators there are always many who admire the prisoner's pluck, if he displays any, and his maudlin boasts that he has been forgiven and is going to glory lead some ignorant and brutal men and boys to believe that when life no longer has any charms for them the scaffold can be made the stepping stone to heaven.

Private midnight executions terrorize, not only the prisoner, but they cause the criminal masses to view with alarm the prospect of a doom so swift, silent, and grim—a leap from the darkness of this world into the blacker gulf of the unknown.[107]

Long after Georgia strictly eliminated public executions, the editor of the *Atlanta Constitution* called for still more: banning "public gatherings of any kind" associated with executions. The editor objected to a recent Black religious ceremony outside the jail on the evening before a private execution, arguing that "public gatherings induced by morbid curiosity and sensational orgies, whether the product of religious excitement or otherwise, have no place in the administration of justice."[108]

The presence of women figured less often in the arguments for making executions private than did discussions of disorder, religion, and race. But that may be deceptive, for while it was rare to have commentators expound upon gender as volubly as upon race and religion, there are reasons to think that they simply did not need to expound at length on this subject, for this argument was considered self-evident to many at the time, given the era's gender norms.[109]

Here, too, is a connection to the religious element of the public execution: privacy would divorce the public theater of religion (a realm of both women and men) from the state action of punishment (a male-coded realm). With private executions, all but white men were eliminated from the crowds. In the era of Jim Crow, this segregation ties into a broader racial theme; but it was also an era of male domination in terms of all forms of public authority, and this shift to privacy bolsters that authority as well. Throughout this book are examples of sentences and phrases (which were rarely more fully elaborated upon in the era's reporting) noting the women at executions and particularly the African American women joining in the religious services and calling out. Amid the "most deafening and unearthly religious yells" "of at least a thousand horror-stricken negroes" "the women, especially, showed great excitement."[110] "Many colored women in the crowd began shouting," read one execution report; another progressed "amid the wailing and screamings of the women."[111]

For this era, we can assume it was particularly important that this mixed-gender audience at public executions was likewise a mixed-race one. White women in a crowd led by Black men upon a stage would be particularly charged. As commentator Bill Arp argued, writing about a recent public execution in his neighborhood, this was a disturbing scene:

> No I don't raise my hand in holy horror about men going to see a man hung — but one time ought to satisfy any man, and no time for women and children. . . . There were, perhaps, a thousand white women around the gallows, and some few whose only appropriate place was at home. It is encouraging a morbid and debasing curiosity and women with tender hearts and refined feelings have no business at such places. . . . Some thoughtful persons say that public executions are a warning to the vicious but this was not, for there stood the man with a cigar in his mouth selling a book and showing no sign of fear or repentance — but rather a desire to play the hero to the last. What kind of a warning is that which trifles with death as he did?[112]

How seriously should we take these critiques of public execution as not rough enough? One could certainly try to argue that some middle-class reformers wanted greater civility, and that these "privacy-as-tough" arguments were rhetorical strategies to achieve that end: cover for how a greater civility might appear weak. It makes sense that some southerners would be, as it appears northern and western reformers were, longing for more decorous operations of state power. This might be particularly important to some middle-class reformers in an era with so many lynchings: finding a way to distinguish legal actions of the state from the disturbing extralegal killings that were receiving more and more attention in these decades of the late nineteenth and early twentieth centuries.

This skepticism about the toughness-of-privacy argument would be more compelling if most of the arguments in the historical record were about African American savagery or of the public gallows breeding violence. But those arguments about disorder do not predominate. The many attacks upon Black religion at the gallows, in fact, run askew from any straightforward argument that the incivility of public executions was the issue: religion is itself considered a major civilizing force and therefore its presence would tend to embody civility more than act as a ready foil for it. In contrast, there are obvious reasons why we might question some of the arguments from this era about any rough "disorder" at the public gallows being a motivating force for changing the laws to make punishment more civil. The era is so rife with examples of white southerners calling "disorder" so many elements of Black life that it often appears that the mere presence of Blacks (particularly alongside of white women) defined a situation as disorderly. White supremacist ideology constantly pulled in the direction of interpreting African American actions as subhuman; it would be odd if such arguments were absent here when those arguments appear almost everywhere else.

Far from private execution being a middle-class rejection of an older tradition of justice, these comments about the failings of public execution point to reformers seeing private executions as the rougher remedy. In this region, editorialized the *Atlanta Constitution* (in contrast to effete New York), "a painful and disgraceful death is the proper penalty for a murderer."[113] What changed over time was the perspective of white southerners in regard to what methods would best yield that terror and therefore the benefits of crime control: public or private execution? Legal ones or extralegal lynchings? For the South, this move to the "secret, silent monster" of private execution had many justifications, including for some the civility of administering punishment in a more controlled environment. But it was also clearly a shift in tactics in policing miscreants, particularly African Americans, by clothing "the murderer's fate with a horrible and terrible secrecy."[114]

Electrocution

In the first half of the twentieth century, every state in the South transitioned to electrocution as its means of capital punishment; this tended to be the moment also when the death penalty was centralized in a state penitentiary rather than carried out in a local county jail yard. This technological-cum-humanitarian innovation in punishment began in New York in 1890, and southern states were about average in embracing it: Virginia, in 1908, was the fifth state to adopt electrocution; Louisiana, the last southern state to make this shift in 1940, was the twenty-third of twenty-five states to do so before the 1972 Furman Supreme Court decision ended a phase of the history of capital punishment in the United States.[115]

If electrocution was not invented in the South, it became a particularly southern way to punish: every southern state turned to electrocution, and that was not true outside the region. As early as 1910, southern states were using it, in proportion to the region's share of the nation's population, more than the nation as a whole. By the middle of the twentieth century, fully two-thirds of all U.S. electrocutions were in the South.[116]

Each state in the South, of course, also therefore had a first electrocution, a moment that focused public attention on this transition. This is important in terms of the arguments this attention left in the historical record but also for the "extra" racial skew in these first electrocutions: every state's first electrocution was of an African American man.[117] If capital punishment was habitually skewed in terms of executing Blacks, this was an extraordinary example of that.

Electrocution fostered many shifts. It required a generator, and therefore a technological infrastructure that did not exist earlier. This tended to emphasize the centralization trend in this era: the creation of a permanent death chamber housing the chair and the electrical apparatus that made it possible.[118] In an era of the expanding influence of electricity, inspiring the nation in so many ways, this new technology opened up possibilities in culture (motion pictures), households (appliances, lighting), and whole cities (street lighting), seemingly transforming every side of American life.[119]

Just as in other fields, the introduction of electricity in punishment also necessitated a shift in skills and labor: centralizing executions meant that a job would no longer be performed by local sheriffs but would now be given to a supposedly more expert state official, often a prison warden, aided by electricians.[120] At least one prison warden resigned rather than take up this duty, which his conscience did not allow him to perform.[121] On the other side, a host of local sheriffs in Arkansas endorsed this centralization and therefore the removal of "one of the most undesirable duties of the sheriffs."[122]

Americans had almost utopian ideas about electricity, its "sublime" character, and its possibilities, and these beliefs affected the nature of discussions of the best method of capital punishment. Scientists and doctors argued that with electricity, death was virtually instantaneous and therefore painless: brain function ceased with the first shock. This lent electrocution a humanitarian cast: a modern, technological solution to yet another enduring social problem. But more: it seemed in line with the attitudes toward how society should greet such moments of punishment. Necessarily performed inside in a state penitentiary and before few, professional witnesses, the idea repeatedly invoked by proponents of electrocution was that it was "solemn." The surgeon of the Virginia penitentiary, Charles Carrington, described an electrocution: "What a swift performance an electrocution is, and I can assure you that it is one of the most solemn, awe-inspiring acts any one can take part in. I have witnessed thirty odd during two years, and the last one was just as fearful in its solemnity as the first one. I hope and believe that the solemn judicial inflicting of the death penalty by electrocution in place of the more or less spectacular hanging, will have a powerful deterrent effect on the criminal classes."[123] Elsewhere, Carrington particularly compared the religious elements of the forms of execution: "Absolutely nothing of the spectacular is permitted at an electrocution, and when you eliminate the psalm-singing-forgiving-your-enemies episode that usually, I am told, preceded a hanging, and in its stead institute a solemn, very swift mode of inflicting the death penalty, you have taken a step which will in time be powerfully deterrent on the criminal classes."[124]

This sentiment is repeated throughout the discussions in the South of electrocution and is worth closer consideration. "Solemn" is so repeatedly referenced—often multiple times in a single passage, as in the Carrington quote above—and it is a very particular word.[125] Solemnity speaks to self-control, a certain attitude of reverence, and perhaps awe, another word frequently deployed in editorials and reports from the period about electrocution. It is joined often by "quiet," which is an especially odd concept to put into play in terms of electrocutions.[126] Hangings had no engines, generators, or electrical currents: just a trap swinging open and a fall. An electrocution would be, in fact, far noisier in its operation. But that is surely not the point to these observers: what was quiet was the crowd, or lack of one. These solemn, quiet, hidden electrocutions were the opposite, in other words, of the white perceptions of the noisy, chaotic, public gallows.

This discussion of electrocution overlaps with the broader discussions of public versus private executions that were happening at the same time, and for many southerners, as with the rest of the nation, electrocution seemed to be the deft (and trendy: a new technology) solution. In fact, for two-thirds of southern states, the bill mandating electrocution as the method of capital punishment also was the bill that removed executions from local county authority and placed them in the hands of the state.[127] For three of these states (Alabama, Florida, and Texas), it also appears to be the moment when public or semipublic executions become more uniformly private. In that way, the discussions about a transition to electrocution were about much more than a new technology: for much of the South, this was the moment when capital punishment was transformed into a more distant and bureaucratic event.[128] This was disturbing to many, upsetting local mores and to some, eliminating a key element of crime prevention.

Opponents of Virginia's 1908 bill to use the electric chair (the first bill in the South for electrocution and to centralize capital punishment) were particularly focused on how it centralized executions in Richmond, arguing that local hangings were a "time honored custom" in the state and region that "served to impress the negroes, and in this way to prevent more of the 'unmentionable crimes.'"[129] After Texas passed a bill for electrocution and centralization in 1923, state senators objected, saying it was "in contravention of all rules of civilized treatment of prisoners by hauling them hundreds of miles over the state subject to the gaze of the public" and that next of kin would be inconvenienced.

In contrast, those in favor of the centralization of executions in Virginia made the typical arguments for civility of this new technology, but they also raised a (very different) racialized argument. Private electrocution's "swift, quiet, and mysterious" nature would have a good effect on African Americans. As one editor put it,

> With the negro, who constitutes so large a proportion of the criminal population of all Southern States, this argument is undeniably important. The *Times Dispatch* has long contended that the publicity, the excitement and the general hurrah-and-holiday air attending the old-time hanging were a positive allurement to the negro. His strong theatrical sense reveled in the final melodrama in which he was the conspicuous central figure. The electric execution wholly does away with that. The time set for turning on the death current is unannounced, the public is rigorously eluded, and the whole affair is conducted with secrecy and mystery, well calculated to inspire terror in the heart of the superstitious African.[130]

For some, electrocution appeared to be the perfect remedy for the problems public and local executions presented: "The general sentiment of the people is, therefore, against the public execution of criminals in this state. . . . The most awful feature of electrocution is its solemn privacy — no uplifting of the criminal before the rabble; no gallows speech to be applauded by the multitude, but the gloom of towering prison walls and the awful silence of the cell of death."[131] An early electrocution in South Carolina included an official telling the thirty-five witnesses allowed to attend how to behave, in essence coaching them in civility: "The occasion was a most serious one and urged that everyone in the room maintain perfect silence."[132]

Religion continued to be present, but the nature of those religious moments were transformed from public and communal to solitary. One South Carolina man condemned to the chair gave a ten-minute speech that was so affecting to the thirty-five witnesses that many in the crowd were weeping— silently.[133] Other reports mention that hymns were sung or a prayer given, and in one case that, when asked if he could give a statement, the condemned was told, "Say anything you wish, Lee," whereupon the condemned asked for a song, "Till We Meet Again." But in the geography of electrocution's death chamber, the song was sung only by the condemned and the chaplain as the mask was affixed in preparation for the switch to be flipped.[134] Religion was there, but reports of electrocutions were as likely to focus on the speed of the operation, or of their quiet. In North Carolina's first electrocution, "He was crying bitterly, but not loudly. There was none of that sensational shouting or hysterical screaming that have so often attended hangings. Morrison appeared not to notice the witnesses. He kept his eyes firmly upon the Cross in his hand, except for a brief moment when he looked at the chair. If he had looked at the auditors he would have seen no member of his race there to witness his death."[135]

Not only were there no crowds except the professional witnesses allowed by law, electrocutions typically received more limited coverage in the press than hangings, not due to any small interest among the public but due to gag orders on the press coverage in many states. In Virginia, for instance, papers were allowed to only print that the execution took place and when it did so.[136] This is best seen, perhaps, as accomplishing two things at once: another effort to make executions less public and a defense against the publicity of something very disturbing that the state was doing. Electrocutions, after all, were not pleasant to behold, describe, or read about: more akin to reading the notorious opening pages of Michel Foucault's *Discipline and Punish* than a proponent of electrocution would wish to admit.[137] Hangings, of course, were likewise disturbing, with a "successful" one snapping the condemned's neck and with others ending in slow strangulation, not to mention an occasional, even more horrible misadventure with the noose. If a goal of each of these punishments was a fast, painless death, that goal was only sometimes reached in terms of either technology.[138] The first electrocution (William Kimmler in New York in 1890) was widely reported, and the trend in the reporting was that it was so botched an operation that it drew into question whether any other electrocution would ever be attempted.[139] It is not, then, accidental that so many future electrocutions limited the access of the press.

In an electrocution, just what did happen behind closed doors and witnessed by so few? In Virginia, witnesses and attendants were taken to the death chamber, and after the condemned was allowed a final short prayer, he was marched the six or eight steps into the death chamber, where the attendants situated him in the oak chair, adjusting straps and buckles to keep him still, and affixing electrodes with copper cables to his head and a leg, a process that reportedly took, in all, less than a minute. At the signal from the attending doctor, the current was switched on for about sixty seconds, varying in intensity through that time, reaching the maximum voltage (2,220 volts) three times in the course of that minute. "After the current is cut off the heart action for a few seconds is tumultuous, churning violently. This most quickly slows off and in a few more seconds the subject is pronounced dead. He died from shock, paralysis of the respiratory centers and of the heart."[140] Being a new technology, many of the early reports overtly specify that it worked; that fact was still in question, clearly: "The electrical apparatus had been thoroughly tested, and no hitch occurred to mar the execution. Morgan received no burns or disfigurements, and he appeared to be dead after the first shock."[141]

In theory, the first blast of electrical current killed all sensation, making brain death virtually immediate, even if the heart beat on briefly. Humane, then. In practice, electrodes might not be placed correctly, and even if they were, the violent spasms of the body, even when not accompanied by smoking flesh at the electrode sites, was very disturbing to many witnesses.[142]

The marriage of modern technology to privacy and civility? Electrocution was a much more mixed development in the history of the nation and the South: equal parts merciful and horrendous, hidden from view. In the first full year of the chair's use in the South, after Virginia had electrocuted sixteen men, the surgeon at the Commonwealth's penitentiary penned a notably haunting phrase capturing this duality, if perhaps inadvertently: "I believe more thoroughly than ever that electrocution is the most humane and feasible method of inflicting capital punishment. It is very swift, very solemn, and very awe-inspiring in its every horrible detail."[143]

WHEN THE SOUTH BANNED public executions, whites continued to enact the state's power through the gallows. But privacy eliminated the possibility of both disorderly crowds and the communal religious services, even if it took more than a generation for all public elements to fade away. When a minister accompanied a condemned man to the scaffold (or, still later, the electrocution chamber) after public executions were strictly and effectively proscribed, his audience would be merely a dozen or so white men. *Both* kinds of crowds—the mixed-race, mixed-gender ones at (local) public executions and the white, male ones at (eventually centralized) private executions—are important to keep in mind. The former crowd was a feature of public executions perceived as problematic, its boisterous character and religious enthusiasms challenging the legitimacy of the retributive "lesson" to be learned at the scaffold. The latter crowd—tending to be composed of doctors and other respectable white males (a "professional audience"), especially after the transition to electrocution—conferred a controlled and solemn legitimacy to the process.[144]

Scholars as well as white commentators on lynching at the time have argued that, in rape cases in particular, whites might have been reluctant to allow trials to proceed—particularly if it meant forcing a white woman to relive publicly in court the horror of her assault. Such reluctance, the idea went, might have led lynch mobs to wrest the accused out of the ambit of the law in order to preclude that second shaming of a victimized woman.

Evidence in this study from execution days in the South suggests a different (yet related) motive for these white mobs: even a successful conviction of a capital case would end in ways they could not fully control. In the era of public and quasi-public executions, a convicted rapist or murderer could be expected to proclaim publicly and before thousands of whites and Blacks that he was redeemed, that he would soon be in Christ's enfolding arms, and that he would—whether he denied his guilt or blamed the crime on the ill effects of alcohol and bad company—see them all in heaven. The scaffold was a stage for African American actors to display in the era of Jim Crow their sacred authority. When hangings became private in the South, they also became Jim Crow, male executions, and one of the central pillars of the Black community, the church, lost a very visible and public moment of devotion, contrition, catharsis, and subversion.

This era witnessed not just the end of slavery, the whipping post, transportation out of the state, and overtly racist "black codes" in southern law, not to mention the slow, steady rise of Black mobility, landowning, literacy, and (for a time, at least) voting. Even in the realm of capital punishment, the white-controlled southern states seemed ill-equipped to force the scene at the public gallows to tell the story they wanted told. This entirely unsatisfying ending of the "lesson" of lethal punishment became increasingly unacceptable to the white South.

Capital punishment was a key element in this wider system of racial supremacy: the ultimate penalty—death—in a system of penalties and restrictions. Unlike in the North, southern condemned were overwhelmingly Black men, and joining them on the gallows were Black ministers, challenging the narrative of punishment and white supremacy. "In many states of the union the masses are largely composed of an inferior race. They are ignorant and superstitious and fear death while they do not dread life imprisonment, believing that escape or pardon will some day set them free," wrote the editor of the *Atlanta Constitution* in 1893. "The only way to control certain dangerous classes of our population is to convince them that death will follow the crime of murder as surely as the night follows the day."[145] But not just death: it needed to be a lesson that was quiet, and solemn, and filled with horror and awe; a moment empty of the redemption narrative of the camp meeting that typically subverted the lessons of the public gallows.

In this era, whites responded to the fraying systems of white authority with a host of measures to bolster their control: disfranchisement, for instance, and de jure segregation. This response extended to official state punishment regimes. In these years, whites invented the convict lease system and devised new laws and punishments for petty crimes like vagrancy. Whites also took control again of death as a punishment, both by extralegally wresting Black men entirely from the system of justice through lynching and by ensuring whites dominated the story of legal executions by segregating executions away from public crowds, away from women, away from African Americans, and performing them behind walls.

Privacy made executions both "lily-white" and male. And they were designed to deepen the horror such moments of punishment could offer. As with seemingly all else in this era in the South, the shift from public to private execution had much to do with race and gender and deploying what some believed would be a more effective means of control. In ways that echo how progressivism in the South was almost equal measures liberal and profoundly racist, the changes in the punishment regime of the South in this period were similarly viewed as progress *and* as doubling down on the horror that punishment needed to provide to be effective with the criminal class. "Laws that would suit the situation in Denmark, Sweden and North Dakota would be a positive menace to Georgia," wrote the *Atlanta Constitution*. "As long as we have the negro in the south and the vicious white man, so long will we need to safeguard our womanhood and law abiding citizens with the protection that capital punishment alone affords."[146]

Public execution had offered the condemned a platform from which to proclaim their devotion, as well as a focal point for communities to emphasize his sanctification. Religion played a provocative role in these moments in terms of challenging the public authority of the white, southern police state after the Civil War. Privacy, centralization, and electrocution stripped away this public authority, placing the mechanisms of lethal, state punishment more firmly in the hands of white men. Not only would they control and witness these punishments, but privacy and electrocution were expressly envisioned as terror-inducing. Given the white South's belief that private executions and electrocutions would be horrifying, the turn to privacy in legal executions in the South had more in common with lynching than with civility. At the time of the South's first electrocution, a newspaper editor captured this: "It is a melancholy satisfaction to know that this gruesome punitive engine is in successful operation."[147]

Afterword

> At the root of the American Negro Problem is the necessity of the American white man to find a way of living with the Negro in order to be able to live with himself. And the history of this problem can be reduced to the means used by Americans—lynch law and law, segregation and legal acceptance, terrorization and concession— either to come to terms with this necessity, or to find a way around it, or (most usually) to find a way of doing both these things at once. The resulting spectacle, at once foolish and dreadful, led someone to make the quite accurate observation that "the Negro-in-America is a form of insanity which overtakes white men."
>
> —JAMES BALDWIN, "Stranger in the Village," 1953

> Hanging certainly does not seem to have a deterrent effect. But a castrated negro would be an object of derision to all the negro men and boys, and particularly to the women. It would not interfere with his usefulness as a working animal. Geldings and oxen are as valuable as entire animals.
>   This is certainly better than lynching, and more effective.
>
> —DR. B. W. GREEN, *Virginia Law Register*, 1903

> The Negroes refused to believe the evidence of white witnesses or the fairness of white juries, so that the greatest deterrent to crime, the public opinion of one's own caste, was lost, and the criminal was looked at as crucified rather than hanged.
>
> —W. E. B. DU BOIS, *Souls of Black Folk*, 1903

The last legal public execution in the South was of Rainey Bethea in front of an estimated 10,000 to 15,000 people in Owensboro, Kentucky, in 1936.[1] On that day, Bethea was reserved on the scaffold, with his final religious ceremony a private, quiet talk and prayer with a Catholic priest. The enclosure was only a four-foot wire fence, and the position of the gallows allowed for a view from all who chose to come to the 5 A.M. hanging. Thousands of visitors arrived in Owensboro the night before, some sleeping out in the open at the gallows site. The crowd cheered and yelled when the trap was sprung, with one paper qualifying this boisterous behavior by assuring readers that "it was not ill-natured or violent, but rather appeared to be enjoying the 'hangman's holiday.'"[2] This article admitted, however, that there was a "lapse in decorum" when bits of the hood were ripped off of Bethea's corpse by the crowd as his body was removed from the scaffold.

This execution brought national (and negative) attention to Kentucky, galvanizing a movement within the state to end the local (and public) execution for rape. It was "Kentucky's Disgrace," according to an editorial in the *Louisville Times*.[3] In response to the outcry over Bethea's execution, the judge who next sentenced a man to death in Kentucky for rape required that the enclosure effectively make the hanging private.[4] Even so, the sheriff responsible for that hanging was quoted as being "horrified by the execution," saying that he was determined to join the growing movement to reform the law. One further hanging of a man in the locality where he committed the crime occurred before a revision to the law was passed in 1938; in this hanging, too, the enclosure was effective in limiting the witnesses. Rainey Bethea would remain the last condemned man in American history to be legally hanged in the open.[5]

IF PUBLIC EXECUTION WERE EVIDENCE of a rougher justice persisting in the legal system of the South—a legal analog to lynching—then several things might be considered likely to follow: that public execution was more prevalent in the more frontier-like parts of the South; that those most antagonistic to African Americans would fight to retain public executions; that public execution would be considered by the condemned and particularly by African Americans as an additional horror; and that African Americans' executions would be more public than the executions of white condemned. Not one of these potential relationships finds support in the historical record. Instead, whites were executed publicly in very much the same proportions as Blacks, and there appear to be no frontier versus settled geographical trends to find. If there are trends to any of these issues, they are both subtle and equivocal.

But other trends are more clearly supported by the historical record. White conservative Democrats were the politicians most in favor of eliminating the public gallows; Republican allies of African Americans were more conflicted or even in favor of keeping the gallows public.[6] In addition, the perception of public execution by African Americans was clearly *not* that it was some sort of extra horror. The historical record abounds with evidence that, as horrible as any execution might be, the public nature of it did not make the event more so. Quite the contrary, in fact. These moments force us to consider how powerful were religious ideas in the lived experience of African American communities. These trends suggest we need to reposition public executions in the punishment regime in the South, and in that way, complicate the national story of capital punishment.

Lynching, in particular, appears in a different light in the context of all the things whites and Blacks in the South were saying and thinking about punishment in general and about legal executions in particular. It is important that whites in the South claimed, among other arguments, that lynching was necessary because of the failure of the legal system to adequately assure justice. This study does not, of course, support that contention: the injustices of the South ran in the other direction, skewed in multiple ways toward white prejudice. But what it reveals is at least as important to our understanding: just how fundamentally the capital punishment regime of the South was failing to terrorize the African American underclass to the extent white supremacists believed was required.

By putting public, legal executions in the South at the center of the analysis, we see just how much the sacred African American gallows experiences challenged white authority and its punishment regime. This challenge had many elements. As segregation became more and more thorough in the South, white and Black women were in attendance along with Black and white men at the public gallows. Playing the central roles on this "stage" at a public execution were Black men—the condemned and ministers—and the participatory nature of the religious services gave still more weight to their authority. In 1852, the minister of the African Church in Richmond preached at the gallows when a Black woman condemned for murder was publicly hanged. But in 1852, the pastor of that church was a white man, Rev. Dr. Robert Ryland, founder of Richmond College.[7] By 1870, that congregation, as throughout the South, was led by African American ministers, who stepped into the role of confessor, consoler, and minister to the condemned of their race. Now the authority of God's word on the stage of a scaffold in front of perhaps thousands of white and Black congregants was coming from the booming voice of a Black minister. Clear and bold claims of equality in the eyes of God—the radicalism of Christ's teachings bolstering the personification of their challenge to white authority as they stood before the whole community—made these moments at the scaffold particularly charged.

This was contested terrain, and white supremacy was failing to dominate in that contest. In the same generation that developed the de jure segregation of Jim Crow, the generation that chained so many Blacks and poor whites to the land with debt peonage born of the sharecropping regime and that stripped the franchise from the African American and the white underclass, the punishment regime of the South was likewise changing to better ensure white control. Lynching was prominent, the convict lease system was at its height, and public, multiracial, gender-inclusive executions were becoming private, white, male ones. Already in complete control of the mechanisms of southern governance by the late 1870s, the white South in the next generation jiggered with the machinery of punishment to yield what they thought might be the best output of social-order-through-terror-and-control under white supremacy.

Both of the developments in lethal punishment in this totalitarian (in terms of the African American population) regime—lynching and privacy in executions—were meant, at least in part, to ensure the underclass was adequately terrorized. That lynching was intended to accomplish this is perhaps obvious. What is revealed here is that the failure of legal, public punishment to terrorize is a starting place we did not have for understanding the grim horror of southern lynching: if the legal punishment regime were accomplishing not just the goals of justice in the South but also the goals of white supremacy by provoking terror and promoting the racial order as effectively as the slave regime had done, fewer white southerners would have found utility in resorting to mobs.

Legal punishment in the South was in the hands of whites: white juries (especially after 1880), white police (especially after Reconstruction), and white lawyers, judges, prosecutors, legislators, and governors. Justice was bent in the directions they wanted to bend it. And bend it they did, with new vagrancy laws, with penalties assigned by white juries armed now with wide discretion, and with new penalties for rape and attempted rape, among other things. Chain gangs were supported by new laws for a range of crimes to allow for punishment not merely on the basis of the crime but on the basis of who the criminal was. In most of these "innovations," as with the death penalty, the South charted a distinct course from the rest of the nation in terms of punishment.

A state expects its judicial system to do more than to deal with a crime after it has occurred: it also helps to shape the nature of an orderly society by strictly drawing lines about what was acceptable, curbing future disorder in a preventative way. And in the South, amid the congeries of social changes emerging in the generations after Appomattox, whites demanded not just justice from its justice system but likewise control. Was the punishment regime of the postbellum South accomplishing the curbing effects that every legal system strives for in terms of preventing crimes by showing they will be penalized? More: was it accomplishing the curbing effects that a white supremacist state requires to keep the underclass firmly in its place?

At least in terms of the second contention, no. And the failures of capital punishment in this way were important preconditions to the extralegal brutality of this moment. To us and to African Americans at the time, lynching was simply evil: criminal brutality condoned by white society not in one instance of passion but in thousands of instances over the course of generations. It was simply among the worst acts ever committed in the United States.

To southern whites, participating in or at least condoning this horror? Whites in the South were used to public executions, accustomed to the pervasive use of the lash, and coached to deem African Americans as much like animals as like themselves. From this profoundly racist world view, lynching was much less shocking than it is for us, for whites' skewed assumptions of justice were built from the norms of nineteenth-century public punishments. This meant, particularly, punishments upon Black bodies: the whipping post and the public noose had been regularly deployed as legal, normal, state-sanctioned punishments, performed in the open. This was not in the distant past, but recently, an inheritance from the previous generation. What shocks and horrifies us were, for many white southerners in the late nineteenth century, normalized in the white supremacist culture in which they were raised. Hurting Black bodies in public in the antebellum South was a key element of maintaining public order, and whites of the postwar South inherited this norm.

What had changed in the late nineteenth century was not racism, nor violence practiced brutally and in public, from the perspective of southern whites. What had changed were rules that made these things no longer legal; what had changed (little by little) was the place African Americans were holding in society. To these racist southern whites, what was out of keeping with tradition was having physical, public punishments now—newly—illegal. What was traditional? The public nature of violence.

We can even presume that, for many southern white supremacists in this moment, those who believed it natural and right that whites be in complete control, lynching was an improvement upon the more mixed-messaged, mixed-race, mixed-gender, legal, public executions with preaching and hymns and confession and seeing-you-all-in-heaven. And white southerners wrested from African American ministers and condemned the authority and the sanctification of the public gallows and its theater of redemption, replacing it with a death penalty regime as segregated as was almost everything else in this era. Both private executions and lynchings were more like what punishment—from the skewed norm inherited from the malignancy of the totalitarian police state of the antebellum South—was meant to be.

MORE THAN ONE HUNDRED YEARS separate us from the period this book studies. By the time I was born in the midst of the civil rights movement, two generations of Americans lived and worked and changed the nature of the South and the nation in terms of race and in terms of gender. As a result, we do not live with the same issues . . . quite. Historians often stretch to make connections between their topics in the distant past and the present day. I dislike that impulse, for the lives that intervened between us and the era under study here *mattered*, and their efforts deserve our respect and attention. Public defenders did not exist; then they did. Rights of defendants verged upon nil; then they were written into the law. Lynching declined radically, chain gangs were ended, and the pace of capital punishment dropped decade by decade in the twentieth century. De jure segregation and disfranchisement were overcome. Generations confronted racism and sexism, and they did so not just in the face of opposition, but in the face of violence; the world we inhabit, due to their effort and sacrifice, has been transformed.

Yet, if this work on legal capital punishment is haunted by the horrors of lynching in its own era, it is likewise haunted by the ways our own echo chambers today allow for slices of our society to believe in internal logics that are resistant to facts, that are self-reinforcing, and that not only are impervious to other views but also actively promote worldviews that are uninterested in knowing what other views (and realities) exist. Whites north and south at the turn of the twentieth century offer us an object lesson in the horrors that can yield. Racism today remains a disturbing issue in America's justice system and in its practice of capital punishment. Modern drug laws and prejudice in their application have made our prison system—doubling in terms of convicts and then doubling again in the generations after 1960—a mockery of justice about as glaring as the chain gangs and convict lease systems of the late nineteenth-century South.[8]

Fear, again, is palpable, present on the left and seemingly pervasive on the right, spinning storylines of a nation under siege. There is less violence now than in the South of five generations ago, and the violence we have has changed its nature. But there are just the sort of rhetorical gestures to tribalism and to some Americans being treated like people and others treated as less-thans, not worthy of being heard or being considered, really, citizens. I did not write this study with an intent to be timely; I would prefer these issues to remain firmly in our past. Yet here we are.

We have a usable past, and it teaches us of complexity as well as of change. Even with such a narrow slice of experience as capital punishment in the post–Civil War South, it is not just black and white, not just justice and injustice. Just as our lives today are not simple, neither were the lives we study from the past; this slice of the past under investigation here involves race, gender, religion, justice, fear, and more, all combining and roiling through communities in messy ways.

Each generation inherits a world, then passes on a different one. If there are struggles today that echo the struggles from more than one hundred years ago, it is also true that change is inevitable, and that change is pervasive. Laws can and will and have been changed. Gender roles and mores change. Race relations have likewise never been static; they, too, change. And so with capital punishment, which has changed in sweeping ways in the last century: downward, upward, and now sharply downward again. A decades-long decline ended in the U.S. Supreme Court banning the death penalty in the United States as cruel and unusual in the 1970s. A revised procedure, allowed by the court in 1976, led to a quarter-century surge (mirroring roughly the massive spike of incarceration) to a modern high of ninety-eight executions in the United States in 1999.[9] Since then, the use of the death penalty has fallen almost every year: all six of the six years with lowest numbers of those legally executed in the United States (20, 23, 25, 22, 17, and 11) were from 2016 to 2021.[10] Almost all of those executions were in southern states. In 2021, Virginia became the twenty-third state to abolish capital punishment—and the first state in the South ever to do so.[11]

If today's rhetoric and divisions confuse the issue at times—making histories like this one far more relevant to today than we would like them to be—these shifts in our world can remind us that, in fact, we do not live in the 1890s South and that our children can, indeed, inherit from us a better world. But history, including the history of crime and punishments, also shows that the arc of the moral universe does not necessarily, inevitably, bend in that direction. In our worst moments, we manage to bend it awry. It requires a tremendous amount of effort—in politics, in shaping the stories that frame our understandings of our world, in movement building, in making connections with people not like ourselves—to patiently, steadfastly, and actively bend that long arc toward justice.

Notes

If the Espy file has been the standard starting point for any work on capital punishment in the United States, it is also very incomplete for the South in this era, as the work of Daniel Hearn and Lewis Laska amply demonstrates. Throughout this work, I use their lists of executions for six states of the South together: Hearn, *Legal Executions in Georgia*; Hearn, *Legal Executions in Kentucky*; Hearn, *Legal Executions in North Carolina and South Carolina*; Hearn, *Legal Executions in Virginia*; and Laska, *Legal Executions in Tennessee*. When data from them all are compiled together in figures or text, they are cited, for convenience, as "Hearn and Laska."

Introduction: Re-centering

1. Historians have long used "redemption" as the word for this emergence from Reconstruction regimes. I believe this has too many positive connotations for what was a brutal episode. Here I use the term "reconquest," which is not perfect but at least communicates the violence of the moment.

2. Some of the most important work in southern history will be studies of just these elements of legal, state-sanctioned punishment; particularly important will be those scholars investigating courtrooms, jury deliberations, and how the law was twisted well before the punishments were rendered. These studies may simply transform our understandings of the period. Twenty-seven Black men and no white men were executed for attempted rape in Virginia between 1894 and 1920, Daniel Hearn found (*Legal Executions in Virginia*). How did they get there? That question points toward juries and policing and the law, and these issues seem at least as important as the ones pursued in this study about the nature of their executions and the stories told about them. But that will be a different project, for this study's sources and its focus on executions illuminate little about courtrooms and jury deliberations.

3. Kotch (*Lethal State*) has offered the most thorough exploration of capital punishment in the South, focused on North Carolina, and centering on the era of state authority over the death penalty, which began in 1910 in that state. He briefly treats developments there between 1880 and 1910, but most of the work concerns later developments, and his findings and even themes differ substantially from this work. More consonant with my findings is his article "Making of the Modern Death Penalty," which parallels a number of arguments here in terms of the importance of religion at the gallows and many of the dynamics of both public and private execution. Miller's "Hanging, the Electric Chair, and Death Penalty Reform" nicely situates a number of themes in terms of the transition to electrocution in the region.

If discussed at all in the wider scholarship of the South, public execution is mentioned in passing or as a context for lynching. Brundage, for instance, calls public execution a "surrogate ritual for lynching" (*Lynching in the New South*, 255–56; see also 40). Pfeifer similarly references public executions as examples of a persistent tradition of rough justice, one ambiguously connected to lynching impulses (*Rough Justice*, 80, 121). Vandiver makes similar comparisons (*Lethal Punishment*, 10–11). George Wright claims that "Afro-Americans consistently cried out against public execution" (*Racial Violence in Kentucky*, 245), but the evidence I found was for objecting to injustice rather than to the public nature of these events. The first chapter of Wood's *Lynching as Spectacle* has terrific insights on the white experience of the public gallows, linking that tradition to the white lynch crowds. But none of these studies investigates the changing dynamics of executions on their own terms or the African American experience of these moments.

Most other scholars of the South and of lynching do not discuss public execution at all—they are, after all, pursuing other prey—or if they do, it is to paint a picture of the scene at the gallows (as in Ayers, *Vengeance and Justice*, 247–48). Often these are the most extreme examples, the ones with violence and disorder and that, therefore, received the most press and that seem (deceptively, I argue) the most telling in terms of race, violence, and the region. See, for instance, Wright, *Racial Violence in Kentucky*, 231–33. Wright does not specifically study public executions, but he describes a number of executions with public and lynching-like behavior. This scholarship has tended to reinforce the impression that whites dominated southern public execution crowds. They did not.

Numerous studies mention in passing public execution in the South (Bowers, *Legal Homicide*, 8; Banner, *Death Penalty*, 143, 154–55; Bessler, *Death in the Dark*, 44, 46, 60, 69–70 [this volume discusses England's transition to private execution more than the U.S. South]; Allen and Clubb, *Race, Class, and the Death Penalty*, 74–75, 79), but the two best works on the transition from public to private execution tell a northern or national story without reference to the South: Masur, *Rites of Execution* and Linders, "Execution Spectacle." Linders includes the South (but I would argue misplaces the interplay of religion and race in the region's experience) in a later article on gender and the end of public execution: "What Daughters?"

4. For those victims of lynch mobs who were devout, a central fear was the prospect of death *unprepared*. Some condemned on the gallows speak to this directly: "I might have been carried away unprepared without a moment's warning. The thought makes me shudder" (*New Orleans Daily Picayune*, 27 January 1882). For similar wordings, see *Florida Times-Union*, 5 March 1910. While a very rich literature has emerged on white southern religious justifications for lynching, more needs to be done to develop an understanding of how religion and lynching also have dramatic connections in terms of the African American victims and community. An important element of the fear and horror of the South's devout population of African Americans would be this lack of preparation, as they were so often killed without any elements of sanctification that defined the good death of the penitent saved. For the literature on religion and lynching, see the work of Donald Mathews, particularly *At the Altar of Lynching*.

The analysis of African American religion in the South started early, including Du Bois, *Negro Church*, and Faduma, "Defects of the Negro Church." Historians have continued to reframe this theme in the history of the South, though none make the religious exercises at the gallows central to their work; most do not mention it. See

Higginbotham, *Righteous Discontent*; Sobel, *Trabelin' On*; Dixie and West, *Courage to Hope*; Montgomery, *Under Their Own Vine*; and Giggie, *After Redemption*. Histories of religion in the South more generally include Harvey, *Redeeming the South*.

5. The ideology of the white South has long attracted the attention of historians, and it continues to do so. Early influential examples include Fredrickson, *Black Image in the White Mind*; Southern, *Malignant Heritage*; Williamson, *Crucible of Race*. More recent studies include Silber, *Romances of Reunion*; Prince, *Stories of the South*; and on the North, Muhammad, *Condemnation of Blackness*. The ideology of African American thinkers has likewise drawn much attention, including Williams, *They Left Great Marks*. Many of the most important studies of the South in this period include among their topics this study of ideology: Litwack, *Been in the Storm* and *Trouble in Mind*; Ayers, *Vengeance and Justice*; Wyatt-Brown, *Southern Honor*; Rable, *But There Was No Peace*.

6. While she tells a more national story and misses the importance of religion in the experience of public executions, Annulla Linders has produced the best work on gender and executions in print, valuable work this study attempts to build upon. See her "What Daughters?"; (with Gundy-Yoder) "Gall, Gallantry, and the Gallows"; and "Execution Spectacle."

On the crime of rape in the South, important work for this study includes Sommerville, *Rape and Race*; Feimster's *Southern Horrors*; Dorr, *White Women*; Freedman, *Redefining Rape*; Bardaglio, *Reconstructing the Household*.

Works of importance to this study on gender in the South include Gilmore, *Gender and Jim Crow*; Edwards, *Gendered Strife and Confusion*; and Hunter, *To 'Joy My Freedom*.

7. *Atlanta Constitution*, 5 September 1891. In this execution, the convict and ministers were not the only African Americans before the crowd: "Forming a square about the scaffold was a detachment of fifty-one men of the colored troops of the city."

Chapter One: A Camp Meeting

1. Roger Lane, for instance, speaks of punishment as "a deterrent to weak wills who might otherwise be tempted" (*Murder in America*, 79).

2. Davis, Gardner, and Gardner, *Deep South*, 527. They continued, "People begin to blame the courts for being too lenient, and to say: 'It's time we had a hanging, that's the only way to stop all these killings.' (Even the sheriff and the judge explain that an occasional hanging is necessary to keep down Negro crime . . .)."

3. Romans 6:23. Scriptural passages in this chapter are from the Revised Standard version of the Bible.

4. Matthew 26:26.

5. Donald Mathews pursues this idea of religion guarding against whites seeing them as beasts without a soul (*At the Altar*, 40).

6. Newspapers in the late nineteenth and early twentieth centuries could be flippant in titling articles on executions, demonstrating the era's much greater tolerance for public violence: "Hempen Harvest" (*New Orleans Daily Picayune*, 1 December 1883), "A Bad Necktie" (*Louisville Courier-Journal*, 22 February 1879), "Rope Stretched" (*Atlanta Constitution*, 10 July 1903), "Duly Fridayed" (*Atlanta Constitution*, 26 January 1888—executions in many states were scheduled for Fridays), "Tight Rope

Exhibition" (*Mobile Daily Register*, 24 August 1874), or "End of His Rope" (*Nashville Daily Advertiser*, 16 April 1887).

7. This study is based largely on the newspaper reports of 1,358 southern executions. Some I could clearly identify as public, private, or having a semiprivate mix of attributes from descriptions of events in newspapers, the only sources that speak to the issue of whether executions were in public or not. Many other reports of executions in the period were too ambiguous to clearly show whether the executions were public or private; still more I did not find or have not sought. A starting place for this search was "The Espy File," started by M. Watt Espy, which lists a variety of information for about 15,000 U.S. executions from 1607 to 2002. Of the Espy file's 2,740 executions in the South between 1866 and 1920, 2,465 of them took place before southern states centralized executions and/or turned to electrocution, moments that ended the possibility for an execution to be public in any meaningful way.

8. *Atlanta Constitution*, 5 October 1893.

9. I have found several dozen references to "mostly" or "predominantly" Black crowds at public executions, and even more that reference the African American crowds congregating outside the jail walls, if a barrier was involved. For a series of Georgia examples (but little interpretation) of "mostly Negro" executions, see Coulter, "Hanging," 25–45. Similarly, crowds in Texas might be "mostly Mexican," *Galveston Daily News*, 8 July 1879 and *Dallas Morning News*, 31 July 1897. In addition, many more dozens of articles emphasize the prominence of African Americans in the crowds (but don't specifically claim them a majority) either by describing the crowd as being composed of "every hue" or something similar or by describing the Blacks in the crowd in ways that imply a large number. The references throughout this chapter cite many of these instances of Black participation. For a few representative citations of "mostly negro," see *Florida Times-Union*, 14 December 1907; *Raleigh News and Observer*, 4 May 1895; *Richmond Dispatch*, 13 June 1874. For references on Black crowds outside walls, see *Mobile Daily Register*, 7 September 1883; *Arkansas Gazette*, 27 June 1885; *Charleston News and Courier*, 24 August 1878. In contrast, I have only found a handful of cases when whites clearly outnumbered Blacks at the execution of a Black man; see, for example, *Atlanta Constitution*, 2 September 1892; *Charleston News and Courier*, 5 May 1877.

10. Privacy in executions made the crowds much whiter (see chapter 6). When Greely Phillips was privately hanged in 1905, he made a speech to, as he put it, "my good white friends," who were the only ones allowed to witness the event (*Atlanta Constitution*, 6 May 1905).

11. One convict even took over part of this role: reading his own death warrant. *Dallas Morning News*, 31 July 1923. More than one was allowed to select the hour of his own hanging (*Daily Democrat*, 5 February 1899; Coulter, "Hanging," 29), and another was allowed to give the signal for the trap to be sprung (*Houston Daily Post*, 25 March 1899).

12. Among the dozens of articles that use this sort of exasperated language ("of course," "as usual," or "etc., etc.") are *Nashville Daily American*, 9 April 1881; *Atlanta Constitution*, 13 May 1891; *Galveston Daily News*, 1 June 1878; *Florida Times-Union*, 5 March 1910; *Raleigh News and Observer*, 31 October 1879; *Birmingham Age-Herald*,

21 July 1894; *New Orleans Daily Picayune*, 16 January 1886; *Norfolk Virginian*, 26 March 1879; *Petersburg Daily Index Appeal*, 23 June 1883.

13. When reading a single report of an execution, one might be tempted to dismiss this religious element as a sort of script: expected of everyone, and for form's sake, the condemned and crowd adhered to it, and then the press reported it. For an interpretation of scaffold speeches as ritualistic, see Schwarz, *Slave Laws*, 95. But after reading hundreds of such reports and finding this religious element in a vast majority of public executions, described in a variety of ways by dozens of different papers and editors, I am convinced that these religious exercises were central both to the participants and to the historical meaning of these events. In spite of my initial skepticism of white newspapers reporting on the hangings of Black criminals, after evaluating the reporting from dozens of different papers across the region (and comparing with reports from northern and African American papers when available), I conclude that reports of southern executions were not typically freighted with the defensive and political baggage that was common in the strident reporting on lynching. This does not mean that the whites writing these reports were not racist, but rather that they rarely seemed concerned about the nature of the scene they were reporting. In addition, the vast array of different papers, editors, and perspectives on the theater of the scaffold provides this study with a breadth of sources — if, sadly, inevitably, mostly white ones — that allows a check upon any one editor's prejudices. Throughout, I have attempted to be mindful of the construction of these narratives by white editors and reporters and to compare them when possible against other sources.

14. Harper, *End of Days*, 9, 20–21. At least by the second decade of the twentieth century, public executions were more rare and noted not just locally but at times nationally, creating a different dynamic for these reports, including more defensiveness. Yet even here, it is unclear how much the southern white press was spinning these stories compared with how northern papers critical of the South's public executions were spinning them; neither side would be devoid of its politics. A double execution in Starkville, Mississippi, in 1915 was public, with vendors supplying the large crowd, and the condemned asked for the audience to sing hymns. The southern white press presented this as almost commonplace; the *Chicago Defender* (21 August 1915) titled its commentary "Roman Orgies Repeated" and spoke of the condemned as "on exhibit." Other northern papers likewise characterized this scene as exploitation of horror, and the *East Mississippi Times* (13 August 1915) responded with both an editorial and a front page story printing excerpts from the *New York World* and the *Chicago Tribune* to make fun of them. The *Hattiesburg News* (7 August 1915) as well as the *Atlanta Constitution* (7 August 1915) interpreted the scene as normal and noted that the crowd was a mix of the races.

15. *Atlanta Constitution*, 16 July 1892. See also 20 February 1892.

16. *Nashville Daily American*, 21 February 1880.

17. *Arkansas Gazette*, 8 November 1902; *Charleston News and Courier*, 27 October 1906.

18. Newspaper reports regularly described the convict moving to a corner of the scaffold where Blacks were gathered in the crowd for the singing, praying, and

preaching: The sheriff in one execution requested that "the lower side be reserved for the darkies. As it was a darkey who was to be hung he thought their wishes should be regarded." *Atlanta Constitution*, 1 November 1884.

19. Durham, North Carolina, "realizes that a hanging is more than an occasion or an event: it is an epoch. From what I saw of the two convicts, a glimmer of this pre-eminence had filtered through to their steel-barred cells: they were something more than doomed, in that they felt their immortalization in Durham history." *Raleigh News and Observer*, 8 February 1908. Edward Ayers speaks of these moments being powerful, memorable theater, and Donald Mathews characterizes their special nature as timeless, quasi-participatory, and transgressive, a particularly nice formulation to keep in mind (Ayers, *Vengeance and Justice*, 248; Mathews, *At the Altar*, 125).

20. *New Orleans Daily Picayune*, 14 January 1893. See also *New Orleans Daily Picayune*, 8 September 1883.

21. It appears that once convicts were condemned to die for their crimes, white sheriffs tended to treat prisoners with respect. Prisoners usually remarked on their kindly treatment, which included tobacco, special meals, freely admitting visitors, family, and clergy and at the gallows allowing them to have their say and sometimes to say goodbye to all their friends; a line of people shaking hands with the condemned was not unheard of. While it would be easy to make too much of this generosity— after all, the central act here was to kill the convict—this behavior seems an expression of the paternalism of southern whites. The sheriffs were on display before thousands, too, and demonstrated their humanity (and sometimes their feelings) at the same time that they clearly expressed their power.

For an example of the sheriff passing a hat for contributions to the (Black) condemned's family, see *Richmond Dispatch*, 4 August 1883. For a similar story, see *New York Times*, 9 April 1872. A later study emphasized the humane treatment of the condemned: Davis, Gardner, and Gardner, *Deep South*, 528–33.

22. *Birmingham Age-Herald*, 8 June 1895. One condemned asked the governor (not the usual process) for two hours on the scaffold to talk. The governor responded that "he could have four hours if he wanted them" (*Atlanta Constitution*, 30 October 1900). "They made no confession, but for fully three hours and a half previous to the fatal moment were engaged giving vent to ravings about their hopes of salvation" (*Charleston News and Courier*, 24 August 1878).

23. *Atlanta Constitution*, 17 July 1886. One Mississippi sheriff allowed the condemned to pick the hour of execution (*Daily Democrat*, 5 February 1899). See also *Atlanta Constitution*, 28 October 1893 and 18 December 1897 for other examples of a sheriff's generosity.

24. *Richmond Dispatch*, 31 May 1869; *Atlanta Constitution*, 2 December 1893. One paper referred to a condemned being "'toned' up for the end" at the scaffold. *Raleigh News and Observer*, 9 February 1907.

25. *New Orleans Daily Picayune*, 17 July 1886.

26. *New Orleans Daily Picayune*, 17 July 1886, 20 February 1892; *Houston Daily Post*, 29 October 1898.

27. *Charleston News and Courier*, 1 September 1893.

28. *Atlanta Constitution*, 2 March 1894; see also *Atlanta Constitution*, 23 July 1892. While it would be helpful to have more African American sources reflecting on these moments (see note 29 below), the fact that white papers report on these moments in so many different ways seems helpful: some making fun of the religious enthusiasms, some simply describing the scene; some surprised at an execution lacking the religious element, and some describing the crowd (or reporter) moved by what they saw. The authors of these execution reports were not merely relaying journalistic boiler plate, in other words; they were describing in a great variety of ways the scenes they found at the gallows. Crucially and unlike their reports of lynching scenes, white papers rarely appear to have been defensive about these events: public executions were acceptable in the late nineteenth century (though not later), and it appears that they could be openly, frankly, and variously narrated.

29. The few Black papers that existed in this era rarely covered the executions of Blacks. Not only were those African American papers typically weeklies (which, as a rule, focused less on local news of any sort, including executions, than did dailies), but reports of Black executions would merely emphasize Black crime, which was not a goal of these papers. On the rare occasions when they did cover an execution (often when white injustice was clearly in play), they described the religious nature of Black executions in similar terms to the white papers: see, for instance, *Huntsville Gazette*, 18 August 1883, 29 August 1885, 1 March 1890; *Richmond Planet*, 18 March 1905, 24 August 1912; *Baltimore Afro-American*, 21 August 1915; and the Black monthly, *Voice of the Negro* (January 1906): 14–16, 61–62. For more on what Black papers covered in this era, see Trotti, *Body in the Reservoir*, 111–44, and Davis, "Black Press."

30. *Richmond Planet*, 11 March 1905. See also the *Planet*'s coverage in 1896 of the hanging of Solomon Marable, executed in the Lunenburg murder case investigated by Suzanne Lebsock (*Murder in Virginia*). Although a private execution (he says, "Well, gentlemen, you is all strangers to me here"), Marable's final statement to the small crowd hearkened back to public executions a generation before in Virginia: "Jesus is standing by me on the right-hand side. I've got a free ticket to glory. Prayer is the gate and the faith, the key which will unlock the door. I will wear a crown of glory" (*Richmond Planet*, 11 July 1896; see also 25 July 1896).

31. *Atlanta Constitution*, 26 July 1897.

32. *Raleigh Observer*, 15 June 1878.

33. *Arkansas Gazette*, 27 July 1901. For a list of questions the audience asked a condemned man, see the *Galveston Daily News*, 23 August 1879.

34. *Atlanta Constitution*, 2 June 1883. For other similar examples, see *Richmond Dispatch*, 31 May 1869; *Nashville Daily American*, 3 June 1882.

35. *Atlanta Constitution*, 16 July 1892; *Atlanta Constitution*, 26 April 1884; see also *Atlanta Constitution*, 2 December 1893. One member of the crowd at an execution took the words of the dying man (an African American convicted of murder) and set them into a poem, "Daniel's Dying Testimonial," quickly publishing it and reportedly selling it widely (*Atlanta Constitution*, 16 July 1892).

36. *Louisville Courier-Journal*, 2 February 1878.

37. Higginbotham, *Righteous Discontent*. While Higginbotham's book deals more with the talented tenth of women leaders in the Black Baptist faith than with the broader overall experience of women in religion, it provides ample evidence of the prominence of women in the faith and how the church provided women with important public roles (16).

38. *Florida Times-Union*, 28 January 1911.

39. *New York Times*, 9 April 1872; see also 11 April 1874. *Dallas Morning News* (10 March 1900) writes of the execution commencing "amid the wailings and screamings of the women." The *Charleston News and Courier* (14 July 1877) reported that women perched upon housetops in the neighborhood overlooking the jail walls "struck up a horrible wailing howl. . . . At every moment the women in the neighborhood increased the weird and awful moan which they had started, and thereby added greatly to the horror of the scene."

40. *New Orleans Daily Picayune*, 31 August 1889; *Arkansas Gazette*, 26 May 1883.

41. *Galveston Daily News*, 28 August 1880.

42. For a rare example, see *Huntsville Gazette*, 8 August 1891.

43. "Was there anything in the history of the courts of his own community to give him even the slightest hope of justice?" wrote William Pickens about a "Desperado" in *The Crisis* 3 (1911): 75. On African American views of justice in general, see Du Bois, *Souls of Black Folk*, 113-14; Work, "Negro Criminality in the South," 78; Trotti, *Body in the Reservoir*, 124-30.

44. *New Orleans Daily Picayune*, 6 June 1885.

45. A *New York Times* story (15 March 1878) about a Tennessee execution found it notable that Blacks in the area also thought the convict was guilty; that was clearly not the norm. "The most talked about subject of the period was clearly violence," according to a national study of the Black press in the era (Davis, "Black Press," 173). Frederick Douglass thought that "we should be about as well situated for the purposes of justice if there were no Constitution of the United States at all; as well off if there were no law or law-makers, no constables, no jails, no courts of justice, and we were left entirely without the pretense of legal protection, for we are now at the mercy of midnight raiders, assassins, and murderers, and we should only be in the same condition if these pretended safeguards were abandoned. They now only mock us" (*Three Addresses*, 60).

46. Historians have choices in how to interpret sources. We could choose to discount this evidence, believing, for instance, that this represents something like a fig leaf offered by white newspapers to cover the power and violence of the moment: to make the shocking punishment more palatable to white newspaper readership. Or we could interpret it as a racist white skew in the sources: white texts demeaning Black experience by presenting them as more childlike and absurd in believing heaven was within reach of criminals like these. Yet Occam's Razor and common sense dictate that the best interpretation of this wealth of evidence of religion woven throughout the history of the public gallows would be to believe them. After all, in a deeply religious and perilously beset community, the hope of redemption was, in fact, central to African Americans of the South. Those beliefs were expressed openly in these moments; how could they not be?

47. Philip Schwarz makes this point in "Transportation of Slaves from Virginia," 219.

48. *Louisville Courier-Journal*, 23 June 1888.

49. *Birmingham Age Herald*, 31 October 1914.

50. *New Orleans Times Democrat*, 17 May 1879.

51. *Nashville Daily Advertiser*, 9 April 1881; Laska, *Legal Executions in Tennessee*, 234. In the Nashville execution, the condemned was baptized in a nearby creek before the execution, an event itself witnessed by more than five hundred.

52. *Atlanta Constitution*, 5 July 1891. The *Constitution* continued, "Washington, it will be remembered, was greatly disappointed that he was denied a public execution. He intended making a confession on the scaffold had he been executed in public. Friday, however, he refused to say anything."

53. *Arkansas Gazette*, 7 May 1892.

54. *Galveston Daily News*, 8 May 1880.

55. *Galveston Daily News*, 18 February 1882.

56. *New Orleans Daily Picayune*, 27 November 1875.

57. *Dallas Morning News*, 21 June 1908; *Arkansas Gazette*, 15 July 1913.

58. Often, the scholarship pursues this role of religion in these moments, contrasting, say, the "mock heroism" of a recalcitrant condemned man against the "successful" execution of a truly penitent, somber, and prayerful one (Kotch, *Lethal State*, 62).

59. Davis, Gardner, and Gardner, *Deep South*, 528-30, 533.

60. Raboteau, "Blood of Martyrs," 26. Ephesians 6:5: "Slaves be obedient to your masters." Under slavery, Black preachers could be whipped for preaching "the freedom of the soul" (Sobel, *Trabelin' On*, 169).

61. One element of this, however, was very common: when confessing either the crime they were condemned for or for their sins in general, the condemned on the gallows would almost always blame bad company and bad liquor and warn others to keep away from them. Sometimes they would reference the devil in particular or, interestingly, bad women. These messages, if not accompanied by the sanctification of the condemned and his call to see all in heaven, would be just the sort of conservative message whites thought most appropriate.

62. Montgomery, *Under Their Own Vine*, 262; Davis, "Negro Church," 97-98. Several studies at the time by African American scholars express these concerns, such as Holloway's "Black Belt County, Georgia," 58; Faduma, "Defects of the Negro Church," 4-5, 14-17; Du Bois, *Souls of Black Folk*, 119-29.

63. In fact, just as some African American congregations were moving from emotional evangelicalism to a more staid and learned style of worship in the 1890s and the decades thereafter, there was a strong countervailing movement: the new Holiness churches emphasized the emotional, physical styles of worship the middle class found so problematic, and they grew like wildfire around the turn of the twentieth century. For more on this Holiness movement, see Giggie, *After Redemption*, 165-93.

64. Harvey, *Redeeming the South*, 162, 178; Davis, "Negro Church," 87-89. Harvey also sees a gendered element here: that self-control was an important part of a vision of masculinity at this time, and religious emotional enthusiasms were not considered seemly in that way (165). One educated minister said to an interviewer, "I'm sorry you

heard me in this kind of a church. I have to talk that way to these people" (Davis, "Negro Church," 87).

65. Litwack, *Been in the Storm*, 461. "God is a Negro, God is not white," preached Bishop Turner of Atlanta. Black religion was superior, many devout African Americans would agree, and the suffering of the race was "merely a prelude to victory," they hoped (Mathews, *At the Altar*, 112–13).

66. Harvey, *Redeeming the South*, 121; Giggie, *After Redemption*, 181.

67. Montgomery, *Under Their Own Vine*, 287.

68. Former slave, quoted in Raboteau, "Blood of Martyrs," 34.

69. Sobel, *Trabelin' On*, 172.

70. Matthew 5:3, 5–6.

71. Raboteau, "Blood of Martyrs," 30.

72. Matthew 5:8, 10–11.

73. Romans 5:3–5; Mathews (*At the Altar*, 112) probes the role of suffering in African American religion.

74. Harper, *End of Days*, 28–29.

75. Higginbotham found that by 1916, the third largest denomination in the United States, behind only the Catholic faith and the Methodist Episcopal denomination, was the National Baptist Convention, USA, the national organization for Black Baptists. This was the largest denomination for any race in many southern cities (6–7). Myers and Sharpless estimated that among Black congregations, 10 percent were a variety of faiths (many of them middle-class Black congregations) with the remaining 90 percent of congregations evangelical churches: 30 percent of all rural African American churches were Methodist and 60 percent were Baptist ("'Of the Least and the Most,'" 56).

76. "It is variously estimated that from thirty to one hundred negro men and women were shouting and rolling and tumbling about upon the ground during this speech and the subsequent proceedings" (*Galveston Daily News*, 3 May 1879).

77. Montgomery, *Under Their Own Vine*, 295–96; Harvey, *Redeeming the South*, 124–25.

78. Northern reporter quoted in Harvey, *Redeeming the South*, 118.

79. Harvey, *Redeeming the South*, 115. Scholars of religion make it plain that both whites and Blacks partook of this sort of emotional display, and many denominations that employed camp meetings participated in this sort of emotional sanctification. Even more broadly, in the era of the second Great Awakening, much of the energy of the camp meetings across the nation centered on individuals admitting their sinful ways, rising to a catharsis of self-loathing that led to a recommitment to Christ. This style persisted among evangelical churches of both races, and in particular it proved very resilient in the South (Harvey, *Redeeming the South*, 77–78). This emotional, joyful expression of "bringing down the Holy Spirit" continues in some African American congregations to this day (Walter Pitts, "Keep the Fire Burnin'," 200).

80. Acts 2:13.

81. Acts 2:2–4.

82. Acts 2:33.

83. Acts 2:38–39.

84. Montgomery nicely calls this an "ego-shattering" moment (*Under Their Own Vine*, 19).

85. Davis, "Negro Church," 97–98. Davis observed in 1940 that "ecclesiastical doctrine receives little emphasis in the low-status Negro churches; in nine out of ten sermons in these churches, one hears neither an analysis of church creed nor an exposition of ethical doctrine." Instead, "the creed preached in the great majority of churches" was composed of "a literal acceptance of the Bible, belief in a patriarchal God, in a conventional Heaven and Hell, and in the efficacy of conversion, and of open testimony in church thereafter in assuring the 'saved' of heavenly salvation."

86. Montgomery, *Under Their Own Vine*, 267; Myers and Sharpless, "'Of the Least and the Most,'" 70. Montgomery calls conversion "the climax of the individual's progression from sinner to child of God."

87. Romans 3:23–25.

88. Montgomery, *Under Their Own Vine*, 20. Du Bois (*Souls of Black Folk*, 127) likewise contrasts the realities of African American life to the promise of religion.

89. Montgomery, *Under Their Own Vine*, 275. Sobel (*Trabelin' On*, 246) calls this promise of redemption "the core of all visions of the future" for African American Blacks in the South in this era.

90. Acts 2:38; emphasis added.

91. Davis, "Negro Church," 86. According to Sobel, "In the new Black Baptist Sacred Cosmos, belief was replaced by knowledge. The converted black had been to Heaven, and *knew* God and *knew* Jesus and *knew* himself saved. . . . The New Testament promise of redemption had become the core of all visions of the future" (*Trabelin' On*, 245–46).

92. Raboteau, "Blood of Martyrs," 32. Du Bois followed this line of thought more than a century ago: *Souls of Black Folk*, 126.

93. Smith, *To Serve the Living*, 21. Likewise, Eugene Genovese sees African American religion in the era of slavery as a mixture of western and African traits, or, perhaps better, how some Christian stories and traditions fit easily into the inherited worldview of African Americans and others did not. For instance, the importance of Moses/exodus and the redeemer Jesus, who suffered for men, and how African religions have no version of original sin, which he finds significant in how that is not typically stressed in Black churches (*Roll, Jordan, Roll*, 246–52).

94. Schwarz, *Slave Laws*, 212n55.

95. Harvey, *Redeeming the South*, 12.

96. Myers and Sharpless, "'Of the Least and the Most,'" 63; Raboteau, "Blood of Martyrs," 24. On the gallows, Solomon Marable said, "Jesus is standing by me on the right-hand side. I've got a free ticket to glory. Prayer is the gate and faith the key which will unlock the door. I will wear a crown of glory. I am speaking to all. Color makes no difference to me" (*Richmond Planet*, 11 July 1896).

97. Myers and Sharpless, "'Of the Least and the Most,'" 61–62.

98. Harvey, *Redeeming the South*, 177–78. For many whites, of course, this local authority now in the hands of African Americans was considered a problem: a child-race now without the needed oversight of whites and devolving into primitivism (Harvey, *Redeeming the South*, 37).

99. Du Bois, *Souls of Black Folk*, 121–22.

100. Sobel, *Trabelin' On*, 166, 169.

101. *Birmingham Age-Herald*, 21 July 1894; *Atlanta Constitution*, 19 February 1910.

102. *Arkansas Gazette*, 16 July 1891; *Louisville Courier-Journal*, 11 December 1886; *Raleigh News and Observer*, 4 May 1895.

103. *Charleston News and Courier*, 24 June 1882.

104. *Raleigh News and Observer*, 19 June 1887. For another example: "Councill held a cross with the figure of Christ in clasped hands and repeated often: 'As Christ died for love of me, I die for love of Christ'" (*Charlotte Observer*, 3 November 1901). See also *Galveston Daily News*, 3 May 1879.

105. In fact, of more than 1,300 execution reports I've collected, plus the detailed reports of executions in Tennessee from Laska, only 150 specific Bible verses or hymns were referenced by name. Hundreds more gave the fact of Bible readings and/or hymns without expending the ink to elaborate on specifics. In this section of the chapter, every quotation is from either hymns or Bible verses I have found referenced in execution stories. Some execution reports offered more than one reference to a hymn or Bible verse, meaning that I have found records of 66 times that a Bible passage was referenced specifically and 175 instances of hymns referenced by name.

106. *Richmond Dispatch*, 27 August 1897.

107. *Richmond Dispatch*, 15 September 1883.

108. *Florida Times-Union*, 28 January 1911.

109. Taylor Banks, in *Huntsville Gazette*, 18 August 1883. This was not the only instance: a long poem by the condemned was published in the *Charleston News and Courier*, 7 August 1886; and another in Tennessee in 1906 (Laska, *Legal Executions in Tennessee*, 231).

110. Written in 1771, "There Is a Fountain Fill'd with Blood" can be found in Baptist, Methodist, and Presbyterian hymnals in the following year. Several Bible verses reference Jesus washing sins away, as well as a fountain in which sins will be washed away (Zechariah 13:1; Julian, *Dictionary of Hymnology*, 1160; Mickel, *Triune Hymnal*, 32).

111. Others with more than two mentions are "Amazing Grace," "Death Cannot Make My Soul Afraid," and "I'm Goin' Home to Glory to Die No More" with five mentions by name; "Did Christ O'er Sinners Weep?" with four; and "How Firm a Foundation," "Just as I Am," "Come Ye that Love the Lord," "If I Must Die, Oh Let Me Die with Hope in Jesus's Name (or Blood)," "Show Pity, Lord, O Lord Forgive," and "Alas and Did My Savior Bleed" with three.

112. With hymns, there is often a great deal of repetition, and the sentiment or theological statement tends to be clear and straightforward. Bible passages are more complex, particularly when an execution report merely mentions the chapter cited rather than the verse, and many sentiments and themes might be broached in a single chapter. In this section I try to make the most straightforward connections between the texts I cite and the moments of execution, but we must understand that this sort of exegesis can result in more than one interpretation.

113. The others mentioned more than once in an execution report were Psalm 51 ("Cleanse me from sin . . . ," 4 times), John 3 ("For God so loved the world . . .") and Job 14 ("If a man die, shall he live again?") each mentioned in three reports, and Luke 23 (crucifixion story, "forgive them . . . ,"), Psalm 130 ("There is forgiveness

with thee . . . ,"), Romans 10 ("for man believes . . . and confesses . . . and is so saved"), and Romans 13 ("let every person be subject to governing authorities") each mentioned twice. Most reports mention only that there was a reading from the Bible, not what reading it was.

114. Psalms 88:4; Job 14:4; Psalms 90:7.

115. *Galveston Daily News*, 3 May 1879.

116. *Louisville Courier-Journal*, 23 June 1888. One minister called a convicted rapist a "dear one" and asked angels to come guard over him (*Galveston Daily News*, 3 April 1897).

117. Psalms 116:11; Psalms 14:3.

118. "Nearer My God to Thee"; "What a Friend We Have in Jesus"; "Jesus My All to Heav'n Is Gone."

119. Revelations 21:4-5.

120. "Jesus, Lover of My Soul"; "And Let This Feeble Body Fail"; "Jesus, the Sinner's Friend."

121. "And Must This Body Die?"

122. Acts 20:28; Acts 7:59-60.

123. Luke 23:43.

124. Mathews, "Lynching Is Part of the Religion," 177-82; Raboteau, "Blood of Martyrs," 22-39. One condemned said he "would rather be on the scaffold with the faith and belief of his eternal happiness than to live in ten thousand worlds like this" (*Raleigh News and Observer*, 12 March 1887).

125. *Louisville Courier-Journal*, 4 February 1899.

126. "Just as I Am."

127. Psalms 51:2; Matthew 6:12-13; John 3:17.

128. "There Is a Land of Pure Delight"; "Why Should We Start, and Fear to Die?"

129. "Come Ye that Love the Lord"; *Atlanta Constitution*, 2 December 1893.

130. Some of the historical scholarship characterizes these religious moments in terms of it being a ritual, a performance, and thereby as something that supported rather than confronted the power of the white state. Amy Louise Wood, for instance, very nicely characterizes much in terms of southern public executions, but I would argue that religion at the gallows had a different effect (*Lynching and Spectacle*, 33-41).

131. Laska, *Legal Executions in Tennessee*, 148.

132. *Charleston News and Courier*, 14 July 1877 and 10 July 1880 ("absent the usual religious orgies"), and many examples from the *New Orleans Daily Picayune*. Note that most Catholic priests, unlike evangelical Baptist ministers, would have been white throughout this period. Whether that or the firmer control over liturgy held by the Catholic faith mattered more in this, it is clear that executions of Catholic condemned did not typically include the camp meeting elements so commonplace otherwise. This might also apply to Episcopal devotions at the gallows, though I have seen few of those. By 1892, the denomination's *Book of Common Prayer* advises ministers to "use such devotions as he shall judge proper" and specifically: "It is judged best that the Criminal shall not make any public profession or declaration" (318).

133. *New Orleans Daily Picayune*, 8 September 1883; see also *Galveston Daily News*, 13 January 1894. Gallows days were important for Black ministers, for only on religious

holidays and at revivals might they have such an opportunity to make an impression upon thousands in their communities. They would be judged by how aptly they led the services, and particularly by how well they were able to offer the crowds what they desired: an emotional connection to God's redemptive plan for us all, as well as bearing witness to the readiness of the sinner's soul to meet his fate.

The tension between the rational Christianity of well-educated Black ministers (and white ones) and the emotionalism of southern congregations was a long-term trend in both the white and Black churches. I have found one exasperated Black editor expressing his discontent with gallows confessions, emphasizing the class dimension to this tension: *Weekly Louisianan*, 20 March 1876. For a contemporary African American evaluation of religious emotionalism, see Faduma, "Defects of the Negro Church." For similar discussions, see Harvey, *Redeeming the South*, 156–94, and Montgomery, *Under Their Own Vine*, 253–306.

134. *Richmond Dispatch*, 31 May 1869.

135. *Nashville Daily American*, 21 February 1880.

136. *Atlanta Constitution*, 20 October 1883. Taylor Brant was condemned for the crimes of rape and murder.

137. *Atlanta Constitution*, 20 October 1883.

138. Montgomery, *Under Their Own Vine*, 253–306; Sobel, *Trabelin' On*, 139–217.

139. *Atlanta Constitution*, 24 May 1884; *Galveston Daily News*, 13 November 1880.

140. *Richmond Dispatch*, 23 April 1881. Similarly: "Women in the adjoining yard, who had evidently been listening for the fatal sound, almost simultaneously with the fall of the trap broke out into loud lamentations" (*New Orleans Times Democrat*, 28 January 1882).

141. *Richmond Dispatch*, 26 March 1873.

142. *Arkansas Gazette*, 26 May 1883.

143. *Arkansas Gazette*, 26 February 1897.

144. *Louisville Courier-Journal*, 4 October 1884; see also *Dallas Morning News*, 17 April 1900, 21 June 1908; *Vicksburg Herald*, 12 February 1905. Others similarly report the condemned particularly requesting to address the crowds gathered at private executions: *Nashville Daily American*, 1 November 1884; *Louisville Courier-Journal*, 10 June 1893. One paper went on about the condemned men being "evidently pleased to see the interest they excited," complete with minstrelsy-like dialect: "Great Lord, look at de people. Dey is settin' up in de trees like turkey buzzards" (*Richmond Dispatch*, 26 March 1879). "There's enough of 'em to look at me die," said another convict when noting the dozens who climbed up to look over the enclosure (*New Orleans Daily Picayune*, 24 September 1904), but another convict said he "would be glad if more people than is here now could hear me" as he spoke on the scaffold (*Atlanta Constitution*, 19 February 1910). One condemned at a public execution hoped that "fifty thousand people will see him hung" (*Atlanta Constitution*, 12 March 1878). More generally, the enthusiasm of so many of the condemned for participating in the ceremonies at the gallows offers good evidence of their complaisance about the public nature of the execution.

145. The importance of being well prepared for death (of dying well) in the nineteenth century is chronicled in Faust, *This Republic of Suffering*, 6–10, 27–30. Sutton

Griggs provides perhaps the most peculiar evidence of the symbolic meaning of the gallows in his novel of a secret Black underworld, *Imperium in Imperio*. Not only does a main character in this novel find a Good Death in honorable execution at the end of the novel, but he is also initiated into the mysteries of the Imperium via a faked hanging, dropping through the trap and falling into an underground headquarters of Black power and authority (184–87, 261).

Chapter Two: Beyond Executions

1. Page, *Negro*, 97, 100.
2. Thomas, *American Negro*, 177, 223, 227. He also wrote (106) that "the negro represents an accentuated type of human degradation. Beyond this, there is a wide divergence of opinion as to whether he is a normally constituted but unawakened member of the human family, a survival of an earlier type of man, or a specific type of indurate degeneracy."
3. Sommerville, *Rape and Race*, 201. Felton earns a thorough treatment in Feimster's *Southern Horrors*.
4. Terrell, "Lynching," 853, 859, 865; Tolnay and Beck, *Festival of Violence*, 3; Brundage, *Lynching in the New South*, 58.
5. Tolnay and Beck, *Festival of Violence*, 48–49. Capital punishment always had a formal charge; with lynchings, rarely. So "reasons" for lynchings are at times elusive and often were not standard crimes. This category of sexual norm violations includes rape, attempted rape, and any other similar motives, as coded by the researchers.
6. "Only *one-third* of the 728 victims to mobs have been *charged* with rape, to say nothing of those of that one-third who were innocent of the charge," Wells wrote in *Southern Horrors*, 61 (emphasis in original). Wright found that accusations of rape and attempted rape accounted for approximately 28 percent of Kentucky lynchings, although when limited to African Americans, the proportion for these crimes was higher (Wright, *Racial Violence in Kentucky*, 77). Fitzhugh Brundage (*Lynching in the New South*, 67–72) found much higher percentages of lynchings in Georgia (60 percent) and Virginia (50 percent) for sexual infractions in the 1880s, but those numbers fell dramatically in ensuing decades, so that murder allegations outnumbered other alleged crimes when considering the period 1880 to 1930 overall.
7. Brundage, *Lynching in the New South*, 62–63.
8. This number adds together all of the listings which the Espy file codes as rape, attempted rape, or either of those crimes along with other crimes ("Espy file"). In states covered by Hearn and Laska, I add in their additional listings for sexual crimes. Started by M. Watt Espy, the Espy file lists a variety of information for about 15,000 U.S. executions from 1607 to 2002. Espy himself believed it to have only three-fourths of all executions, particularly before the twentieth century. A supplement of over 4,000 additional executions was made available in 2008, but that supplement has very limited information and is therefore much less useful at present. Blackman and McLaughlin ("The Espy File") compared the original Espy file with this supplement to show the ways the original Espy file was not simply rife with inevitable minor errors but also flawed more substantially in terms of its incompleteness. In this study, I use

the original Espy file for some figures but defer to the much more complete data from Hearn and Laska when possible.

Where there are discrepancies between the coding of the Espy file and the description in the newspaper coverage I have found in the non–Hearn and Laska states, I have followed the newspapers: I eliminated one execution because a newspaper reported that the condemned received a respite on the date of execution and it is unclear whether he was later executed (Sam Wright, Louisiana, 9 February 1900) and one where the crime reported in the newspapers was murder with no mention of rape or attempted rape (Victor Johnson, Mississippi, 21 January 1902). These discrepancies between the Espy file and the newspaper evidence illustrate the difficulty in this work: not only identifying that an execution occurred but requiring information on the charge that can be difficult to discern.

9. Bowers, *Legal Homicide*, 36–37.

10. In fact, many statutes were written with "female" specified in terms of victim. For important studies of sexual crimes in the South, see Feimster, *Southern Horrors*; Freedman, *Redefining Rape*; Sommerville, *Rape and Race*; Dorr, *White Women*.

11. "Sexual crime" in this chapter includes any charge of sexual assault: rape, attempted rape, or one of those crimes along with another crime.

12. Espy file. In addition, the Espy file includes as condemned for sexual crimes, six Hispanic men in Texas and one Native American man in North Carolina, as well as three other men coded as race unknown.

13. Project HAL lists the lynchings studied by Tolnay and Beck. Adding up all of the lynchings from 1882 to 1920 coded as having sexual motives in this database for the ten states Tolnay and Beck studied plus those in Virginia collected by Fitzhugh Brundage (*Lynching in the New South*, 270–79) for that period yields 846 lynchings for sexual motives, with 805 of them African American men, 33 white men, and 8 race unknown. Texas is not included due to the lack of dependable statewide lynching lists.

14. George Wright's work on Kentucky (*Racial Violence in Kentucky*, 12–13, 231, and passim) and Margaret Vandiver's work on Florida and Tennessee (*Lethal Punishment*, 89–102) pursue this idea of "sham justice" being not far removed from lynchings. I find it difficult to evaluate whether the cases they find are representative of an important trend or are exceptional, notable for how they diverge from the norm.

15. *Daily Democrat*, 6 August 1897. While the typical coverage was longer than this, there are many examples of this sort of abbreviated coverage, for instance: *Montgomery Advertiser*, 15 February 1913; *Atlanta Constitution*, 7 February 1903; *Vicksburg Herald*, 2 August 1902.

16. Most of the almost 200 execution days for sexual crimes evaluated in this study are these sorts of reports: between one-third of a column and a column and a half of print, usually with a section on "The Crime" at the end and the particulars of the condemned's last day, march to the gallows, speeches (if public), and drop at the front of the article. Most of the notes in this chapter refer to such examples; for a few representative ones, see *Mobile Daily Register*, 16 September 1899; *Florida Times-Union*, 30 July 1910; *Charleston News and Courier*, 21 August 1897.

17. *Louisville Courier-Journal*, 3 April 1880. Many issues in the two weeks before this hanging also dealt with the case and the proposed changes in the law.

18. *Louisville Courier-Journal*, 15 August 1936; *Louisville Times*, 14 August 1936.

19. *Galveston Daily News*, 3 April 1897.

20. Any Espy file entry that lists the crime as either murder or murder and another crime (e.g., "murder/robbery") is counted in the percentage here for murder; any with rape or rape and another crime (except murder, which is included in the murder category) is counted here in the rape percentage; only those condemned who are *only* listed as condemned for the nonmurder/nonrape crimes are counted in the 3.6 percent figure. There are surely errors in the record here; in fact, I found a number of Espy entries where the crime listed was in conflict in some way with the characterization in newspaper reports on execution day. For more on problems with the Espy file, see chapter 4.

21. Hearn and Laska.

22. Colvin, *Penitentiaries, Reformatories, and Chain Gangs*, 233–34.

23. Clarke, *Lineaments of Wrath*, 121. Clarke quotes (109) a southern businessman in 1883 using rather arresting prose: "Before the war we owned the negroes. . . . But these convicts: we don't own 'em. One dies, get another."

24. *Code of Virginia* (1887), 885.

25. Bowers, *Legal Homicide*, 11.

26. No executions for treason occurred in this period, so it is not treated in this study.

27. State laws change with every meeting of the state assemblies, making the tracing of changes to state criminal laws a challenge. I found postwar codes (generally two per state) that allowed me to draw these conclusions, but I am concerned that there might be twists and turns in terms of punishments in any given state that this general survey of state laws might have missed. Even with my examples, there were some other crimes that could earn the death penalty in these states, even if never used: insurrection (Florida), for instance, or arson at night (Mississippi).

28. The Espy file sometimes lists composite crimes such as Robbery/Murder. In this accounting, I considered only those without murder or rape listed in Espy.

29. The other two states with fewer capital crimes on the books? Florida had the smallest actual population of African Americans (but a high percentage), and Mississippi had the smallest overall numbers of executions in the South (and one of the highest lynching numbers). Populations are based on an average of the 1890 and 1900 census figures. While the numbers for each state shift somewhat over time, all of these states with fewer executions for other crimes would be among those with comparatively low percentages of African Americans no matter what years were chosen. Averaging the 1890 and 1900 census figures: Kentucky (13.8 percent African Americans), Texas (20.4 percent), Tennessee (24 percent), and Arkansas (27.7). Florida was quite different, the third-highest percentage (50.8 percent) in the South, behind only South Carolina and Mississippi. It also had the smallest population of any southern state, both overall and in terms of African American population: 269,699 African Americans, averaging the two census figures. Mississippi is still more of an outlier here, but it was the state in the South that deployed the legal death penalty the least overall, so having no executions for these other crimes is no outlier in that way (Espy file; Hearn and Laska; Carter, *Historical Statistics*, 1:180–379).

30. Bowers, *Legal Homicide*, 9. Of the four U.S. states to permanently abolish capital punishment in the nineteenth century (a few other states ended the practice briefly), none had a sizable Black population: Maine (1,451 African Americans in 1880, 0.22 percent of the state's population); Wisconsin (2,702, 0.21 percent); Rhode Island (6,488, 2.35 percent); Michigan (15,100, 0.92 percent). These are four of the fourteen smallest Black populations among U.S. states in 1880, and that probably underplays how extraordinarily white they were compared with the rest of the nation, for five of the other states with small African American populations were in the West, where other racial populations than African Americans would have been more numerous. The average percentage Black population (0.66 percent) of these states without the death penalty would have to be multiplied by 21 to get close to the average Black population (14.27 percent) of the states in the United States that retained the death penalty in the nineteenth century (Carter, *Historical Statistics*, 1:180–379).

In fact, looking ahead, this trend continues. Only one state (West Virginia) that eliminated capital punishment in the twentieth century (before the 1972 *Furman* decision) had a Black population (in 1960) above 26,000 or a Black percentage of the population above 3 percent. North Dakota had 777 African Americans in 1960 (0.12 percent of the state's population); Minnesota, 22,263 (0.65 percent); Hawaii, 4,943 (0.78 percent); Iowa, 25,354 (0.92 percent); Oregon, 18,133 (1.03 percent); Alaska, 6,771 (2.99 percent); West Virginia, 89,378 (4.80 percent). (Carter, *Historical Statistics*, 1:180–379).

31. The Espy file lists ninety-five executions for crimes other than murder and rape, and Hearn and Laska add an additional twenty-four, all but one of which is in these three states. If under 4 percent of the South's executions overall were for these crimes between 1866 and 1920, almost 9 percent of executions were for crimes other than murder or rape in North Carolina, South Carolina, and Virginia.

32. I have found newspaper reports that differ from the Espy file's data in their characterizations of the crimes condemned were executed for. In this table, I am taking the Espy file's information at face value. This is an area difficult to deal with: knowing an execution took place is one thing; determining the charge for which a criminal was condemned requires qualitative evidence that is not always forthcoming or trustworthy: Does a newspaper characterize the crime right? Does the newspaper use euphemisms ("assault" rather than "rape" that might or might not imply a sexual crime?) or just mention murder when the charge might have been robbery and murder? Where I have newspaper reports phrasing things differently from how the Espy file categorizes them, I frankly don't know how to interpret this: trust the primary source of the newspaper, or figure that shortcuts and mistakes in the press are commonplace, and trust the researchers who compiled the Espy file? See chapter 4 for more on this problem.

33. *Raleigh Observer*, 17 May 1879.

34. *Montgomery Advertiser*, 28 March 1903. Later that year, the *Birmingham Age-Herald* (8 August 1903) printed a longer article on two highwaymen hanged and the many questions the crowd asked of them, but still this was less than a column and conformed to the "meet you all in heaven" religious nature of these moments.

35. None of the additional executions for these crimes from Hearn and Laska were of whites.

36. The Espy file mentions attempted rape for three executions in North Carolina, but each of these three was listed as "Burglary/Attempted Rape": it was the Burglary part that made this a capital crime. Attempted rape was not a capital crime in North Carolina (*Code of North Carolina* [1883], 428–29). In his study of North Carolina, Seth Kotch argues that burglary often implied sexual danger (*Lethal State*, 43). Virginia and South Carolina each had higher rates of execution for attempted rape; North Carolina had higher rates for burglary. Those facts might not be so different from one another.

37. This figure is the total of all women listed in the Espy file for southern states executed between 1866 and 1920, minus two who were not, it turns out, women, and with two added in from Hearn and Laska that the Espy file missed. In another telling demonstration of how any historical list of lynchings or executions will have its errors, two executions in the Espy database are listed as being women, but newspaper reports are clear that they were men: Ada Hiers, 29 July 1893, in South Carolina, and Florence English, 22 November 1895, in Georgia. (See *Charleston News and Courier*, 29 July 1893, and *Atlanta Constitution*, 23 November 1895.) Of the more than 1,300 executions centering this study, no evidence arose of any condemned being a woman when the Espy file called her a man, which should give some sense that this is not, at least, a runaway problem.

This is, of course, with a gender binary in mind; the historical record offers nothing that would help us to understand any condemned who might have had a more fluid gender identity.

38. Chapter 5 gives overall execution numbers (and rates) for all of these states. Georgia (seven women executed) had the largest overall execution numbers, Virginia (six women) was third, and South Carolina (three) was sixth, with Louisiana (two) and North Carolina (two) fourth and seventh in overall execution numbers. Alabama and Kentucky had fewer executions both in terms of women and in overall numbers: one woman executed in each, and fifth and ninth in overall capital punishment tallies. Texas is the exception to this pattern: one of the most active in using capital punishment (second), but in this era apparently never legally executing a woman.

39. Of the two whom I did not find (Annie Middlebrooks, 1866, and Ellen Osgood, 1878, Georgia), the first was Black and the second was listed as race unknown. It may be important that both entries were early and both were only in one of the two data sets available: the former only in Hearn and the latter only in the Espy file. Many local executions are quite easy to miss, particularly in these early decades.

40. The *Richmond Dispatch* (29 September 1891) covered the execution of Henrietta Murrell with about one-third of a column of print, writing that she believed herself saved, and that she claimed innocence. The execution was private, and the paper described something of the crime of burning down the house, killing the children of Lucy Rowe.

41. *Raleigh News and Observer*, 23 January 1892. See also *Louisville Courier-Journal* (12 February 1868; both Espy and Hearn call the condemned in this 1868 execution "Susan," but this letter addressed her as Eliza). Despite her killing a three-year-old in her care, Eliza was described with great compassion in the brief letter published by the *Courier-Journal*.

42. *Atlanta Constitution*, 2 May 1874.
43. *Atlanta Constitution*, 20 October 1883.
44. *Atlanta Constitution*, 23 November 1895.
45. *New Orleans Daily Picayune*, 1 August 1885.
46. "Finis for Five," *Atlanta Constitution*, 21 October 1882.
47. Charleston *News and Courier*, 24 June 1882.
48. See *Mobile Daily Register*, 13 October 1888; *Charleston News and Courier*, 8 October 1892. *Raleigh News and Observer*, 13 January 1882; *Charleston News and Courier*, 24 June 1882.
49. Hodes, "Sexualization of Reconstruction Politics," 410–12. She writes, "White women of the lower classes could not count upon white ideology about white female purity and black male aggression to absolve them of illicit sexual activity" (410).
50. *Lexington Morning Herald*, 16 July 1896.
51. *Atlanta Constitution*, 3 May 1873.
52. *Atlanta Constitution*, 3 May 1873. Emphasis in original.
53. *Atlanta Constitution*, 3 May 1873.
54. This is certainly not always the case, as the Mary Snodgrass case shows. The chief competing cultural stereotype to the innocent victim in stories of women and crime was of the depraved, corrupting woman. But in the South, that type was most often deployed in terms of women of color, and, overall, white womanhood was a powerful force in bending story lines toward virtue. For more, see Trotti, *Body in the Reservoir*, 54–65 and 89–94; Halttunen, *Murder Most Foul*, 172–207 and passim; Cohen, *Murder of Helen Jewett*, 38–68, 87–100, 126–86; and Cohen, "Beautiful Female Murder Victim," 277–306.
55. *Richmond Times-Dispatch*, 22 March 1916. Seth Kotch nicely treats this case in *Lethal State*, 95–96.
56. Harris, "'Commonwealth of Virginia vs. Virginia Christian,'" 928.
57. They later wrote the governor that their strategy was a "mistake of judgment" that they rued. Why? Not because she should have the right to speak on her own behalf but rather that her speaking would reveal her ignorance and might have provided an avenue for an appeal to the Supreme Court (Harris, "'Commonwealth of Virginia vs. Virginia Christian,'" 931–32).
58. *Crisis* 4 (1912): 236–39. This article notes with disgust that nowhere in the state was there a reformatory for African American girls.
59. Harris, "'Commonwealth of Virginia vs. Virginia Christian,'" 933–34.
60. *Crisis* 4 (1912): 236, 239. The article argues that Christian "was a product of Virginia far more than of the colored race" (236).
61. *Richmond Planet*, 22 June 1912; even that was a reprint from a white daily, a not-uncommon occurrence in this era.
62. *Richmond Planet*, 13 July 1912; this was the most complete coverage her story received in the *Planet*.
63. *Richmond Planet*, 24 and 31 August 1912.
64. *Richmond Planet*, 27 July 1912.
65. The *New York Times* (16 August 1912) characterized it as the governor of Virginia "besieged by petitions and letters from all over the country, imploring him to com-

mute the sentence." The following day, reporting on the electrocution, the *Times* specifically referred to the "entreaties of several Chicago persons."

66. This required clear commentary in newspapers and therefore is dependent both on the accuracy of those reports and on papers giving enough column-inches to include this information, and many reports did not. Therefore, while I have a source base of newspaper coverage of more than 1,300 executions in this era, I do not have clear evidence of the public versus private nature of those events for even a majority of those cases.

67. The white percentage of condemned executed in public was higher in 1881–85, 1886–90, and 1901–5 (Espy file).

68. Espy file; Hearn and Laska. The more thorough data from the studies of Hearn and Laska add about 10 percent to the white executions in the Espy file. They also add more accurate data for some executions that Espy included, and in several cases those data included that the condemned was Black instead of Espy's coding of either "white" or "unknown."

69. *Atlanta Constitution*, 18 December 1897.

70. *Richmond Dispatch*, *Richmond Times*, and *Atlanta Constitution*, 28 October 1893.

71. *Richmond Dispatch*, 26 July 1895.

72. *Galveston Daily News*, 30 August 1879. In another, "more than half of the crowd" of 3,000 took up the hymn "There Is a Fountain Filled with Blood." (*Atlanta Constitution*, 21 October 1893). See also *Arkansas Gazette*, 7 December 1895; *Atlanta Constitution*, 18 June 1887.

73. *Vicksburg Herald*, 23 July 1902. Another: "He assumed the role of a prophet of evil, predicting unknown woes to come as a retribution for his execution." *Atlanta Constitution*, 9 June 1883. For a later example, see also *Louisville Courier-Journal*, 20 April 1935.

74. Wanting private: *Nashville Daily American*, 23 November 1878. For another instance, see Laska, *Legal Executions in Tennessee*, 137. In contrast, another white condemned, Hanvey, "specially requested that his execution be in public." (*Atlanta Constitution*, 6 June 1882). Attempting suicide: *Houston Daily Post*, 14 January 1899; *Louisville Courier-Journal*, 16 February 1907. See also Laska, *Legal Executions in Tennessee*, 129, 172, 176. Seth Kotch found an example of a white condemned who attempted suicide to avoid being the first to die in North Carolina's electric chair (*Lethal State*, 205).

75. The ways that press sensationalism of both white and Black murders in the South changed over time is the subject of Trotti, *Body in the Reservoir*.

76. *Richmond Dispatch*, 14 and 15 January 1887; the case and execution are explored in Trotti, *Body in the Reservoir*, particularly 181–85. Overall, the *Dispatch* published 172 stories on Cluverius's murder over eighteen months between the discovery of Lillian Madison's body in the city reservoir and his execution for the crime.

77. Trotti, *Body in the Reservoir*, 43–79.

78. Images of the condemned, the sheriff, the crowd, the gallows, and more became increasingly commonplace in coverage of white condemned. For two good examples, see *Louisville Courier-Journal*, 1 August 1889; *Atlanta Constitution*, 19 June 1897. For more on the changing roles of images in the southern press, see Trotti, *Body in the Reservoir*, 145–80.

79. *Savannah Tribune*, 24 April 1897.

80. Du Bois, "Black Social Equals." Du Bois's essay, written in response to Page's "Great American Question" in *McClure's*, was rejected. Strikethroughs are in the original.

Chapter Three: Shooting the Sheep-Killing Dogs

1. Lears, "Concept of Cultural Hegemony," 592; Aune, "'Power of Hegemony,'" 64.

2. "South Hysterical on the Negro Problem," *Alexander's Magazine* 3 (1907): 225.

3. Responding to Thomas Nelson Page's 1907 essay (an excerpt of which opened the chapter), Mary Church Terrell wrote a blistering, never-published essay, which included the line, speaking of his view of the old-time Negro: "And this is the only type of Afro-American which Mr. Page seems genuinely to admire—a type which he regards as he would a horse that had rendered valuable service as a burden bearer all his life and which should be fed and sheltered—not shot—in its old age, for the good it had done" ("Concerning Mr. Page's Article"). In 1864, the final report of the American Freedmen's Inquiry Commission treated mulattoes like cross-species mistakes: "The mixed race is inferior, in physical power and in health, to the pure race black or white" (quoted in Fredrickson, *Black Image in the White Mind*, 173). In 1902, Andrew Sledd observed that whites in the South saw an African American as "either nothing more than the beast that perishes, unnoticed and uncared for so long as he goes quietly about his menial toil (as a young man recently said to the writer, 'the farmer regards his nigger in the same light as his mule,' but this puts the matter far too favorably for the negro); or, if he happens to offend, he is punished as a beast with a curse or a kick, and with tortures that event the beast is spared; or, if he is thought of at all in a general way, it is with the most absolute loathing and contempt. He is either unnoticed or despised" ("The Negro: Another View," *Atlantic Monthly* 90 [1902]: 67).

4. Quoted in Carrigan, *Making of a Lynching Culture*, 124.

5. "I'se happy ter know that I'se ter die like Jesus Christ—ter save sinners. I'se a 'zample and when I'se gone the folks will say, 'He's gone ter rest; he give his life as a 'zample'" (*Birmingham Age-Herald*, 21 July 1894).

6. *New Orleans Daily Picayune*, 24 April 1891, 25 February 1893.

7. *Atlanta Constitution*, 26 June 1897. Another called the "religious enthusiasms" of a condemned man "almost maniacal" (*New Orleans Daily Picayune*, 20 February 1892).

8. Davenport, "Religion of the American Negro," 373.

9. Quoted in Johnson and Johnson, "Church and the Race Problem," 330.

10. *Atlanta Constitution*, 16 July 1892. They interpret this business as his bid to delay the proceedings. Most of what I have found seems to trend in the direction of being afraid of people out of control, that Black religious enthusiasms were akin to insanity. But we should not dismiss the ways whites might see a deeper, more revolutionary danger to Black religion. Especially in terms of condemned criminals as the focal point for gallows religion, there are many ways Christian rhetoric and traditions could pose rather substantial challenges to white power.

11. Watson, "Churches and Religious Conditions," 120.

12. Bruce, *Plantation Negro*, 93–110. For further examples, see Litwack, *Been in the Storm*, 458–62.

13. Tucker, *Relations*, 17.
14. Quoted in Montgomery, *Under Their Own Vine*, 286.
15. Thomas, *American Negro*, 209–10.
16. Sobel, *Trabelin' On*, 166; Greenberg, *Confessions of Nat Turner*, 48 and passim. Nat Turner rebelled against slavery in Virginia in 1831, killing over fifty whites in his neighborhood; dozens of Blacks, including Turner, were hanged in the wake of this most-deadly insurrection. Denmark Vesey planned a rebellion in South Carolina in 1822 that was crushed before it occurred.
17. Page, *Red Rock*, 160–61.
18. Quoted in Davenport, "Religion of the American Negro," 375.
19. Harvey, *Redeeming the South*, 33. These churches, of course, *were* sites of Black power and authority, and even potentially dangerous to the racist regime: they supported their community, and it is through their doors that most of the leaders of the civil rights movement would emerge in later generations.
20. *Louisville Courier-Journal*, 24 July 1883.
21. Davenport, "Religion of the American Negro," 375. He refers to an argument that there was a time in human development before the invention of a moral code and the primitive Africans lived there still. "An animal in every respect. . . . He was simply non-moral" (Norwood, *Address on the Negro*, 8).
22. Bruce, *Plantation Negro*, 97–99.
23. Quoted in Johnson and Johnson, "Church and the Race Problem," 350.
24. Cox, "'Half-Bacchanalian, Half Devout,'" 241–67.
25. Davenport, "Religion of the American Negro," 370. This sort of thinking remains in evidence in the research materials in the Schomburg Collection of the Library of Congress. See Johnson and Johnson, "Church and the Race Problem," 339, 350. These sentiments are in line with the general perception among whites that African Americans were apt to be superstitious, believing in terrorizing forces invisible to view. See Bruce, *Plantation Negro*, 11–25; Howard Odum, *Social and Mental Traits*, 268–73. Edward Ayers has a number of telling quotations from the nineteenth century revealing the white understanding of Black psychology and what would work best to keep Blacks in line. See *Vengeance and Justice*, 247 and passim.
26. Cox, "'Half-Bacchanalian, Half Devout,'" 256.
27. Quoted in Cox, "'Half-Bacchanalian, Half Devout,'" 254.
28. Fredrickson, *Black Image in the White Mind*, 75, 86, 137.
29. Fredrickson, *Black Image in the White Mind*, 252–53. Some believed, an idea that persisted quite a while, that mixed-race offspring, as with mules, would be less fit and perhaps sterile.
30. Burroughs, *Tarzan of the Apes*, 57, 63.
31. Quoted in Kotch, "Making of the Modern Death Penalty," 198.
32. "The Negro Religion," *New York Times*, 6 August 1883. They are referencing the execution of Charles Lee in Virginia for the crime of murder.
33. Bruce, *Plantation Negro*, 132, 80.
34. Eugene Genovese explores how in the antebellum period, whites saw danger in Black religion. Whites sought to control it, including supervising Black funeral services; in the 1800s, especially after 1831, more laws were passed to forbid Black

preachers from preaching to slaves (*Roll, Jordan, Roll*, 189-90, 196, 164-65, 257-61).

35. "Did our prognathic, dolichocephalic cannibal come to us with brutal instincts molded by centuries of crime on every lineament of his visage and yet clothed in the beautitude [*sic*] of sexual purity? No! . . . It is reversion pure and simple and these figures [of rising Black crime in the late nineteenth century] simply point again to the superb moral influence of slavery. In the hands of a gentle people, the Negro came quite near the gentleman" (Barringer, "Negro and the Social Order," 189).

36. Thomas Piketty estimates that the monetary value of U.S. slaves in 1860 was approximately the value of all of the agricultural land in the United States. That wealth evaporated five years later (*Capital in the Twenty-First Century*, 160).

37. The editor of the *Richmond Dispatch* phrased it oddly nine years after the Civil War ended the antebellum regime, but he was getting at the naturalness of the racist view: "A negro is a negro, and he will never be aught else. Wherever he is, he must either be a barbarian or else he must have a white man to look up to and almost worship" (3 June 1874).

38. Psychological studies show not only that human understandings of the world are as emotional as they are rational but also that we focus less on what is the norm and more on what is different, changing, and, particularly, threatening. Change — those things a culture or subculture perceives as shifting in the world around them — has an outsized place in our worldviews, particularly when the change is perceived as negative. Fear likewise fosters outsized attention in the human mind. See Kahneman, *Thinking, Fast and Slow*.

39. The only firm data are from the last decades of the century, but to get from near zero literacy during slavery to those levels of literacy (52 percent) found in 1900, the era would have to average something like a 10 percent rise each decade. The percentage was 39.3 in 1890. (Bureau of the Census, *Negroes in the United States*, 41-42).

40. Schweninger, *Black Property Owners*, 164, 170, 174, 180. In 1870, the twelve states of the South under study here had 16,935 Black farms and 3,228 Black homes. In 1890, this rose to 108,381 farms and 100,839 homes; by 1910 those numbers were 201,348 farms and 199,556 homes. These houses and farms would have been smaller, cheaper, and more marginal than white farms and houses, but the progress is clear. In percentage terms, this growth in Black ownership would have been one of the fastest changes in the economy of the South, with the growth of Black ownership far outpacing white growth in ownership in this era.

Note that land ownership may have risen dramatically in percentage terms, but that was from a base rate of almost no ownership: the proportion of total farm wealth in the South in the hands of African Americans was still only 6 percent in 1910, for instance (Schweninger, *Black Property Owners*, 184). Even with this metric of farm wealth, it should be noted, African American owners were gaining on white ones: this was up from Blacks controlling only 5 percent of farm wealth in 1900, and, of course, close to zero in 1860. In fact, farm ownership among southern African Americans rose between 1890 and 1910 from 21 to 24 percent; white ownership in that period fell from 65 to 60 percent (183).

41. Hunter, *To 'Joy My Freedom*, 28.

42. W. E. B. Du Bois earned the first Harvard PhD ever awarded a Black man in 1895; George Washington Carver earned his master's in science the following year. John Mitchell became an editor and banker and spoke before a national meeting of bankers, and Madam C. J. Walker became a millionaire through her beauty product empire. Marshall "Major" Taylor won the world championship sprint event in bicycling in Montreal in 1899, almost a decade before Jack Johnson won his boxing championship and a fourteen-year-old African American girl, Maria Bolden, won with a perfect score the first-ever national spelling bee ("Colored Girl Wins Big Spelling Bee," *New York Times*, 30 June 1908; Ward, *Unforgivable Blackness*; Alexander, *Race Man*; Lowry, *Her Dream of Dreams*; Taylor, *Fastest Bicycle Rider in the World*).

It is notable how most African Americans lived in the South but most of these figures did not, or did not stay there. From this quite incomplete list of Black excellence, only Carver and Mitchell found a way to have successful careers and remain in the South.

43. Terrell, "Plea for the White South," 7.

44. Quoted in Williams, *They Left Great Marks on Me*, 25.

45. Ayers, *Vengeance and Justice*, 241.

46. Prince, *Stories of the South*, 210–11. Martha Hodes wrote, "Now, for the first time, black men possessed political power, as well as opportunities for greater economic and social power. White Southerners thus conflated those powers with a newly alarmist ideology about black sexuality. Armed with such an ideology, they hoped to halt the disintegration of their racial caste system" ("Sexualization of Reconstruction Politics," 415).

47. Page, *Negro*, 64. In the original article, Page finished this passage with "destroyed all within reach." Was "desolation" his attempt to tone it down? (Page, "Negro . . . Third Paper: Its Present Condition," 98.)

48. Edwards, *Gendered Strife and Confusion*, 95; Ayers, *Promise of the New South*, 153–58; Ayers, *Vengeance and Justice*, 250–52.

49. Norwood, *Address on the Negro*, 20–21.

50. Ayers, *Vengeance and Justice*, 191 and passim; Schwarz, *Twice Condemned*.

51. Ramsey, "Negro Criminality," 107.

52. Page, *Negro*, 155. Another writer phrased it, "The mawkish sympathy sometimes manifested for our criminals is the sign rather of a weak head than of a soft heart, and its indulgence is as injurious to the best interests of society as the hallelujahs of the scaffold are to the propagation of a sound and honest religion" (Barton, "Punishment of Crime," 159).

53. Willcox, *Negro Criminality*, 20. "Juramentado" refers to a Filipino willing to die to kill invaders; today, some Americans might use "Jihadist" or "Islamic terrorist" in a similar fashion.

54. Work, "Negro Criminality in the South," 75. Prisoners per 100,000 Black population likewise doubled: 136 to 284 (75). Chapter 4 of this study starts with a quotation from Governor James Vardaman in this style.

55. Muhammad, *Condemnation of Blackness*, passim. The heart of this wonderful book is the use of statistics in the national (and particularly northern) conversation about race in the late nineteenth and early twentieth centuries. I found in southern sources many parallels to what Muhammad found in (mostly) northern ones.

56. Page, *Negro*, 74, 125.

57. Walter L. Hawley, "Passing of the Race Problem," *Arena* 24 (1900): 474.

58. Dr. B. W. Green, "Punishment for Rape," *Virginia Law Register* 8 (1903): 848. "During the negro's single generation of freedom and so-called education and advancement," another wrote, "these revolting crimes [rapes] have originated, and, according to statistics recently published, have increased instead of diminished" (Walter Guild, "A Plea from the South," *Arena* 24 [1900]: 486). This idea of a connection between education and crime seeped into the wider public enough that a student in a class in Mississippi wrote that "ninety per cent of the crime committed by blacks was by those that had had schooling" (Carl Holliday, "The Young Southerner and the Negro," *South Atlantic Quarterly* 8 [1909]: 119).

59. Work, "Negro Criminality in the South," 75. It is particularly here that Muhammad's work (*Condemnation of Blackness*) is so helpful, for the North was perceived by all as a sort of "best case" for Black advancement, and the "failure" of Blacks to thrive in the North was pitched as proof positive of inherent problems of character in African Americans, particularly in terms of criminality.

60. Khalil Muhammad is brilliant at critiquing racial statistics in this era: presented as objective and color-blind, they became a "strategy of communication" and a "durable signifier of black inferiority," a social science movement toward "statistical Anglo-Saxonism" (*Condemnation of Blackness*, 2–33).

61. Page, *Negro*, 84.

62. George Allen Mebane, "The Negro Vindicated," *Arena* 25 (1900): 453.

63. Mebane, "Negro Vindicated," 453–55; Roland P. Faulkner, "Crime and the Census," *Annals of the American Academy of Political and Social Sciences* 9 (1897): 63.

64. Faulkner, "Crime and the Census," 66; "A Side-Light," *Horizon* (1 January 1910).

65. Terrell, "Lynching," 854.

66. Terrell, "Lynching," 864.

67. Gilbert Stephenson, "Education and Crime among Negroes," *South Atlantic Quarterly* 16 (1917): 15. In addition to these straightforward critiques of the statistics, they also miss a number of more subtle factors that we know affect crime: solving for age (crime is committed disproportionately by the young, and the Black population of the South was younger than the white) and class (poverty pushes the poor toward crime, and so the only fair comparisons would be between the Black rates of crime and a similarly class-profiled subset of the much-more-wealthy white population). African American writers pushed back particularly strongly against this link between education and crime. Mary Church Terrell explains how it is the illiterate class in the Black community that contribute to the criminal class ("Lynching," 856), and George Allen Mebane calls the idea "absolutely baseless" and shows that "not one of the hideous crimes . . . has ever been traced back to a graduate of any of our great industrial schools" ("Negro Vindicated," 462).

68. W. S. Scarborough, "Lawlessness vs. Lawlessness," *Arena* 25 (1900): 482.

69. James R. L. Diggs, "Is It Ignorance or Slander: An Answer to Thomas Nelson Page," *Voice of the Negro* (1904): 231–32.

70. Quoted in Emberton, *Beyond Redemption*, 168. Chesnutt wrote this in 1905.

71. *New Orleans Weekly Pelican*, 11 May 1889.

72. Quoted in Muhammad, *Condemnation of Blackness*, 272.

73. *Weekly Louisianan*, 9 July 1881.

74. John Mitchell, "Mr. Page and Negro Immorality," *Richmond Planet*, 9 July 1904.

75. Here the whipping post is of particular interest. This physical punishment is low cost — requiring no long-term incarceration — and in line with the consideration of Blacks as being a lower order; responsive, then, to the supposed nature of animals in requiring physical correction. It was a central part of the punishment regime of the antebellum slavery system, and therefore, familiar. It did not become a major part of the postbellum punishment regime, but was ever-present as an oft-introduced potential reform that might solve the problem of criminality in the Black population. While I have found little in the scholarly literature on the persistence of other forms of public punishments than the gallows, in my work I have stumbled across a number of telling notices in newspapers and in legislative journals concerning the whipping post. Most Republican regimes after the war banned it. While it never again became widespread, southern whites had many discussions about the efficacy of the return of this punishment in the wake of their reconquest of the South, and it was briefly reintroduced in at least Virginia. See, for instance, *Mobile Daily Register*, 14 September 1878; *New York Times*, 2 February and 1 May 1882; *Richmond Dispatch*, 31 July 1869, 26 July 1877, and 17 May 1881.

Proposals to exact physical punishment upon the bodies of African Americans were not limited to the whipping post. Castration was proposed as a penalty for conviction on the charge of rape, a proposal that went far enough in 1910 in Kentucky as to be voted on in the House (*Journal of the Kentucky House* [1910], 328–29). This may or may not have been influenced by William Hannibal Thomas's book published earlier in the decade. He not only specifically recommended whipping as an effective punishment (jail was considered "no punishment for negroes") but also suggested emasculation as a remedy for the crime of rape (*American Negro*, 222, 234–36).

76. *Richmond Dispatch*, 17 September 1870. Four Black men died on the gallows at Isle of Wight Courthouse for the murder of one white man.

77. Quoted in Williams, *They Left Great Marks on Me*, 134.

78. Edward E. Wilson, "Thomas Nelson Page on the Negro," *Alexander's Magazine* 3 (1907): 296; for a similar argument, see "The South Hysterical on the Negro Problem," *Alexander's Magazine* 3 (1907): 223–26.

79. John Mitchell, "Mr. Thomas Nelson Page and the Negro Question," *Richmond Planet*, 19 March 1904. After another volley from Page in 1907, Mitchell elaborated: "Northerners will listen to them and after listening are disposed to believe. The cause of this is that the Negro cannot state his side of the question through the same channels that this distinguished gentleman uses. . . . [It is] essential that the Negro's side of the controversy should be presented to the conservative elements of the North. As the matter now stands the case is being judged by ex-parte statements, with now and then a scintillation of the truth being observable in a few of the justice-loving magazines and daily newspapers of the North" (John Mitchell, "The Great American Question," *Richmond Planet* [16 March 1907]).

80. Page, *Negro*, 31, 36, 43, 44, 95, 124, 194–95.

81. Page, *Negro*, 80, 112, 174.

82. *New York Times*, 10 December 1904.

83. *Nation* (5 October 1905): 280–82.

84. *Outlook* (12 May 1906): 87.

85. *American Journal of Sociology* 11 (1906): 698–99.

86. *American Academy of Politics and Social Sciences* 25 (1905): 141.

87. Diggs, "Is It Ignorance or Slander," 230. In response to similar claims by Page in 1907, Du Bois emphasized how Page's fear of social equality was also insulting to southern white women: "Is there imminent danger of their accepting Negro husbands? Are they in fact besieged by ignorant black suitors? Do black men stand ready to burst in upon soirees and receptions? Nonsense! The sight of half a dozen stalwart bullies astride a poor black boy, blandly informing the public that if they let him up, he will marry their daughters is perhaps the most perfectly ludicrous thing imaginable, even to the new wealth-bred cowardice of this land" (Du Bois, "Black Social Equals," 6).

88. Terrell, "Lynching," 853.

89. Terrell, "Lynching," 859, 865; Diggs, "Is It Ignorance or Slander," 228, 232.

90. Du Bois, "The Southerner's Problem" *Dial* (1 May 1905): 316; Terrell, "Lynching," 274; Diggs, "Is It Ignorance or Slander," 228.

91. Du Bois, "Southerner's Problem," 317; John Mitchell, "The Negro: The Southerner's Problem," *Richmond Planet*, 26 March 1904; Mitchell, "Mr. Page and the Negro," *Richmond Planet*, 9 April 1904; Diggs, "Is It Ignorance or Slander," 229.

92. John Mitchell, "Mr. Thomas Nelson Page and the Negro Question," *Richmond Planet*, 19 March 1904.

93. *Voice of the Negro* (1905): 274; "The Pessimism of Page," *Voice of the Negro* (1904): 216; Diggs, "Is It Ignorance or Slander," 230. *Argumentum ad populum*, Latin for "argument to the people," means that something was true because people choose to believe it.

94. Muhammad, *Condemnation of Blackness*, 3.

95. Williams, *They Left Great Marks on Me*, 107 and passim.

96. Du Bois discussed with *Collier's* the possibility of a regular column called "Along the Color Line" or "Voice of the Darker Millions" for African American views to be featured each month; *Collier's* declined, siting space restrictions (Du Bois papers, reel 1, frame 629, Du Bois handwritten draft; Richard Jones to Du Bois, 3 February 1904.) Similarly, Richard Gilder, editor of the *Century*, declined to publish Charles Chesnutt's "The Negro's Answer to the Negro Question" despite its being "a timely paper." The problem is that it was "so timely and so political—in fact so partisan—that we cannot handle it. It should at once appear somewhere" (quoted in Smith, *Richard Watson Gilder*, 71).

97. *N.W. Ayer and Son's Newspaper Annual* (1904), 599, 603, 606.

98. Shapiro, "Muckrakers and the Negroes," 77. See also Southern, *Malignant Heritage*, 32–54.

99. Quoted in Dewey Grantham, "Introduction to the Torchbook Edition," in Baker, *Following the Color Line*, viii.

100. Quoted in McHenry, "Toward a History of Access," 395–96; see also Watson, "Churches and Religious Conditions," 65–90.

101. Silber, *Romances of Reunion*, 113.

102. This exchange is in the Du Bois papers and is substantially reprinted in *Correspondence of W.E.B. Du Bois*, 1:128–29. McClure responded to Du Bois only after receiving from him a heated reply to his office's boilerplate form letter sent in answer to Du Bois's first query: "We have had a good many requests to print replies to his article, but have uniformly refused because we do not wish to open our pages to a controversy." Du Bois made this treatment into a part of his critique by printing it in *Horizon: A Journal of the Color Line* 1 (1907): 3.

African Americans continued to push back against this white supremacy message in Black publications: John Mitchell again responded in the *Richmond Planet* (9, 16 March 1907), as does Carrie Clifford in the *Colored American Magazine* ("The Great American Question" 12 (1907): 364–73), and *Alexander's Magazine* did so twice, including this gem: "To write a review of an article by Thomas Nelson Page on the Negro is like delving into a charnel-house" (Wilson, "Thomas Nelson Page on the Negro," 295).

103. Page, "Great American Question," 565–72.

104. The African American activist Anna Julia Cooper wrote that Blacks were "the most talked about" but rarely were allowed to talk, left as "the dumb skeleton in the closet provoking ceaseless harangues" (Prince, *Stories of the South*, 219–20). It wasn't just writers who were shut out. African American reformers and researchers were likewise without the resources afforded whites; instead of leaders, they were "so marginal as to be nearly invisible" (Muhammad, *Condemnation of Blackness*, 144).

105. Ray Stannard Baker's "Along the Color Line" series (essays between 1905 and 1908 in *McClure's* and the *American Magazine*, collected as *Following the Color Line* in 1908) is something of an exception to this generalization if only for presenting the situation in more complex, nuanced ways.

106. Silber, *Romances of Reunion*, 93–123. Silber argues that modern life and its problems (immigration, labor strife, urban corruption, and more) in the North is the apt context for how many northerners found a positive "moral alternative" in the myth of the South.

107. Litwack, *North of Slavery*, 268–76 and passim; for the continuation of racism in the North: Silber, *Romances of Reunion*. When the Republican Party gained power in state houses in the 1850s, they did not introduce bills to expand the franchise to African Americans; an Illinois Republican said, "We, the Republican Party, are the white man's party"; an Ohio Republican wrote, "The 'negro question' is a *white man's question*, the right of free white laborers to the soil in the territories. . . . We have no Sambo in our platform. . . . We object to Sambo. We don't want him about. We insist that he shall not be forced upon us" (Litwack, *North of Slavery*, 90–91, 269, 270).

108. Muhammad, *Condemnation of Blackness*, 122.

109. Quoted in Fredrickson, *Black Image in the White Mind*, 180–81. A New York opponent of Reconstruction was as virulent as any southern apologists would be a generation later: "The negro is not the equal of the white man, much less his master; and this I can demonstrate anatomically, physiologically and psychologically too, if necessary. Volumes of scientific authority establish the fact" (quoted in Fredrickson, *Black Image in the White Mind*, 191).

110. This is commonplace. The human brain is naturally biased toward confirming already-held notions. People "seek data that are likely to be compatible with the beliefs they currently hold" (Kahneman, *Thinking, Fast and Slow*, 81).

111. Southern, *Malignant Heritage*, 67–81; Shapiro, *White Violence and Black Response*, 103–6. This follows Elaine Frantz's insight about the KKK as "a convenient and disposable container in which to place evidence of southern violence" and how whites had "a collective desire to avoid thinking about the plight of freedpeople" (*Ku-Klux*, 208).

112. Quoted in Muhammad, *Condemnation of Blackness*, 52. Hoffman's book is at the center of Muhammad's investigation of the northern conversation on race in this era: the beginning of the use of statistics to argue for innate Black criminality. Many in the North were saying the same things white southerners were saying.

113. Terrell, "Who Are the Negro's Best Friends."

114. Norwood, *Address on the Negro*, 14.

115. Lipscomb and Bergh, *Writings of Thomas Jefferson*, 2:192.

116. Lipscomb and Bergh, *Writings of Thomas Jefferson*, 15:249.

117. Poole, "Confederate Apocalypse," 44. In 1907, John E. White wrote, "We are dominated by the Negro in our thoughts and in our feelings, of a truth, more dreadfully than we ever were in our state governments during Reconstruction"; ("Need of a Southern Program on the Negro Problem," *South Atlantic Quarterly* 6 [1907]:184). Seth Kotch makes similar arguments about mobs in this era revealing the fragility of state power in the South (*Lethal State*, 25).

118. Mitchell, "Nationalization of Southern Sentiment," 107–13. Lyman Abbott, northern pastor, progressive, and former secretary of the Freedman's Bureau, demonstrated how far northern views were changing in this era when he wrote, "The Southerner understands the Negro better than the Northerner does and likes him better" (quoted in Southern, *Malignant Heritage*, 36).

119. Quoted in Muhammad, *Condemnation of Blackness*, 28.

120. Ray Stannard Baker likewise puts racial conflict in the South in the context of empire, claiming, in fact, that "the tangle of race problems" in the Philippines makes the southern situation "simple" in comparison (*Following the Color Line*, 292).

121. *Afro-American*, 22 January 1916.

122. Douglass, *Why Is the Negro Lynched?*, 32.

Chapter Four: Counting the South's Legal Executions

1. Many studies simply look at executions under state authority, and as that data set for the South starts in 1908, it both misses the earlier high point of execution in the late nineteenth century and draws attention to the modest rise in execution in the Great Depression. Both Margaret Vandiver (*Lethal Punishment*, 20) and Seth Kotch (*Lethal State*, 50–55) write of the 1930s being the high point of execution. Vandiver's data sets start at different moments in the late nineteenth century, and while Kotch treats the late nineteenth century, most of his study is focused on the period after North Carolina's centralization of executions in 1910.

2. For recent studies that speak of executions in some way coming out of lynchings or replacing them, see Pfeifer, *Rough Justice*, 146, 152; Kotch, *Lethal State*, 18, 23–4, 29, 58; Vandiver, *Lethal Punishment*, 87–88, 175. Every statistical evaluation of this dynamic has contradicted this, concluding "that executions and lynchings were largely independent forms of social control" (Tolnay and Beck, *Festival of Violence*, 111). See also Bailey and Tolnay, *Lynched*, 18. Much of the scholarship uses counts rather than rates, which misses the sizable rise in populations over time, a rise resulting in more crime and therefore, inevitably, in more punishments as well. This can lead to the mistaken impression that lynching's decline in the early twentieth century coincided with a rise in legal executions.

3. After the Supreme Court's 1972 *Furman v. Georgia* decision (408 U.S. 238) halted the use of the death penalty, states rewrote their laws to abide by the Court's interpretation of what capital punishment procedures would be constitutional. Between 1976 and the end of 2021, the states that have used the death penalty the most were in the South: Texas (573), Oklahoma (114), Virginia (113), Florida (99), Missouri (90), Georgia (76), Alabama (68), Ohio (56), North Carolina (43), South Carolina (43), Arizona (37), Arkansas (31), Louisiana (28), and Mississippi (22) (Death Penalty Information Center, "Death Penalty in 2021" and "Facts about the Death Penalty").

4. The rest of the South from 1976 to 2021 = 539; all states outside the South = 410. Half of those (204) are from two states (Oklahoma and Missouri) bordering what this study considers the South (Death Penalty Information Center, "Death Penalty in 2021" and "Facts about the Death Penalty").

5. Approximately three times more African Americans have been executed since 1976 as their share of the population would dictate (Death Penalty Information Center, "Facts about the Death Penalty").

6. In their study of lynching in ten southern states, Tolnay and Beck found 2,596 lynchings between 1882 and 1920, 2,282 (88 percent) of which were of African Americans. Their data are available as Project HAL on the web.

7. Ending capital punishment before 1920: Michigan (1846–), Rhode Island (1852–), Wisconsin (1853–), Iowa (1872–78), Maine (1876–83, 1887–), Colorado (1897–1901), Kansas (1907–35), Minnesota (1911–), Washington (1913–19), Oregon (1914–20), South Dakota (1915–39), Arizona (1916–18), Missouri (1917–19) (Bowers, *Legal Homicide*, 9).

8. According to the Espy file, 952 people were executed in the United States between 1840 and 1859; of that number, 583 were in the twelve states of the South. Those states had an 1860 population of just under 9.9 million people, which was 31 percent of the total U.S. population of just over 31.4 million (Espy file; Carter, *Historical Statistics*, 1:180–359).

9. Schwarz, *Twice Condemned*, 15.

10. Even without considering the smaller population of the South, these twelve southern states accounted for more than 52 percent of those executed in the nation in those decades. According to the Espy file, 1,111 of the 2,118 executions performed in the United States between 1880 and 1899 were in the South. These twelve states were approximately 17.5 million (or 28 percent) of the U.S. population of 63 million in 1890. (Espy file; Carter, *Historical Statistics*, 1:180–359).

11. My choice of dates and my choice of states have created a subset of these data unique to this study. The dates 1866–1920 were chosen to capture the era when the South shifted to private execution without complicating matters by attempting to bring in either the tumultuous era of the Civil War or the Great Depression. One could argue that the decade of the 1920s would profitably belong in this study, particularly because several southern states moved to centralize executions in their state penitentiaries in that decade. But even by 1910, most executions in the South were private, and so 1920 seemed the appropriate endpoint to this work.

12. The most populous states in the nation at this time, New York and Pennsylvania, had very large numbers of executions (358 and 452, respectively) between 1866 and 1920, and the booming frontier state of California likewise used capital punishment very frequently (303). The other four states would land at the bottom of the list of southern states and executions in table 4.1, even though their populations were much larger than that of most southern states: Missouri (167), Illinois (145), Ohio (139), and New Jersey (135). Populations in 1920: New York (10.4m), Pennsylvania (8.7m), California (3.4m), Missouri (3.4m), Illinois (6.5m), Ohio (5.8m), and New Jersey (3.2m). Texas (4.7m) was the only southern state in 1920 among the ten states with the highest populations. The twelve southern states in this study accounted for only 31 percent of the nation's population in 1860 (9,882,328 out of a U.S. population of 31,443,321), a share that fell to 26 percent by 1920 (27,523,584 out of a U.S. population of 106,021,537) (Carter, *Historical Statistics*, 1:180–359).

13. Some sources mistakenly claim Tennessee to have briefly abolished the death penalty when it ended capital punishment for most crimes, including murder, in 1915 (reinstating it in 1919), but even in that singular moment, the state retained the death penalty for rape as well as for convicts accused of murder while in prison, and used it for the former: *Acts of Tennessee* (1915), 5–7; *Acts of Tennessee* (1919), 27–28; Vandiver, *Lethal Punishment*, 156–64; Galliher et al., "Abolition and Reinstatement of Capital Punishment," 556–58.

14. It is well established in the literature that the South has perennially led the nation in violent crimes. See Lane, *Murder in America*, 149–51, 229, 235, 255, 321, 342, 350; Roth, *American Homicide*, 329–54, 411–34.

15. Redfield, *Homicide, North and South*, 12, 28–30. The ten northern states were the states of New England, New York, Pennsylvania, Michigan, and Minnesota; their population, together, was 17 million; Texas in 1870 was just over 800,000. For another regional analysis of homicide at the time, see B. J. Ramage, "Homicide in Southern States" *Sewanee Review* 4 (1896): 220–21. This penchant for violence in the South has been the subject of a number of studies, including Ayers, *Vengeance and Justice*; Frantz [Parsons], *Ku-Klux*; Emberton, *Beyond Redemption*.

16. A smaller contributing factor might be that the proportion of its population in the demographic most likely to be violent was also slightly higher: violence most often arises from young men, and the South in the late nineteenth century was younger than other regions. The South in this era was not more male than other regions, although the population profiles of some violent frontier areas (South Georgia, for instance) *were* slightly skewed toward males in the late nineteenth century. But every southern state was in the nation's top fifteen states in the proportion of its

population that were teenagers in the 1890s and in the bottom fifteen in the proportion in their thirties. Every southern state had a median age more than five years younger than the least violent region, New England. The only states in the nation with median ages under nineteen were seven states in the South (*Twelfth U.S. Census, 1900, Special Reports*, 146, 161). Young white men coming of age in the late 1880s were entering into their demographically most-violent phase of life, and had been coached to violence by its successful deployment in Reconstruction. Edward Ayers posits something similar (*Vengeance and Justice*, 241).

17. Roth, *American Homicide*, 329–38, 421. In her terrific book on the South after the Civil War, Carol Emberton makes the very important point, built from Primo Levi's formulation, that "'useless violence' isn't really useless" (*Beyond Redemption*, 186). The violence itself becomes the point, degrading and dehumanizing its victims. This goal seems particularly apt for these periods.

18. Wyatt-Brown, *Southern Honor*, 368.

19. Roth, *American Homicide*, 352. Emberton makes particularly compelling arguments linking freedom, ideas of masculinity, and violence: "a tangled relationship between freedom and violence" (*Beyond Redemption*, 135). In this period, a sort of "manly violence" prevailed, but she hearkens back as well to Frederick Douglass's formulation of "a slave is a man without force" (107). Freedom in some sense *meant* fighting to many in these generations.

20. Compare New York's rate of executing whites (0.059 in the 1890s) with table 4.7 for whites in the South: roughly half the rate generated from Hearn and Laska's data. (Hearn, *Legal Executions in New York*; Carter, *Historical Statistics*, 1:180–359).

21. Numbers of most things (jobs, houses, stores, crime, punishment) track population sizes, barring other dynamics. Florida, with its small population in this period, would be toward the bottom of any list of states in mere counts of any of those things (jobs, stores . . .); Georgia and Texas, with their large populations, would be toward the top (as in table 4.1). But this would tell us little about jobs or stores or, in this case, capital punishment; it would mostly tell us that these states had more people and everything that comes with them. Rates, then, subtract out this population-dependent dynamic, leaving a more telling pattern of the intensity of the use of the death penalty.

22. Kahneman, *Thinking Fast and Slow*, 79–88. Our brains play a host of tricks on us in terms of trends, numbers, and their interpretations. Of the many ways our brains are inherently *logical-ish* rather than forthrightly rational, two stand out as important to this discussion of the quantitative data of executions. The first is the substitution error: allowing the data we have ready access to—like numbers of executions or lynchings—to stand in for data that we want (but don't have). In terms of the WYSIATI problem ("What You See Is All There Is"), our brains *actively bend the data* that are readily accessible toward how they might be most helpful. We have no numbers for other important ideas like "segregation" or "white supremacy" or "fear." Our brains may tend to privilege the numerical information we have, perhaps even (at least unconsciously) to make numbers and their resulting trends stand in for more than they can reasonably bear.

The second is the law of small numbers and its relationship to our (mis)understanding of how randomness works. Small data sets can be erratic, and we readily impose reasons (a story) to data that actually have no patterns (Kahneman, *Thinking Fast and Slow*, 109–18). In general, huge populations will end up toward the middle of whatever variable is measured, for divergences from the mean will be more effectively canceled out within larger groups. In contrast, smaller populations will be more scattered throughout the bell curve of possible results of whatever is being measured. This is common sense, but when we are offered data with some diverging from the mean, we tend to see patterns anyway: to find meaning in whatever data we are given. This might be in part because we have an innate drive for story, for turning the world around us into narratives that have cause and effect (Kahneman, *Thinking Fast and Slow*, 168–74). Flipping a coin 1,000 times *means* that there will be four or six heads (or ten or twelve) in a row at some point, not indicating anything about that moment of flipping the coin but merely demonstrating that that is what randomness is. We know this, but our intuitive minds, when greeted with eight flips of a coin in a row that are all heads, will begin to consider how something is making that happen. Randomness consists of randomly distributed nonuniformities, but we rarely intuit it in that way. In terms of this study, *all* of these numbers of executions (and of lynchings) are small numbers—just several hundred incidents in each decade among a population of millions. With the South divided into 1,200 counties, perhaps only one-third of those counties had even one execution in any given decade. Such data are *supposed* to look weird and nonuniform; that's what data *are*.

23. Who knows where this phrase originated: "There are three kinds of lies: lies, damned lies, and statistics." Mark Twain attributed it to Benjamin Disraeli (Mark Twain, "Chapters from My Autobiography—XX," *North American Review* [5 July 1907]: 471).

24. There is an active element to the building of lists, policing what is in or out, and in interpreting them. Just as any other source is not "truth," numbers built from the past are meaningful, helpful, but exactly as in need of context and interpretation (good building) as any other sources. Do we believe the newspaper in a distant town in a different state that describes an execution? Or do we decide that because the local paper failed to mention it, the execution was a fiction? This is less of an issue in terms of legal capital punishment, a category that tends to be more or less clear in the record of the past (if laborious to research), as long as we can find those records. This is a much larger issue with other deathly violence like lynchings: just which murders fit into this category is an act of judgment, and often a challenging one.

25. Blackman and McLaughlin, "Espy File," 221. A supplement to the Espy file of over 4,000 additional executions was made available in 2008, but that supplement has very limited information and is therefore much less useful at present. Blackman and McLaughlin compared the original Espy file with this supplement in order to show the ways the original Espy file was not simply rife with inevitable minor errors but also flawed more substantially in terms of its incompleteness.

26. In addition, my rather accidental review of Espy file entries (I attempted no thorough review but did look at newspaper reports for approximately half of the South's executions the Espy file had in this period) found twenty-three condemned listed with race unknown in Espy where the newspapers give that information; twelve condemned listed in Espy as being one race, when the papers say another; two con-

demned listed in Espy as being women, when papers list them as men; two listed in Espy as offense unknown when papers gave the offense; thirty-five executions that the newspapers say occurred on a different day (usually one day away from what was listed in Espy), including several without a date where the newspaper offers one; one name unknown when the newspaper gave the name; and more than 130 entries where names were spelled differently between the Espy file and newspapers.

I failed to find in the regional press some executions reported in the Espy file, which could mean either that an entry has an error or that the paper did not cover the hanging. The file includes executions well before 1863 under West Virginia when they, of course, were Virginia executions, and it includes a host of executions from forts in the Indian Territory with the count of Arkansas. For this project, I have started with the original Espy file, subtracted all executions under federal jurisdiction as well as those four respited convicts, and added forty-two executions that I have found but that are not listed in the Espy file. Much more importantly, for many calculations, I have abandoned the more problematic Espy file data for the whole South and instead use the more complete data for half of the South that are available from the work of Hearn and Laska.

27. For the six southern states with new numbers from Hearn and Laska, there were almost no additions to any state list from the moment of centralization to 1920. Georgia has many additions all the way through 1920 because it did not execute under state authority until 1924; Espy and new lists are identical after centralization in Kentucky, South Carolina, Tennessee, and Virginia; Hearn adds only one execution to Espy's list for North Carolina (Zachary Taylor Love in 1911) after centralization (Espy file; Hearn and Laska).

28. Espy file. According to William Bowers, the states that had centralized capital punishment under state authority before 1900 were California, Colorado, Connecticut, District of Columbia, Indiana, Iowa, New Hampshire, New York, Ohio, Vermont, and West Virginia. Four others had abolished the death penalty (Maine, Michigan, Rhode Island, and Wisconsin), and many other western and northern states centralized in the first decade of the twentieth century (Idaho, Massachusetts, Nebraska, Nevada, New Jersey, North Dakota, Oregon, Utah, and Washington). (*Legal Homicide*, 46–47). As an example of how few new executions we can expect to discover in the era of state authority for these states, Hearn found only one execution that was not already in the Espy file from 1890 (when New York centralized) to 1920. (Espy file; Hearn, *Legal Executions in New York*).

29. Blackman and McLaughlin, "Espy File," 215. They also note that while the South accounts for only 41 percent of the original Espy file, it accounts for 71 percent of the supplement. Reconstruction is a particular low point in completeness of the original Espy file, and that, along with late adoption of executions under state authority in the South, may account for a large proportion of the "missing" executions in the supplement as well as possible future additions yet to be found.

30. These books are "registries," and they are very accurate and helpful but also very peculiar documents. Aside from some nonscholarly or even argumentative editorial commentary and wordings characterizing crimes and punishments (in one introduction, Hearn says he opts to "not use politically correct phraseology," and in another, he calls opponents of capital punishment naïve and another perspective

"twisted liberalism" [Hearn, *Legal Executions in North Carolina and South Carolina*, 7; Hearn, *Legal Executions in Virginia*, 3]), they include not just the facts of the execution (date, place, name, race, crime) but also citations from newspapers and local records that scholars can turn to. This is exceedingly useful.

To the extent that my own research can do so, it verifies these new lists as much more accurate than the original Espy file: for these six states, I found twenty-four executions not on Espy's original list; every one of them was on these new lists. I found two executions of men whom Espy listed as women; these lists have them as men. My findings don't agree with these new lists for every date of execution or race of the condemned, but almost: I found twenty-three instances from these states where the Espy file had a date different from what I found in newspapers; the new lists had twenty-two of them correctly listed. I found six cases where Espy had condemned of one race and newspapers said another, and fourteen cases where Espy did not identify a race but the newspapers did. The new lists differed from mine in only three of those cases, each of which apparently involved a Native American condemned who was racially classified in varied ways in sources of the time. My research in newspapers verifies one in the Espy file that Laska has for another year (Arthur Pearson was executed in Tennessee in 1906, not in Laska's 1908), and one execution the Espy file has in Virginia (Mary Snodgrass in 1896) that Hearn omits. I cannot speak to the research methodologies used in Hearn and Laska or the degree to which portions of a state might be more fully enumerated in these lists than others. It is bound to be true that despite "comprehensive" being in these titles, other executions occurred that they did not find. There are also bound to be typos and inconsistencies introduced in these lists as with any. That will always be true. These registries are a huge step forward in the study of capital punishment: every scholar who has been using the original Espy file should add these new lists into their work if they are available for the state under study.

A more pervasive problem for some scholars using Hearn and Laska is the fact that many condemned were charged with multiple crimes or aggravating factors in a crime; these registries list only one crime for each entry, although some discussion in their text can give perspective on some aggravating factors. It would be a mistake to interpret their italicized categories of charges as strict coding categories; they rather appear to be commonsense identifying words for the crime as it appears in their sources. As such, they will not offer multiple charges, which may leave researchers in a conundrum: an execution called "murder" but then described in terms of its motive being "sexual assault" (Hearn, *Legal Executions in Georgia*, 39) leaves us with unanswered questions.

31. Of the "new" executions found in Hearn and Laska, 98 percent were of African Americans.

32. In this, Blackman and McLaughlin appear to have underplayed a major category of errors in the Espy file. Blackman and McLaughlin were looking through all of American history and every region, focusing on overall, persistent flaws, including military executions, a British bias, and missing Native American executions, among others. The undercount of African Americans and of the South overall, it appears, was at a scale at least as dramatic. A bar graph (Blackman and McLaughlin, "Espy File," 215) shows the South dominating the whole figure of new executions, but the

caption misidentifies southern states, and this dramatic preponderance of new executions for the South in the supplement is not a central part of their evaluation (216-18).

33. States with no executions of African Americans in the 1890s were the New England states; Michigan, Minnesota, and Wisconsin in the Midwest; and Iowa, Nevada, and Oregon in the West. There may be more African Americans executed that the Espy file does not identify, not merely in terms of executions missing in its file but in terms of the several dozen entries in the Espy file listed as "race unknown." Espy file.

34. These states had the following counts and rates of executions of African Americans from 1889 to 1899 according to the Espy file: New York (14 executions = 1.6/year/100,000), Illinois (9 = 1.2), New Jersey (8 = 1.3), California (2 = 1.6), Colorado (2 = 2.6), Montana (2 = 12.1), and Washington (1 = 1.8). Espy file. Southern white apologists for the region's racial regime exploited such numbers of Black crime and punishment in the North: see chapter 3.

So why were these execution rates so high outside the South for Blacks? While the numbers of those executed were low, the populations of African Americans in these regions were *very* small. North and South Dakota each executed a single African American in the 1890s; their estimated 1893 population of African Americans, *combined*, was only 865 people, making their execution rates for Blacks astronomical (26.2 and 17.5, respectively). This is an extreme version of the small numbers problem: each of these states with large rates was also just one execution away from a rate of zero.

35. Bailey and Tolnay, *Lynched*, 209-10. Louis Masur found that those who were hanged in the North tended to be Black or foreign born: "Outsiders were more likely to be hanged," for they earned the least sympathy (*Rites of Execution*, 38-39).

36. With the imperfect Espy counts, Arkansas, Florida, Louisiana, and Texas figure prominently, particularly in terms of executions of African Americans: see table 4.6. If that trend were to hold in terms of newer, better data, there might be a meaningful story to tell about the southern frontier, race, and the death penalty (Espy file; Carter, *Historical Statistics*, 1:180-359).

37. South Georgia and Georgia's coastal regions stand out here in different ways. The coastal counties had relatively few executions, but the population there was smaller than in other regions, yielding a robust rate. As a settled region with a large African American population, the coastal region had particularly low numbers of lynchings, which might be an important context for these numbers (Brundage, *Lynching in the New South*, 130-37). South Georgia, with both large numbers of executed and frontier conditions, was by far the fastest-growing region in Georgia: South Georgia's total population more than doubled between 1880 and 1900; no other Georgia region increased more than 50 percent in that era. Between 1880 and 1920, the African American population of this region grew by 340 percent (from 92,804 to 316,882); it was also the Georgia region with the highest rate of lynching. This sort of demographic disorder can foster more crime and therefore more punishment. (*Twelfth U.S. Census, 1900*, 1:533-34, 561-62; *Fourteenth U.S. Census, 1920*, 3:207-21, 1061-76).

38. Lane discusses this as a national trend (*Murder in America*, 199).

39. Rates of Black execution were many times higher than the overall rates in states of the North (9.5 times more), Midwest (13 times more), and West (11 times more). Intrastate regions in Virginia and Georgia executed Blacks anywhere from 50 percent more to six times more than overall rates of execution.

40. With Hearn and Laska for their six states and the Espy file for the other half of the South, 2,533 executions of Blacks out of 3,199 total executions = 79 percent (Espy file; Hearn and Laska).

41. Hearn, *Legal Executions in Georgia*.

42. Most historians choose equivalent periods to study (generally decades [10s] but sometimes five-year increments), but that has always appeared to me to be arbitrary, applying something like a grid to history. I was concerned that such a rigid imposition would miss dynamics that crossed those arbitrary boundaries. As this work covers a span of time that includes two different eras of extraordinary extralegal violence in the South (Reconstruction and the 1890s), greater utility may be found by crafting the units of analysis to fit those eras, and adjusting the boundaries of measuring. That is what I have chosen to do: eras that make the most sense in terms of this history.

So what I have in this study is Reconstruction (defined here as the eleven years from 1866 to 1876); the era after white Democrats reconquered the South (twelve years from 1877 to 1888); the disordered era of the 1890s when lynchings were so prominent both in fact and in the attention they were beginning to receive (eleven years from 1889 to 1899); and the era of the early twentieth century when lethal racial violence was on its slow decline and when the great migration began to change the nature of race in the region and nationally (twenty-one years from 1900 to 1920). Given the different lengths of these periods, numbers are made comparable to each other and to any other study's numbers by giving them in annualized (per-year) form. This is unconventional, but using decades would make both Reconstruction and the reconquest periods largely disappear into different decades. For this work, being nonstandard was less problematic than the alternative.

43. Hearn and Laska's lists add 120 percent to the Espy file's list for Reconstruction (1866–76), 13 percent to reconquest (1877–88), 44 percent to the 1890s (1889–99), and 18 percent for the early twentieth century (1900–1920). Altogether, 32 percent of the Hearn and Laska lists are of executions not on the original Espy list.

44. These percentages include both new executions and new information on race for executions already in the Espy file, which is why the rise in the number of African American executions can be above 100 percent.

45. The African American share of the southern population was 39.2 percent in 1860, 38.5 percent in 1870, 38.5 percent in 1880, 36.4 percent in 1890, 35.4 percent in 1900, 33.2 percent in 1910, and 30.2 percent in 1920 (Carter, *Historical Statistics*, 1:180–359).

46. From 1850 to 1859, the Espy file lists 338 executions in the twelve states of the South, which had a population (the average of the 1850 and 1860 populations) of 9,257,688, yielding an execution rate of 0.365, very close to that in reconquest (0.344). (Espy file; Carter, *Historical Statistics*, 1:180–359). I would expect this count in Espy to be as incomplete as those for the postwar period and therefore that this surely understates the "real" rate by some indeterminant amount.

47. Rabinowitz, *Race Relations*, 35; Ayers, *Vengeance and Justice*, 185–222.

48. Roth, *American Homicide*, 329–38, 421.

49. Chesson, *Richmond after the War*, 112–14; *Richmond Police and Fire Department Directory*, 22–25. This included African Americans (briefly) sworn in by the Republican faction as deputies, the only time they served on the Richmond police force in the era. There were skirmishes between Democratic-led police and African American citizens, and ultimately the Republican mayor was besieged in a Richmond police station.

50. Reconstruction's rates are probably a little overstated in these figures due to the undercount of the South in the 1870 census. This fact would not affect any *counts* of executions or later *rates*, but an apparent large undercount of the South in 1870 exaggerates the rates for Reconstruction at least somewhat.

Just on the face of it, the census numbers appear erratic: with a typical census growth for the region being above 20 percent each decade, the 1870s census recorded only a 9.4 percent growth from 1860, followed by the 1880 census recording a growth in the South's population of more than 35 percent. For context, the next four censuses after 1880 averaged increases between these two extremes: 17 percent per decade. It "appears evident that the enumeration of 1870 in this area was seriously incomplete, undoubtedly as a result of the unsettled conditions of the Reconstruction period" (Carter, *Historical Statistics*, 1:18). Margo J. Anderson finds that among the problems with administering the 1870 census were political fights over its impact on Reconstruction and shifting notions of citizenship and suffrage with constitutional amendments affecting the franchise: counting African Americans as whole people (rather than three-fifths) as well as Confederates not allowed to vote. The inclusion of a question about suffrage made these already-polarizing issues that much more challenging, as did "extremely poor field procedures" (*American Census*, 72–81). Needed reforms in process and administration were caught in the political crossfire, and few were made in time for this census. Anderson found, for instance, that in 1870 the census had 6,530 enumerators for the South; in 1880, it had 31,382 (*American Census*, 275). Add to this the chaos and violence of the era and African Americans being more mobile than ever before, and the census bureau in 1890 estimated that it missed 1,260,078 people in the South in 1870, about 12 percent of the region's entire population (241). For another take on these developments, see Schor, *Counting Americans*, 86–87.

J. David Hacker wrote a very interesting evaluation of errors in the census in which he argues that this reevaluation actually overstates problems in the 1870 census, finding only a 1 percent to 3 percent error in the nation overall for that year's census. However, he chose to evaluate only the white population, and we might dispute his claim that the South's white population would be a "good proxy" for the South as a whole during Reconstruction, for few people would be harder to locate in the years after the Civil War than landless, newly freed folk whom his analysis did not consider. And there are differences in official census records by race in these years, indicating a skew toward more African Americans uncounted in 1870. In the South, the white population grew 10.5 percent (1870 census), jumping to 34.9 percent (1880); the Black population grew 7.6 percent and 35.3 percent. It appears Hacker was looking at the portion of the South's population somewhat less undercounted in 1870. Less in dispute would be his emphasis on how the big change in the nature of census taking (centralizing the organization, hiring more enumerators) occurred in 1880 and before that, the process was more ad hoc, with little control over field enumerators and with officials viewing the census as filled with political patronage positions (Hacker, "New Estimates," 75–76, 94–95).

Adding in 12 percent more for the South's population would lower any rates of execution generated for Reconstruction; using Hearn and Laska's data, the rate with that added population would fall to 0.339 for their states, very close to the rate in the reconquest era that follows (table 4.4). Because there is no way to effectively identify a corrected number for states, by race, or for counties, all other rates calculated in this chapter for Reconstruction necessarily use the official, flawed 1870 census population figures and are therefore surely underplaying the population for this early era, and thereby overplaying the rates generated from them. It is simply impossible to know by how much.

51. Roth, *American Homicide*, 411.

52. Strauder v. West Virginia, 100 U. S. 303 (1880); Ex Parte Virginia, 100 U .S. 339 (1880).

53. Virginia v. Rives, 100 U. S. 313 (1880).

54. In effect, these decisions helped to bar Blacks from juries a generation before disfranchisement erected yet another barrier, for jurors in many states were drawn from the rolls of eligible voters. In the 1930s, the Supreme Court amended this ruling on race and jury selection. See Davis and Graham, *Supreme Court*, 18–25.

55. Carrigan, *Making of a Lynching Culture*, 146; Rabinowitz, *Race Relations*, 34–41.

56. Edwards, *Gendered Strife and Confusion*, 214–16; Roth, *American Homicide*, 413. While Tolnay and Beck were clear that there was no substitution relationship that they could find between lynching and legal executions after 1890, they pointedly refrained from making that claim for this early era, writing instead that in "1880–89, executions and lynchings were significantly related negatively" (Tolnay and Beck, *Festival of Violence*, 110), meaning that in that era, places with more lynchings had fewer executions and vice versa.

57. "The Gallows for the White Man and Imprisonment for the Negro," *Richmond Dispatch*, 9 October 1868; *Southern Opinion*, 24 October 1868; Emberton, *Beyond Redemption*, 158, 181.

58. In both Virginia and North Carolina, execution rates for African Americans in other periods tended to be around ten times higher than for whites. In reconquest Virginia, it was down to 3.3 times higher; in 1890s North Carolina, 5.7 times higher. As skewed as these figures remain, they are the "most equitable" for each state respectively, and Virginia's was the most equitable of any of the Hearn and Laska states in any period. Give yourself a minute, and you'll realize that you just read that having more than three times more Blacks (proportionately) executed in Virginia was "most equitable." . . . Clearly the main story is the skew everywhere in that direction. In rates built from the Espy file, there are similarly "low" disparities in terms of race, but all of them were in the Reconstruction era, the moment when so much of the South had more years with judges who might side with Black defendants more often.

59. For comparison, the depression era of the 1930s, which is sometimes referred to as the high point of executions for the region (recent examples are Vandiver, *Lethal*

Punishment, 20, and Kotch, *Lethal State*, 23), can be considered so only if we don't take into consideration the rising population of the South, which more than doubled between 1880 and 1930. Using the Espy file (which should be more dependable for this era of centralized executions under state authority), the rate for the 1930s was 0.263, slightly higher than early twentieth-century rates using Espy numbers but considerably lower than late nineteenth-century ones and lower than all rates calculated with the more complete Hearn and Laska data (Espy file; Carter, *Historical Statistics*, 1:180–359). For a comparison with trends in lynching, see chapter 5 and Trotti, "What Counts?," 375–400.

Chapter Five: Uncivil Executions

1. The most important work for this project from this burgeoning field includes Hall, *Revolt against Chivalry*; Carrigan, *Making of a Lynching Culture*; Wood, *Lynching as Spectacle*; Tolnay and Beck, *Festival of Violence*; Brundage, *Lynching in the New South*; Wright, *Racial Violence in Kentucky*; Baker, *This Mob*; Vandiver, *Lethal Punishment*; Pfeifer, *Rough Justice*; Waldrep, *Many Faces of Judge Lynch*.

Recent work on lynching outside the South includes Gonzalez-Day, *Lynching in the West*; Pfeifer, *Lynching beyond Dixie*; Carrigan and Waldrep, *Swift to Wrath*.

2. "New Issue Negroes" was a phrase used by Thomas Nelson Page and other white supremacists in contrast to the "good" African Americans of slavery times. John Mitchell of the *Richmond Planet* used it as well when he wrote "What is true of New Issue Negroes [that they are shiftless, etc.] is also true of the New Issue Whites" (25 June 1904).

3. See Trotti, "What Counts?," 381–85. Some killings simply require a judgment call as to whether the available evidence fits lynching's definition: an irreducible margin of error. Modern scholars insist that their lists remain incomplete: "My lists are not definitive; they are simply as close to definitive as feasible" (Brundage, *Lynching in the New South*, 295). Tolnay and Beck did not claim to include every lynching, sure that new evidence will demand revision (*Festival of Violence*, 261).

4. Tolnay and Beck's data on lynching demonstrate a high point in lynchings between the late 1880s and 1900, paralleling the findings of every other lynching study. Their data are available as Project HAL; for Virginia, see Brundage, *Lynching in the New South*, 270–80; population data from Carter, *Historical Statistics*, 1:180–359.

5. From 1866 to 1920, the Espy file has 78 percent of executions in southern states being of African Americans. But adding in the better data from Hearn and Laska, and limiting consideration to just the half of the South they cover, they found that 82 percent were of Blacks.

6. Factoring in population growth since the Civil War, Kentucky as well as counties in northwest Tennessee had twice the lynching rate in Reconstruction than in the 1890s; the counties around Waco, Texas, had a rate six times that of the 1890s (Carrigan, *Making of a Lynching Culture*, 275–87; Wright, *Racial Violence*, 307–19; Vandiver, *Lethal Punishment*, 196–99). This is more fully explored in Trotti, "What Counts?."

7. Virtually all of the scholarship on lynching in the South is predicated on the notion that the number of lynchings rose in the late 1880s, reached a peak in the 1890s,

and slowly declined over the coming half century. But the very fact of counting—the existence of lists (beginning in 1882)—surely makes counting lynchings easier after that moment than before. The end of the century witnessed a burgeoning number of newspaper stories, commentaries, and ultimately books on lynching. Waldrep shows that this changed the understanding of lynching in the press and public (*Many Faces of Judge Lynch*, 103–26). Wright makes a similar argument (*Racial Violence in Kentucky*, 8). In short, there appear to be no data in the historical record to support the idea that there were more lynchings in the 1890s than in Reconstruction but much data to support the idea that the issue of lynching held a very different role in those two periods. While it is unclear whether quantitative data from an era so chaotic as Reconstruction will ever prove thoroughly convincing, the role of lynching in these early decades is surely worthy of further study.

8. Carrigan, *Making of a Lynching Culture*, 253n8. Wright emphasized how Reconstruction provided particular challenges that might never be overcome: "The vast majority of lynchings . . . for these years are lacking in solid historical documentation (usually the only known details are newspaper accounts of someone's recollection that a lynching happened in a particular county some years ago) and therefore have not been counted" (*Racial Violence in Kentucky*, 42). See Trotti, "What Counts?"

9. Brundage, *Lynching in the New South*, 29–30; Wright, *Racial Violence in Kentucky*, 102–3; Pfeifer, *Rough Justice*, 119–20; Litwack, *Trouble in Mind*, 303–4. Project HAL lists 154 lynchings before 1920 that at least reportedly included African Americans in the mobs.

10. This follows the taxonomy of lynching suggested by Fitzhugh Brundage: private, terrorist, posse, and mass lynchings. Mass lynchings were the largest, most sensationalized, ritualized, and most often sadistic form of lynchings; having the most popular participation, they were always noticed and are central in the lynching scholarship (*Lynching in the New South*, 36–45; on page 40, Brundage mentions this connection to public executions).

11. *Atlanta Constitution*, 2 December 1893; 8 January 1898; 2 September 1900; 30 October 1900. On the lynching of Sam Hose, see Mathews, *At the Altar of Lynching*; Brundage, *Lynching in the New South*, 82–83; and Hale, *Making Whiteness*, 209–15.

12. Perhaps mirroring this difference in valuing the victim, images of legal executions were taken before the hanging; those of lynchings were typically after (Wood, *Lynching as Spectacle*, 36, 71–111).

13. *Charleston News and Courier*, 25 November 1899. Another thanked those at the gallows, ending: "People have let me live long enough to make peace with God" (*Arkansas Gazette*, 24 June 1904).

14. *New Orleans Daily Picayune*, 27 January 1882. Another condemned said that "he was glad indeed that he had not been lynched, but had been given time in which to repent and prepare for the journey into the other world" (*Florida Times-Union*, 5 March 1910). Ministers requested a respite for a white Tennessee man in order for him to better "prepare for death," for the condemned was "not satisfied with his future condition" (Laska, *Legal Executions in Tennessee*, 215, 148).

15. Baker, "What Is a Lynching?," 305. Baker also gives an instance of a mob entering a courtroom, when a minister (brother to the murder victim) pleaded with the mob to let the law take its course. A voice yelled, "We don't want religion, we want blood" (306).

16. Editorial from a white Oklahoma paper quoted in *Chicago Defender*, 1 April 1916.

17. *Chicago Defender*, 1 April 1916.

18. The *Raleigh Gazette* (6 November 1897), an African American paper, reprinted this white justification for lynching from the *Raleigh News and Observer*.

19. Page, *Negro*, 100.

20. Mathews, *At the Altar of Lynching*, 139–77.

21. *Atlanta Constitution*, 5 March 1881; for a similar wording, see *Galveston Daily News*, 12 August 1876. See chapter 1 for a variety of examples of religious calling out.

22. Litwack, *Trouble in Mind*, 286. Du Bois, in Atlanta at this time, wrote of his response to this butchery of Hose and its display: "Something died in me that day" (quoted in Litwack, *Trouble in Mind*, 404).

23. L. J. Brown, "Philosophy of Lynching," *Voice of the Negro* (November 1904): 558–59. Brown continued by imagining the impulses of the savage whites "fighting screaming, and struggling to get a bone of a burned Negro which he will carry home and string around his baby's little neck as an amulet to ward off the great black monster."

24. *Atlanta Constitution*, 26 January 1893.

25. *Raleigh News and Observer*, 4 August 1894. The rope in this hanging had hanged several and was to be sent to a neighboring county where a man was condemned. Several articles end with a sort of brief history of the particular gallows in use: an antebellum hanging, a famous murderer in the 1870s and now this one, say. One paper speaks of the gallows being owned by a local man and used in thirteen executions: *Louisville Courier-Journal*, 10 January 1897.

26. *Atlanta Journal*, 25 January 1889. Short reports from executions would never mention souvenirs; it is the more elaborate reports that give the space to this sort of observation, those setting the scene rather than just reporting that the execution took place. But it is less than clear that this desire was absent in executions that earned fewer column inches; it seems as likely that it is the elaboration of the reporting that makes these comments in the historical record appear from time to time: an artifact of the sources, then, as much as the dynamics of these particular events. While the crowds were regularly foiled from obtaining such totems, the simplest explanation of these events would be that crowds (which were generally mixed-race) at least regularly wanted them.

27. Unclaimed bodies tended to go to local medical facilities, for few other legal opportunities for obtaining cadavers for learning anatomy were available. At times, particular local doctors or medical schools "bought" the body from the condemned, paying for the privilege of having a corpse to practice anatomy. Impoverished condemned men would find this a means to pay for incidentals they needed or desired while awaiting execution. For instance: "Debill sold his body to Dr. T. S. Dekle for $20 and lived comfortably on the proceeds" (*Atlanta Constitution*, 15 June 1889). One paper described the sale of different parts of the condemned's body to different doctors:

"Jim had disposed of his head and body separately to two persons for necessaries he required while in jail" (*Richmond Dispatch*, 12 July 1873).

In a further gruesome history of bodies, the public was barred from viewing the articulated skeleton of presidential assassin Charles Guiteau assembled at the Army Medical Museum, and "great care was taken to see that none of the bones were carried off by relic-seekers." Even with this "great care," hundreds each day in the early 1880s reportedly asked to see the skeleton or the belongings of Guiteau and were disappointed (*Richmond Dispatch*, 27 December 1883).

28. *Richmond Dispatch*, 12 February 1887. "Souvenirs Still in Demand" was the subtitle of this article printed a month after the execution.

29. *Galveston Daily News*, 5 August 1893; see also *Atlanta Constitution*, 25 July 1891.

30. *Louisville Courier-Journal*, 28 March 1885.

31. *Charlotte Observer*, 26 November 1902.

32. *Atlanta Constitution*, 8 December 1905.

33. Laska, *Legal Executions in Tennessee*, 155.

34. Of course, the Christian faith is replete with instances of physical objects being imbued with religious meaning: pilgrimages to cathedrals housing the remains of a saintly figure, sometimes a body part (!) or an article of clothing. A "relic" of a religious rite is therefore another frame to give these moments. But just as newspapers fail to specify the nature of the interest in these objects, little in the historical record points overtly to this sort of interpretation of souvenir-hunting at hangings.

35. Mathews, *At the Altar of Lynching*, 124–26.

36. But there *was* at least one attempted rescue (simply not on an execution day) that led to a shoot-out and further trials and executions. In South Carolina in 1877, a condemned Black man was being escorted to Georgia when African Americans attempted rescue; as a result of this melee, ten men were taken into custody and three of them ended up with the death penalty for that rescue attempt (*Charleston News and Courier*, 5 May 1877). Guards were called out for the executions of those men.

If most executions in the South were of African American men and most newspaper references to fear of rescue involved them, executions of whites also might have extra guards due to fears of rescue. A white woman's execution in Georgia prompted this fear (*Atlanta Constitution*, 3 May 1873), and a white man in the hills of Virginia was successfully rescued; I have not found that he was later apprehended (*Richmond Dispatch*, 30 November 1883). A $500 reward was offered by the Baldwin detectives when John W. Kennedy broke from the Staunton jail two days before his execution in 1904. Both the reward notice and the cards that had already been printed to allow observers into the jail yard for the private execution are in the archives of the Virginia Historical Society ("$500.00 Reward for Escaped Murderer" and Invitation, 1904, to the execution of John W. Kennedy, Sect. 22, Armistead C. Gordon Papers, 1705–1957, Virginia Historical Society, Richmond).

37. The notes for this section contain the newspaper accounts of every execution I have found with this perceived threat of Black rescue. My search has surely missed some of these, and the historical record surely does not contain a complete set of sources documenting all the moments when this was feared. But as this fear was so visceral to whites at the time, I would assume that papers were not shy in both raising

it and showing how the state was confronting it. African American threats and disorder were rarely downplayed; much more often, they were exaggerated.

38. *Alexandria Gazette*, 10 December 1898. Similarly, "a strong guard was posted in and around the jail and every precaution was taken to prevent a rescue of the prisoner. Happily, however, there was no cause for alarm" (*Atlanta Constitution*, 9 October 1875).

39. *Atlanta Constitution*, 9 November 1872. In one case, the fear was that Native Americans would rescue a prisoner. The sheriff did not believe a rescue likely but secured eighty men "to be safe" when it was rumored that 400 Choctaw were in the area and 25 had come to town when one of the condemned men about to be executed was Native American (*Galveston Daily News*, 31 August 1878).

40. *Atlanta Constitution*, 26 August 1884. The *Atlanta Journal*'s coverage (25 August 1884, the afternoon of the execution) was mostly reprints of the hectic series of telegrams between Dawson's mayor and state officials about the deployment of the guard.

41. *Wilmington Morning News*, 19 June 1887; *Raleigh News and Observer*, 19 June 1887. For a similar story, see: *Richmond Dispatch*, 17 September 1870.

42. *Arkansas Gazette*, 26 May 1883. See also *Richmond Dispatch*, 23 June 1883.

43. *Florida Times-Union*, 28 September 1912. This article goes on to outline the steps being taken in the town: streets patrolled by special police that night, and instructions that if the telegraph wires were interrupted, to assume they have been cut and to send assistance to the town.

44. *Louisville Courier-Journal*, 10 August 1907.

45. *New Orleans Times-Democrat*, 20 July 1907; *New Orleans Daily Picayune*, 20 July 1907. For a similar case, see: *Atlanta Constitution*, 9 January 1892. Despite the warning not to attend, the *Picayune* describes the crowd as including every age, gender, and race. The board enclosure was torn down, but it is less clear whether that speaks to the passions aroused by the crowd against the condemned or to the more commonplace determination to see the scene.

46. Hodes, "Sexualization of Reconstruction Politics," 407.

47. *Louisville Courier-Journal*, 10 August 1907; *Atlanta Constitution*, 8 October 1875.

48. *Atlanta Journal*, 20 May 1910. See also surging crowds and bayonets in *Raleigh Observer*, 15 June 1878.

49. *Birmingham Age-Herald*, 21 September 1901.

50. *Atlanta Constitution*, 15 June 1907.

51. *Atlanta Journal*, 1 September 1900. A very similar scene in 1912: a burned fence, two companies of militia holding back a "morbid crowd" of 8,000, some with "children in their arms," witnessing the double execution in a "natural amphitheater," ending with the "great crowd cheered as the negroes went through the trap" (*Atlanta Journal*, 25 October 1912). Papers printed a rebuke of the sheriff for allowing that execution to go forward without rebuilding the fence in this case, but local officials justified it due to the fact that no local men were willing to part with the lumber necessary to rebuild it (*Atlanta Constitution*, 26 October 1912).

52. *Atlanta Journal*, 1 November 1901; *Raleigh Observer*, 10 September 1903.

53. *Louisville Courier-Journal*, 1 August 1906. See also *Vicksburg Herald*, 23 July 1909.

54. *Charleston News and Courier*, 2 March 1906. In the text, this article elaborated that a "lynching was narrowly averted."

55. *Dallas Morning News*, 31 May 1903. This scene also included cheers from the crowd.

56. *New Orleans Daily Picayune*, 2 March 1906.

57. *Louisville Courier-Journal*, 9 May 1885.

58. *Galveston Daily News*, 3 July 1880.

59. *Louisville Courier-Journal*, 1 August 1889.

60. *Arkansas Gazette*, 12 August 1913.

61. *Louisville Courier-Journal*, 10 January 1897.

62. *Atlanta Constitution*, 19 June 1897; *Florida Times-Union*, 7 May 1910.

63. *Huntsville Gazette*, 1 March 1890.

64. *Birmingham Age-Herald*, 21 September 1901. In this case, a Black man thought to be the condemned was shot before the condemned was found, and when a mob tried to wrest him from the courtroom, the sheriff killed a white man. The sheriff stayed away from the execution, not wanting to provoke more violence, and a deputy was responsible for the hanging.

65. Trotti, *Body in the Reservoir*, 79–109, 145–80.

66. With legal executions, the charge is usually clearer, but not always. Most of the Espy file executions coded for rape or attempted rape were confirmed by the newspaper accounts of executions used in this study. But several newspapers called the charge murder when Espy coded them rape, and more often, the Espy file and the newspaper accounts differed in terms of whether a charge was attempted rape or rape.

67. Baker, *This Mob*, 143. Martha Hodes writes of claims of interracial sex in the era of Klan violence: "It is impossible to separate fabricated accusations from observed transgressions, or false admissions given under threat from truthful confessions" ("Sexualization of Reconstruction Politics," 407).

68. A northern Black paper reported that one southern woman recanted her accusations of rape (*Philadelphia Tribune*, 12 December 1914); it is impossible to know how many claims of whites were mistaken or imagined, much less those knowingly misidentifying Black accused.

69. In terms of geography and rape and lynching, the two states that lynched the least overall (Virginia and North Carolina) similarly lynched the least for sexual crimes between 1866 and 1920. They are the only two southern states to legally execute more (54 and 49, respectively) than to lynch (30 and 28, respectively) for sexual crimes. These capital punishment figures are from the original Espy file; Hearn's more complete lists exaggerate this trend: adding nineteen executions for sexual crimes in Virginia and twenty-five more in North Carolina. On the other end of the spectrum (using Espy), Florida lynched (72) seven times more for sexual infractions than legally executed (10), and Mississippi lynched (142) thirty-five times more than legally executed (4) (Espy file; Project HAL; Brundage, *Lynching in the New South*, 270–79; Hearn, *Legal Executions in Virginia*; Hearn, *Legal Executions in North Carolina*).

Trials have overtly stated charges brought to bear; lynchings might or might not be motivated by even an accusation of criminal wrongdoing. These lynching tallies reflect any "reasons" or "offenses" for lynching that imply sexual danger that historians were able to discern: rape, rape and murder, attempted rape, criminal assault (rape), assault (rape), miscegenation, frightening a girl, entering a girl's room, and more are listed in Tolnay and Beck, *Festival of Violence*; Wright, *Racial Violence in Kentucky*; and Brundage, *Lynching in the New South* as justifications for lynching.

70. Sommerville, *Rape and Race*, 210.

71. In the 1890 census, North Carolina had just over 9 percent of the South's population (Carter, *Historical Statistics*, 1:180–359). If North Carolina had an average of fourteen African American men per year going to the penitentiary for sexual crimes, perhaps the wider South averaged something like 140 annually. This is highly speculative, of course. Note that North Carolina and Virginia are at one extreme in terms of southern states and lynching; they may or may not be representative of the South as a whole. More information is needed on Deep South states and incarceration for sexual crimes.

72. Dorr, *White Women*, 5.

73. Some reports do not clearly identify the victim, and I have not pursued every execution for the crime of rape, but I have found 20 instances of the execution of a Black man for raping a Black woman and 162 instances of the rape victim being a white woman. Note the lack of any white man ever executed for raping a Black woman.

74. The Espy file's particularly incomplete data from the Reconstruction exaggerate this: it lists only thirteen executions for sexual crimes in the whole South in that era. The new data from Hearn and Laska significantly adjust these numbers upward (table 5.2), adding twenty-two more executions for sexual crimes in the Reconstruction era that the Espy file missed and seventy more overall, a 20 percent increase. As this is actually a smaller rise than for executions overall, I am concerned that the fact that Hearn and Laska offer one word for each entry's crime might be disguising other cases with sexual assault dimensions. I found twenty-nine cases where "murder" was the word used in Hearn and Laska when Espy had "murder and rape"; in almost every case in their descriptions that follow, Hearn and Laska included the information that a sexual assault was either intended or a part of the crime, but that was not in their classification.

75. Arkansas averaged 1.7 lynchings annually from 1882 to 1899, and 0.9 from 1900 to 1920 (Project HAL).

76. Adding up all of the lynchings for sexual motives from the ten states Tolnay and Beck studied, plus Brundage's numbers for Virginia: an average of twenty-three lynchings per year in the period 1882–88, thirty-four per year in 1889–99, falling to twenty per year in 1900–1909, and to eleven per year in 1910–20 (Project HAL; Brundage, *Lynching in the New South*, 270–79). Compare this with table 5.2 on legal executions: in the 1890s, there were about six lynchings for every legal execution for sexual crimes; in the 1910s, the rise of legal executions for these crimes and the decline of lynching meant that they were almost equal in numbers per year (ten and eleven per year, respectively). Note how different this trend in executions for sexual crimes is compared with executions overall: both lynchings *and* legal executions declined in the twentieth century overall.

77. Tolnay and Beck, *Festival of Violence*, 110.

78. Sommerville writes, "It was not until the turn of the century, when female moral reform made significant strides on rape law reform, that southern white men begin to consider rape a distinctive wrong" (*Rape and Race*, 11).

79. Sommerville, *Rape and Race*, 210; Dorr, *White Women*, 5; Espy file; Project HAL; Brundage, *Lynching in the New South*, 270–79.

80. *Code of Alabama* (1852), 562, 594; *Statute Laws of Georgia* (1851), 787, 987; *General Statutes of Kentucky* (1860), 1:379–80; *Revised Code of Mississippi* (1857), 248, 255, 608, 631; *Code of Tennessee* (1857–58), 509, 524, 830; *Penal Code of Texas* (1857), 163–64, 494, 523–29; *Code of Virginia* (1860), 785, 815. Only in Arkansas, Florida, Louisiana, North Carolina, and South Carolina did antebellum statutes open the possibility of death for a white man charged with rape: *Digest of the Statutes of Arkansas* (1858), 334; *Digest of the Laws of Florida* (1847), 490, 538; *Revised Statutes of Louisiana* (1857), 50, 136; *Code of North Carolina* (1855), 203, 570–73. South Carolina's legal code is particularly difficult to research, and I am concerned I might have missed something here, but the *Statutes* discuss the inheritance from English law of a penalty of death for the crime of rape (*Statutes of South Carolina* (1837), 2:498–99).

81. See previous note for the page references to these laws. The stipulation that the victim of the rape must be white to earn the death penalty for a Black man before the Civil War is a particularly harsh reminder of the ways Black women in the South had no legal protections. See Bardaglio, *Reconstructing the Household*, 66–68, 191; Morris, *Southern Slavery*, 305–10. Writing of the post–Civil War period, Tera Hunter observes, "'Rape' and 'black women' were words that were never uttered in the same breath by white Southerners" (*To 'Joy My Freedom*, 34). Texas and Virginia had death as a *possible* penalty (along with a prison term) for Black men convicted of *attempted* rape of white women; all of the other states offered no discretion in sentencing. Death was the only penalty for either rape or attempted rape of white women. South Carolina's statutes do not mention particular laws regarding the punishment of rape by slaves, but they do mandate death for any second offense of "any felony not already mentioned" (the penalty for a first offense was branding the slave's hand) and death for any penalty where benefit of clergy was not offered (*Statutes of South Carolina* [1840], 7:373–74, 402).

82. Bardaglio, *Reconstructing the Household*, 69. Before the Civil War, punishments in the South for Black-on-white rape included death but also in some cases castration, and most states punished an attempt the same as a rape, something not true for the punishment of whites (Morris, "Slaves, Sexual Violence, and the Law," 310–11).

83. *Revised Code of Mississippi* (1871), 584; *Acts of South Carolina* (1868–69), 175; *Code of Tennessee* (1873), 2:48. Although printed two years after Tennessee introduced death as a penalty for rape, the 1873 code had already been typeset when this law was passed, and so it represents the law in force before the 1871 change; that 1871 change to allow the death penalty for rape appears in a supplementary section to this edition of the code (2:148). Mississippi and South Carolina are the only two states with majority Black populations in this era; while an unprovable correlation, it is tempting to note how they are two of the states to refuse to import the (Black) antebellum penalty of death into the postwar code for rape under Reconstruction governments.

Peter Bardaglio notes that the *Digest* for Texas in 1866 says that the penalty for rape was likewise prison rather than death (*Reconstructing the Household*, 294n55). But as a 10 November 1866 law in the *Acts* for that year shows that death was a possible penalty for rape, and considering that the *Digest* of 1874 references that 1866 act as the statute making the punishment death or a term in the penitentiary in the discretion of the jury, it seems unlikely that there was a different punishment for rape in the intervening years. Digests can include laws previously in effect, and I suspect that explains the language in both the 1866 *Digest* that Bardaglio references and the 1870 one that has similar language: both include the language Texas had for the lighter punishment of rape in the antebellum period (for whites) (*Digest of the Laws of Texas* [1866], 447; *General Laws of Texas* [1866], 161; *Digest of the Laws of Texas* [1870], 447; *Digest of the Laws of Texas* [1874], 1329).

84. *Laws of Mississippi* (1878), 184; *Acts of South Carolina* (1878), 631–32; *Acts of Tennessee* (1871), 50.

85. *Code of Alabama* (1867), 699–700; *Digest of the Statutes of Arkansas* (1874), 333; *Digest of the Laws of Florida* (1872), 217; *Acts of Georgia* (1866), 151; *Acts of Kentucky* (1867), 1:102–3; *Revised Statutes of Louisiana* (1870), 160; *Public Laws of North Carolina* (1868–69), 406; *Acts of Virginia* (1866), 82.

86. Lisa Lindquist Dorr posits a particularly interesting dynamic in terms of attempted rape: the fact that a white woman's honor would be maintained if the crime were a *failed* attempt, for the storyline would then be of fighting someone off and maintaining one's purity. There might have been a pressure in society to aid women by charging attempt even in cases where actual rape had occurred (*White Women*, 65).

87. The Espy file codes one Georgia execution as attempted rape in 1880 (Dan Brigherty), but newspapers call this a rape rather than an attempt. This appears to be a coding error in the Espy file; Hearn agrees (*Legal Executions in Georgia*, 28). North Carolina has three executions for "Burglary/Attempted Rape," and while attempted rape was not a capital crime there, burglary in North Carolina could be. For more on North Carolina and burglary and rape, see chapter 2, note 36 (*Digest of the Statutes of Arkansas* [1921], 847; *Revised General Statutes of Florida* [1919], 2:2637; *Park's Code of Georgia* [1914], vol. 6, *Penal Code*, 112; *General Statutes of Kentucky* [1873], 322; *Code of Mississippi* [1917], 1:631; *Code of North Carolina* [1916], 123, 811; *Complete Texas Statutes* [1920], 175; Espy file).

88. Tennessee's one execution for attempted rape (of a seven-year-old) came in 1897. (*Code of Alabama* [1907], vol. 3, *Criminal*, 889–93; *Code of Tennessee* [1918], 2:2495).

89. *Acts of Virginia* (1894), 29; *Acts of South Carolina* (1909), 206. South Carolina (24) and Virginia (18) had the most executions for sexual crimes in the South from 1910 to 1920 due in large part to executing not only for rape but also for attempted rape (eighteen and five, respectively). (Hearn and Laska).

Louisiana adds a complexity: attempted rape was punished with a term in the penitentiary throughout this period, but the crime of lying in wait and wounding someone in an attempt to murder, rob, or rape could be punished with death, and it is apparently under this statute that six African American men were executed for what the Espy file calls attempted rape (*Revised Statutes of Louisiana* [1915], 1:535; *Acts of Louisiana* [1882], 40).

90. *Acts of Virginia* (1893), 29; Brundage, *Lynching in the New South*, 177. House of Delegates member R. H. Logan from Roanoke submitted this bill on 7 December 1893 (*Journal of the Virginia House* [1893], 64). Note how this law, like so many in the South, left to the jury whether the perpetrator deserved what had been in the antebellum era the penalty for whites (term in prison) or Blacks (death).

91. Alexander, "'Like an Evil Wind,'" 173–206.

92. Hearn, *Legal Executions in Virginia*. For context: attempted murder in Virginia was punished only with a prison sentence.

93. Dunlap, "Reform of Rape Law," 352–72. When Georgia (the last southern state to raise its age of consent law from its antebellum tradition) finally did so in 1918, a history of the women's movement wrote that activists in the state had been working on this issue in Georgia for twenty-three years and always for an age of eighteen; . . . they got fourteen (Harper, *History of Woman Suffrage*, 6:133).

94. For example: "If the woman is fifteen years of age or over, the defendant may show in consent cases, she was not of previous chaste character as a defense" (*General Laws of Texas* [1918], 123). For similar phrasings: *Acts of Tennessee* (1893), 273–74; *Revised General Statutes of Florida* (1919), 2:2640; *Laws of Mississippi* (1914), 219. North Carolina's law included the phrase "provided she never before had sexual intercourse with any male person" (*Public Laws of North Carolina* [1895], 374. Freedman, *Redefining Rape*, 32 and passim, and Sommerville, *Rape and Race*, 201–6). Peter Bardaglio found this sentiment about chastity being essential for a woman to bring a charge of rape in the antebellum period as well (*Reconstructing the Household*, 72–74).

95. Freedman, *Redefining Rape*, 17–19; Sommerville, *Rape and Race*, 4–10; Dorr, *White Women*, 128; Feimster, *Southern Horrors*, 115–18 and passim; Bardaglio, *Reconstructing the Household*, 198. In addition to the class of the victim of sexual assault affecting whether a jury believed the victim's testimony, the length of a sentence given to someone convicted of rape might be shorter if the rape victim were lower class (Sommerville, *Rape and Race*, 5; Morris, "Slaves, Sexual Violence, and the Law," 314–15).

96. Freedman, *Redefining Rape*, 14–17. Many women, so the story continued, *acted* like they were reluctant because they were supposed to act that way, even when they were not reluctant at all. Rich men frequented brothels; many if not most men were sexually active before marriage. Poor women, in particular, were considered fair game to predatory men. It was seen as natural for a man to "sow his wild oats," a phrase that normalized men using less respectable classes of women, avoiding society's censure.

In essence, before the work of the moral crusades of the late nineteenth century (and to a substantial extent continuing thereafter), some degree of active "force" or "direction" on the part of men—or at the very least some degree of a lack of protection for whole classes of women—was considered by most in the nineteenth century to be a normal part of what sexuality was. Rape in the late nineteenth century was, in essence, less distant from the idea of sex than we might imagine or want it to be, at least if the woman was not of the white middle or upper class. Considering the extent to which wives were virtually the property of their husbands (including the legal inability to deny him her own body) perhaps is the context to make this disturbing reality most legible: women were not generally treated as having rights (or in many cases property) of their own, but rather as adjuncts to the men around them (Geddes and Tennyson, "Passage," 145–89).

97. This would imperil white men in particular, for no discussion of the respectability or reputation or class of the woman bringing the charge or the man being charged would be relevant (Freedman, *Redefining Rape*, 125–46; Dunlap, "Reform of Rape Law," passim; Feimster, *Southern Horrors*, 70–74). Freedman quotes a Mississippi man concerned about the threat of these laws for white men: "This would enable negro girls to sue white men." A Kentucky man called raising the age of consent "a terrible weapon for evil . . . when placed in the hands of a lecherous, sensual negro woman" (both quotations: *Redefining Rape*, 142).

98. As late as 1892, 10 was the age of consent for Alabama, Georgia, Mississippi, North Carolina, South Carolina, Tennessee, and Texas; 12 was the age of consent for Kentucky, Louisiana, and Virginia; Arkansas named the age of consent as "puberty," which Mary Odem shows is 12 (*Delinquent Daughters*, 14–15). No southern state had an age of consent higher than 12 before the late-1870s. Florida was the outlier: by 1881, it had a fine or imprisonment as the penalty for carnal knowledge of a female under 16; no other southern state raised its age of consent until the 1890s (*Digest of the Laws of Florida* [1881], 819).

Code of Alabama (1867), 699–700; *Digest of the Statutes of Arkansas* (1874), 333; *Digest of the Laws of Florida* (1872), 217; *Digest of the Laws of Florida* (1881), 819; *General Statutes of Kentucky* (1873), 322; *Revised Code of Mississippi* (1871), 584; *Public Laws of North Carolina* (1868–69), 406; *Statutes of South Carolina* (1873), 711; *Acts of Tennessee* (1871), 50; *General Laws of Texas* (1866), 161; *Acts of Virginia* (1866), 82. Neither Georgia nor Louisiana statutes explicitly define the age of consent in the early years after the Civil War.

99. Starting with the traditional age of consent from antebellum statutes, the following are the ages of consent and the year of each change in them in the laws of southern states: Alabama (10; 14 in 1897; 16 in 1915); Arkansas ("puberty" [12]; 16 in 1893); Florida (10; 16 in 1870s, 18 in 1901); Georgia (10; 14 in 1918); Kentucky (12; 16 in 1906); Louisiana (12; 18 in 1912); Mississippi (10; 12 in 1908, 18 in 1914); North Carolina (10; 14 in 1895); South Carolina (10; 14 in 1896); Tennessee (10; 16 in 1893, 18 in 1901; 21 in 1911); Texas (10; 14 in 1891; 15 in 1896; 18 in 1918); Virginia (12; 14 in 1896; 15 in 1918). Also changing were the penalties, which in most states was a term in prison or a fine, but for young girls in particular, some states had the death penalty for carnal knowledge with a minor. *Acts of Alabama* (1896–97), 960; *General Laws of Alabama* (1915), 137; *Digest of the Statutes of Arkansas* (1894), 572; *Digest of the Laws of Florida* (1881), 819; *Acts of Florida, Extraordinary Session* (1901), 111; *Acts of Georgia* (1918), 259; *Acts of Kentucky* (1906), 255; *Acts of Louisiana* (1912), 380–81; *Laws of Mississippi* (1908), 187; *Laws of Mississippi* (1914), 219; *Public Laws of North Carolina* (1895), 374; *Acts of South Carolina* (1896), 223; *Acts of Tennessee* (1893), 273–74; *Acts of Tennessee* (1901), 29–30; *Acts of Tennessee* (1911), 70–71; *General Laws of Texas* (1891), 96; *General Laws of Texas* (1895), 79; *General Laws of Texas* (1918), 123; *Acts of Virginia* (1895–96), 673; *Acts of Virginia* (1918), 139.

100. Sommerville, *Rape and Race*, 199, 216–17, 239–41; Freedman, *Redefining Rape*, 89–91.

101. *Acts of Tennessee* (1915), 5–7; *Acts of Tennessee* (1919), 27–28.

102. Rape would continue to be a capital crime in the South until the era of the civil rights movement, with its vast changes in values—about punishment, Blackness, whiteness, and more. In 1948, seven African Americans in Virginia were accused of raping a white woman; all were convicted by white juries; all were electrocuted. Between Virginia's first use of electrocution (1908) and this mass execution in 1951, forty-five men were electrocuted in Virginia for rape. All were Black (Rise, *Martinsville Seven*). Three more African American men would be electrocuted for rape before Virginia changed its laws in the 1960s to make rape punishable by imprisonment but not death.

In 1976, the U.S. Supreme Court would end the era of rape as a capital crime for good. In Coker v. Georgia (433 U.S. 584), the Court declared (7–2) that the punishment of death was so disproportionate for the crime of rape as to be cruel and unusual. The dramatic racial disparities in the penalties—imprisonment for whites and so often death for Blacks—figured prominently in this case. More than a century of the South deploying the death penalty for this crime was over.

103. Wyatt-Brown, *Southern Honor*, 458–60.

104. Brundage, *Lynching in the New South*, 256. He also said that lynching drew from the expectations created by public executions, a more modest claim that I think there is good evidence for (40). See also Wood, *Lynching as Spectacle*, 21–38.

105. Pfeifer, *Rough Justice*, 80, 121.

106. For instance, George Wright, *Racial Violence in Kentucky*, 231–33; Ayers, *Vengeance and Justice*, 247–48.

Chapter Six: Make It a Secret Silent Monster

1. D.S.G. C*****, "Death Punishment," *Southern Literary Messenger* (1852): 650.

2. Quoted in Ayers, *Vengeance and Justice*, 215.

3. Quoted in Brundage, *Lynching in the New South*, 73. Racial hatred and sadistic fantasies appear the only rationale for some killings; there is a report of three African Americans killed to "thin the niggers out and drive them to their holes" (quoted in Crouch, "Spirit of Lawlessness," 226).

4. Masur, *Rites of Execution*, 93–116; Banner, *Death Penalty*, 144–68; Bessler, *Death in the Dark*, 40–45. Judith Randle offers a convincing argument for the South's effect (as a negative example) in the North's deliberations over capital punishment. See her "Cultural Lives," 100–103.

Among the far West states, legislators passed statutes against public execution mostly in the 1870s: California (1858), Montana (1871), Oregon (1874), Nevada (1875), Wyoming (1876), and Utah (1878). Colorado (1889) and Washington (1901) transitioned to private execution later. The particular legislation for each state can be found in the published statutes of the legislature of that state or territory for the year given.

5. *Richmond Dispatch*, 11 September 1852. Note that in this era of praising public executions, it would generally have been white ministers leading the religious ceremonies at the gallows.

6. *Atlanta Constitution*, 13 May 1891.

7. *Laws of Mississippi* (1839), 110; *Acts of Alabama* (1840), 150; *Laws of Mississippi* (1850), 105–6; *Acts of Virginia* (1855–56), 36–37; *Penal Code of Texas* (1857), 136; *Acts of Georgia* (1859), 62; *Acts of Florida* (1868), 110–11; *Laws of North Carolina* (1868), 34; *Laws of North Carolina* (1879), 381. The vague nature of all of these early acts is in keeping with norms for the nation. Most early legislation in northern states similarly left much to the discretion of local authorities. See Masur, *Rites of Execution*, 93–116.

8. According to the reports in the *Atlanta Constitution*, between 1884 and 1893, forty executions were public in Georgia, nineteen were private, eight had elements of both public and private (a hybrid phenomenon discussed below), and thirteen I did not find or reports were unclear about the nature of the crowd. According to the *Richmond Dispatch*, between 1870 and the passage of Virginia's privacy laws in April of 1879, eight executions were public, one was private, eight had elements of both public and private, and four I did not find or reports were unclear about the nature of the crowd.

9. For the practical considerations facing smaller towns, see *Galveston Daily News*, 13 November 1880; *Dallas Morning News*, 14 December 1902, 19 October 1909. Both the *Richmond Times-Dispatch* (14 October 1908) and the *Atlanta Constitution* (26 October 1912) pointed to the "more or less public executions in small places" when they later argued in favor of centralizing executions in state penitentiaries.

10. *Acts of South Carolina* (1877), 381; *Acts of Kentucky* (1880), 1:60–61; *Acts of Tennessee* (1883), 139–40; *Acts of Louisiana* (1884), 102; *Acts of Arkansas* (1887), 29; *Public Laws of North Carolina* (1901), 352; *Laws of Mississippi* (1916), 330; *General Laws of Texas* (1923), 111. In addition, states that had written ambiguous laws revised them to strictly prohibit public execution: *Acts of Alabama* (1879), 45; *Acts of Virginia* (1878–79), 380; *Acts of Georgia* (1893), 41–42.

11. *Atlanta Constitution*, 2 March 1895, 8 January 1898, 2 September 1900, 30 October 1900, 2 November 1901, 4 January 1902, 11 October 1902, 24 September 1904, 11 September 1906, 10 June 1911, 17 June 1911, 26 October 1912 (double execution). Others were unclear, for some reports simply neglect to say whether there was a barrier. For example, Alex Williams and his guard were "followed by an immense crowd" to the edge of town, where Williams spoke to them before being hanged. No mention is made of a barrier, but was there one? (15 December 1894).

Virginia strictly prohibited public execution in 1879, but four years later Virginia newspapers reported a public execution as a commonplace: *Petersburg Daily Index Appeal*, 23 June 1883. Similarly, Louisiana prohibited public execution in 1884 but had at least five public executions in the decades following: *New Orleans Daily Picayune*, 14 December 1889, 20 August 1892, 25 February 1893, 11 January 1896, 20 July 1907.

12. Bowers, *Legal Homicide*, 46–47.

13. Using newspaper reports of executions, I estimate that the following states had a rather clear moment of transition. Most were public before this date, and most were private (or, often, a semiprivate mix of public and private elements) after it: South Carolina (1878), Virginia (1879), Tennessee (1883), Louisiana (1884), Arkansas (1887), Kentucky (1887ish: odd pattern here, dwindling numbers of public from 1880 through the 1890s), and North Carolina (1901). There was no specific moment of transition, although there were generally fewer public executions later in the era, in

five states (Alabama, Florida, Georgia, Mississippi, and Texas) at least until the 1920s. Existing scholarship often confuses the dates for the transition to private execution in the South (for instance, Randle ["Cultural Lives," 99], Banner [*Death Penalty*, 155], and Allen and Clubb [*Race, Class, and the Death Penalty*, 74]). Seth Kotch stresses the importance of the transition to state control in North Carolina in 1910, and while this was the definitive endpoint to any public features of executions, the 1901 privacy law, I would argue, is the more important moment of transition there ("Making of the Modern Death Penalty," 195).

14. *Atlanta Constitution*, 5 September 1891. Another had "120 spectators and a crowd of perhaps 8000 outside" (*Nashville Daily American*, 18 June 1892).

15. Grandstand or courthouse steps: *Richmond Dispatch*, 28 October 1893, 7 February 1885, and 28 October 1893; *Birmingham Age-Herald*, 8 June 1895. For window speeches: *Mobile Daily Register*, 2 August 1884; *Birmingham Age-Herald*, 4 January 1913. Another convict spoke to the crowd from the circuit courtroom before going to the gallows: *Arkansas Gazette*, 16 November 1895.

16. *Birmingham Age-Herald*, 22 March 1913.

17. *Atlanta Constitution*, 24 August 1912. Even when outside an enclosure, the crowds might be very close to the action, hearing the voices of those within as well as knowing by the "rattle of the trap as it struck against the supports of the platform" that the hanging had taken place, witnessing the hanging aurally if not visually (*Atlanta Constitution*, 19 June 1897, 18 December 1897; *Richmond Dispatch*, 23 April 1881). Wrote the *New Orleans Daily Picayune* (6 June 1885) on the intensity of a denied-crowd's continued interest: "The crowd continued gazing intently at the walls and windows of the prison, and if glances had been chisels many an orifice had penetrated the brick and mortar."

18. *Atlanta Constitution*, 7 December 1899; *Louisville Courier-Journal*, 6 January 1894; *Galveston Daily News*, 18 November 1893; *Florida Times-Union*, 22 May 1909. For a description of how haphazard these tenting-barriers could be, see Coulter, "Hanging," 50.

19. *Nashville Daily American*, 1 November 1884. In this instance, the newspaper overtly subtitled its article "How the Law Requiring Private Execution Was Evaded" and described how the condemned himself requested permission to address the crowd. Other instances of enclosure after ceremonies include *Arkansas Gazette*, 29 July 1913, 12 August 1913; *New Orleans Daily Picayune*, 14 December 1889.

20. For short fences: *Louisville Courier-Journal*, 9 May 1885, 2 December 1894; *Raleigh News and Observer*, 22 May 1886. Barbed wire, which "answered the purpose" of a required enclosure but "did not, however, shut off the grim spectacle from the view of men and women who gathered": *Florida Times-Union*, 24 July 1920. A strand of rope: *Louisville Courier-Journal*, 21 March 1884. For a scaffold built so high it was even with the fence: *Louisville Courier-Journal*, 6 February 1892; *Arkansas Gazette*, 30 April 1893; *New Orleans Daily Picayune*, 8 January 1898.

21. *Atlanta Constitution*, 19 June 1897; *Richmond Dispatch*, 16 September 1899; *Florida Times-Union*, 30 July 1910.

22. "Something over forty or fifty persons witnessed the hanging from inside the enclosure," reported the *Arkansas Gazette*, "and several hundred from the court house square and from the court house windows. Big, little, old and young climbed

the trees, and all seemed eager to see the execution" (7 December 1901). For similar crowds, see *Charleston News and Courier*, 22 September 1894; *Louisville Courier-Journal*, 28 March 1885 and 14 October 1882; *Atlanta Constitution*, 11 December 1897; *Christian Observer*, 31 January 1906.

23. *New Orleans Daily Picayune*, 24 September 1904. See also the Cluverius execution described in chapter 2 and in Trotti, *Body in the Reservoir*, 182–85; *Richmond Dispatch*, *Richmond Times*, and *Richmond State*, 15 January 1887. The police sergeant in charge of the Richmond crowd was fined $50 by the court for allowing so many to be in the jail yard when the law permitted only twelve to witness an execution in Virginia (*Richmond Dispatch*, 15 February 1887).

24. *Atlanta Constitution*, 19 June 1897.

25. A notice in the *Atlanta Constitution* (6 September 1901) eight years after public executions were prohibited expressed surprise and admiration for a sheriff who "literally" carried out the injunction to hang in private with only "the legal number of witnesses." Similarly, the *New Orleans Daily Picayune* (25 March 1905) noted twenty years after Louisiana ended public execution that "never before in the history of local executions had the strict letter of the law as to the number of witnesses to be present been lived up to."

26. For example: "At 11:35 those who were to be permitted to see the execution passed through the prison into the yard. So eager and excited were the crowd to enter the grim enclosure that the mob almost fought their way by the police in order to get through the gates. Many had their hats destroyed, their clothes torn, and not a few were jammed into the gates" (*New Orleans Times-Democrat*, 11 April 1896). In another example of the intense desire to view these events, ground-floor jail cells were emptied in one case, due to their having a view of the private gallows, "the supposition probably being that many are so anxious to witness a hanging that if the prisoners were permitted to witness one of these elevating and soul-refining exhibitions, the gloomy old place would be overrun with men serving ten-day sentences in the hope that they might be lucky enough to occupy cells fronting on the gallows court" (*New Orleans Times-Democrat*, 14 May 1892).

27. *Montgomery Advertiser*, 24 June 1905. For other reports (among dozens) of African Americans outside walls: *Richmond Dispatch*, 23 April 1881; *New Orleans Times-Democrat*, 28 January 1882.

28. *Nashville Daily American*, 20 June 1885.

29. *Atlanta Constitution*, 5 September 1891.

30. *New York Times*, 11 April 1874. They are reporting on a Tennessee execution. Many of the citations in chapter 1 refer specifically to the religious participation of African American women at the gallows.

31. *Atlanta Constitution*, 2 November 1901, 15 June 1907; *Louisville Courier-Journal*, 20 October 1905; *Daily Democrat*, 24 July 1909. There are many more cases in which a husband, father, or son of the rape victim was present at the execution and mentioned in the coverage. In the 1907 Georgia example cited here, the victim was invited to attend but at the last minute withdrew, and her husband was there instead.

32. *Louisville Courier-Journal*, 15 August 1936; *Louisville Times*, 14 August 1936. According to the *Times*, the Davies County Sheriff, the "matronly," "brown-haired"

forty-two-year-old Mrs. Florence Thompson was appointed to the post at the death of her husband, then the sheriff. She chose not to preside at the hanging for fear that her children would be embarrassed by the publicity of her killing a man.

33. *New Orleans Daily Picayune*, 1 November 1884.

34. *Louisville Courier-Journal*, 2 April 1880.

35. The *Louisville Courier-Journal*, 29 March 1880, 2 April 1880. The subtitle of the first article was "They Cry Out with One Voice: Let Them Be Crucified and in Public Sight." Similarly strong words against private execution occasionally came from legislators and editors, discussed below.

36. *Louisville Courier-Journal*, 19 December 1889. This sentiment was echoed by another editor who called for "star chamber" executions to be abolished: "The public desire to see that everything is fairly and artistically done. Secrecy is repugnant to democratic institutions and ideas. If a man is to be killed as an example to other men, the example loses its virtue if the many-eyed public have to depend upon the certificate a trio of doctors for evidence of the fact" (*Galveston Daily News*, 23 August 1879).

37. *Raleigh News and Observer*, 7 April 1905. In a Tennessee case, there was mixed opinion of the efficacy of privacy in executions, with some appreciating the eradication of excitement and crowds. But "one man said that as the purpose of an execution is, by the horror of it, to deter others from the commission of crime, no good purpose is served by performing a hanging so privately that those who might be deterred know nothing of it. 'These executions to-day,' he said, 'were a shock to no community in the state except this penal community, which is already expiating its offense'" (*Nashville Banner*, 1 October 1909).

38. As the *Southern Quarterly Review* ([January 1842], 5) put it, in newspapers, "the lover of the marvelous and horrible may have his taste gratified by an account of the last duel that took place, the latest murder or suicide that has occurred, with perhaps the dying confession of the felon, and a minute account of all that took place at the time of the execution, accompanied probably by some judicious remarks from the editor against the practice of public executions, as having a tendency to increase, rather than prevent, the frequency of crimes, by the pomp and consequences it attaches to the victim of the violated laws; notwithstanding which sage opinion, he continues to feed the depraved appetite of his readers with all such items of intelligence, seeming to forget that the publicity which he himself thus gives to crime, renders it more interesting and less odious in the eyes of the perpetrator."

39. Trotti, *Body in the Reservoir*, 145–80. One can find images of both white and Black condemned in the historical record, but both the volume of print and the number of images demonstrated how white papers were much more interested in white criminals.

40. *Nashville Banner*, 21 March 1883.

41. This concern about the impact of the press could easily be overplayed, for looking at a flat, static image of a gallows is very little like standing in a crowd watching the drop.

42. *Charleston News and Courier*, 15 February 1878.

43. *Atlanta Constitution*, 12 March 1878.

44. *New Orleans Times-Picayune*, 12 September 1941. Most of the first southern states to centralize executions were in the Upper South: Virginia (1908), North Carolina (1909), Kentucky (1911), Arkansas (1913), and Tennessee (1916), although two Deep South states, Louisiana (1910, briefly) and South Carolina (1912), joined them. Most of the rest of the Deep South did so in the 1920s: Florida (1924), Georgia (1924), Texas (1924), and Alabama (1927). Louisiana reintroduced local hangings in 1918, and so Mississippi (1955) and Louisiana (1957) were the last states to move permanently away from executions in local communities. These two states believed so fervently in local punishment that even when they introduced electrocution (two of the last states to abandon hangings), they each provided for a mobile generator and electric chair so that the punishment could continue to be meted out locally (*New Orleans Times-Picayune*, 12 September 1941).

45. *Atlanta Constitution*, 14 January 1899. For an example of a crowd that had to be staved off with troops with fixed bayonets, see *Raleigh Observer*, 15 June 1878.

46. *Atlanta Constitution*, 9 January 1892. The men hanged were convicted of rioting, and the sheriff was concerned about what crowd might gather.

47. *Atlanta Journal*, 1 November 1901.

48. *Richmond Times-Dispatch*, 11 February 1905.

49. *Arkansas Gazette*, 21 March 1901.

50. *Arkansas Gazette*, 24 March 1901. *Acts of Arkansas* (1901), 105; *Journal of the Arkansas Senate* (1901), 203; *Journal of the Arkansas House* (1901), 350; *Arkansas Gazette*, 21–24 March 1901.

51. *Arkansas Gazette*, 21 March 1901.

52. *Arkansas Gazette*, 24 March 1901.

53. *Arkansas Democrat*, 26 March 1901.

54. *Arkansas Democrat*, 26 July 1901; *Arkansas Gazette*, 27 July 1901; *Arkansas Democrat*, 7 November 1902; *Arkansas Gazette*, 8 November 1902; *Arkansas Gazette*, 26 June 1904. It is unclear whether the rape-murder charge against David Cross resulted in a public or a private execution: *Arkansas Democrat*, 12 December 1902. Espy file.

55. *Acts of Arkansas* (1905), 723.

56. *Louisville Courier-Journal*, 10 February 1920; see also Wright, *Racial Violence in Kentucky*, 194-98. An article on the 10th in the *Journal* is about the regrets that Lockett had for the deaths. His statement emphasizes the sorts of religious values so common in execution narratives: "I'm sorry that anybody would be hurt on my account," that "the death sentence is what I deserve," and that he told a minister that he "did not fear the mob or the death chair, but he did fear going to 'Hell' and that all he wanted was to 'get right with God.'"

57. *Louisville Courier-Journal*, 10 February 1920. There was an inquiry into the riot which did not yield prosecutions (*Louisville Courier-Journal*, 14–15 February 1920).

58. *Acts of Kentucky* (1920), 693–94; *Journal of the Kentucky House* (1920), 1776–79; *Journal of the Kentucky Senate* (1920), 1045–47, 2742–44; *Louisville Courier-Journal*, 17–18 March 1920. All other capital crimes in the state by this time were punished with electrocution in the state penitentiary.

59. *Louisville Courier-Journal*, 17 March 1920.

60. *Louisville Times*, 11 March 1920. Fifty-five people witnessed this electrocution, the most for an electrocution in Kentucky history to that point.

61. Nine men in the coming eighteen years would be executed by hanging before this legislation was again changed. In the coverage by the *Louisville Courier-Journal*, the crowds were described as 1,000 (6 March 1926), 150 (29 August 1926), 7,000 (26 November 1927 [a double execution] — complete with photographs; enclosure was a four-foot plank fence topped with barbed wire), 5,000 whites (18 June 1932 — "no negroes attended"; wire enclosure), 1,500 (20 April 1935 — a white man; again with photographs; eight-foot fence, but scaffold towered above it), 10,000 (15 August 1936 — even though at 5:30 A.M.; more photographs; wire enclosure; this was the execution of Rainey Bethea, discussed in the afterword). The last two hangings under this law were private (18 December 1937, 4 June 1938), as sentiment had turned away again from such spectacles. The *Louisville Times* likewise covered all of these executions, but as it published in the afternoons, its coverage was on the day before each of the days listed in this note.

62. Laska, *Legal Executions in Tennessee*, 197.

63. Alabama — Privacy: *Acts of Alabama* (1878–79), 45; *Journal of the Alabama House* (1879), 96–97; *Journal of the Alabama Senate* (1879), 118; Centralization/Electrocution: *General Laws of Alabama* (1923), 759–62; *Journal of the Alabama House* (1923), 2610–11, 2794–96; *Journal of the Alabama Senate* (1923), 735, 2068–69. Arkansas — Privacy: *Acts of Arkansas* (1887), 29; *Journal of the Arkansas House* (1887), 469; *Journal of the Arkansas Senate* (1887), 112, 150, 229; Centralization/Electrocution: *Acts of Arkansas* (1913), 171–75; *Journal of the Arkansas House* (1913), 232, 348–49; *Journal of the Arkansas Senate* (1913), 142. Florida — Privacy/Centralization/Electrocution: *Acts of Florida* (1923), 175–77; *Journal of the Florida House* (1923), 1049–50; *Journal of the Florida Senate* (1923), 200. Georgia — Privacy: *Acts of Georgia* (1893), 41–42; *Journal of the Georgia House* (1893), 874; *Journal of the Georgia Senate* (1893), 76; Centralization/Electrocution: *Acts of Georgia* (1924), 195–97; *Journal of the Georgia House* (1924), 353–57; *Journal of the Georgia Senate* (1924), 541; Kentucky — Privacy: *Acts of Kentucky* (1880), 60–61; Centralization/Electrocution: *Acts of Kentucky* (1910), 111–13; *Journal of the Kentucky House* (1910), 1477–79; *Journal of the Kentucky Senate* (1910), 623–26. Louisiana — Privacy: *Acts of Louisiana* (1884), 102; *Journal of the Louisiana House* (1884), 424–25; *Journal of the Louisiana Senate* (1884), 372; Centralization: *Acts of Louisiana* (1910), 107; *Journal of the Louisiana House* (1910), 285–86; *Journal of the Louisiana Senate* (1910), 423; Electrocution: *Acts of Louisiana* (1940), 79–81. Mississippi — Privacy: *Laws of Mississippi* (1916), 330; *House Journal of Mississippi* (1916), 264–65, 572–73; *Senate Journal of Mississippi* (1916), 393; Electrocution: *Laws of Mississippi* (1940), 411–13; *House Journal of Mississippi* (1940), 324, 628–29; *Senate Journal of Mississippi* (1940), 441. North Carolina — Privacy: *Public Laws of North Carolina* (1901), 352; Centralization/Electrocution: *Public Laws of North Carolina* (1909), 758–61. South Carolina — Privacy: *Acts of South Carolina* (1877–78), 381; *Journal of the South Carolina House* (1877–78), 145–46; *Journal of the South Carolina Senate* (1877–78), 497–98. Centralization/Electrocution: *Statutes of South Carolina* (1912), 702–3; *Journal of the South Carolina Senate* (1912), 257. Tennessee — Privacy: *Acts of Tennessee* (1883), 139–40; *House Journal of Tennessee* (1883), 564–65; *Senate Journal of Tennessee* (1883), 634–35; Centralization: *Acts of Tennessee* (1909), 1810–12; *House Journal of Tennessee* (1909), 223–24; *Senate Journal of Tennessee* (1909), 555–56, 647; Electro-

cution: *Acts of Tennessee* (1913), 515-16; *House Journal of Tennessee* (1913), 1441; *Senate Journal of Tennessee* (1913), 1232-33; Texas—Privacy/Centralization/Electrocution: *General Laws of Texas* (1923), 111-14; *Texas House Journal* (1923), 1434-36; *Texas Senate Journal* (1923), 221-22. Virginia—Privacy: *Acts of Virginia* (1878-79), 380. Centralization/Electrocution: *Acts of Virginia* (1908), 684-86; *Journal of the Virginia House* (1908), 470-71; *Journal of the Virginia Senate* (1908), 747-48. This is not a complete list of votes in states, for some states set up "soft" laws against public executions earlier; the votes in this list are the most consequential state votes for privacy.

64. Arkansas—return to public: *Acts of Arkansas* (1901), 105; *Journal of the Arkansas House* (1901), 350; *Journal of the Arkansas Senate* (1901), 203; end of public: *Acts of Arkansas* (1905), 723-24; *Journal of the Arkansas House* (1905), 759; *Journal of the Arkansas Senate* (1905), 271-72. Kentucky—return to local: *Acts of Kentucky* (1920), 693-94; *Journal of the Kentucky House* (1920), 1776-79; *Journal of the Kentucky Senate* (1920), 1045-47, 2742-44. Louisiana—return to local: *Acts of Louisiana* (1918), 227-28; *Journal of the Louisiana House* (1918), 821-22; *Journal of the Louisiana Senate* (1918), 557-58. Tennessee—abolish (most) capital punishment: *Acts of Tennessee* (1915), 5-6; *House Journal of Tennessee* (1915), 371-76, 930-32; *Senate Journal of Tennessee* (1915), 602-3; reinstate capital punishment: *Acts of Tennessee* (1919), 27-28; *House Journal of Tennessee* (1919), 175-76; *Senate Journal of Tennessee* (1919), 162-23, 164-65. Tennessee retained the death penalty for rape, and the legislative journals are quite interesting in terms of amendments proposed to this bill (limiting the abolition to cases of murder based only on circumstantial evidence, having it take effect in 1999, taking the vote on the bill to the people of Tennessee), and in terms of the explanations for their votes in the affirmative. In addition, the governor returned the bill without his signature, saying that it would "increase crime and encourage mob law," but as this message was received after five days of its passage in the legislature, the bill was already law.

65. If all projects shift while they are in progress, this is a place where I first thought this project would offer an important and novel set of data that might reveal new trends. It is possible that other researchers with more sophisticated statistical tools than I command will be able to wring greater meaning out of these data, and I offer a bounty of citations to give them a path to that end. I have my doubts. The silver lining: in doing this research, I accumulated the qualitative data on justifications made by competing sides in these debates that provide what I consider to be the more meaningful evaluation below.

66. At various times in compiling and trying to interpret these data, I believed that I might discern the starts of trends in tables and maps comparing the votes of legislators with their counties ranked by size, by founding data (a possible stand-in for how settled a given county might be), or by state subregion. The most tenacious of those beliefs (the one most common to occur to me, and therefore perhaps the most promising to follow up on if any researchers with greater statistical acumen might want to pursue this) was that cities tended to vote more for private and centralized executions and rural areas for public and local ones. Even this possible trend in city representatives being for privacy (which ultimately I did not find at all clear) would simply track those areas most likely to already have jail yards built and therefore already to perform executions within a barrier. In other words, even if this were a trend,

it might simply be a trend of all legislators voting for the process in their area to remain the same. This trend was noticed at the time: "We content ourselves, in the fastidious cities, with hiding the gallows out of sight" ("The Gallows in America," *Putnam's Magazine* [February 1869]: 227). At no time did I actually become convinced that this was anything more than how randomness in data doesn't result in uniformity but rather in randomly distributed nonuniformities.

67. *House Journal of Tennessee* (1883), 564–65; *Journal of the Louisiana House* (1884), 424–25. That is 13 percent and 19 percent in favor of keeping public execution among Democratic House members in Tennessee and Louisiana, respectively. Of the state houses for which I have been able to find party affiliations (a much more difficult undertaking than I imagined), only the Tennessee Senate in 1883 had a higher proportion of Democrats (22 percent, or 4 members) in favor of retaining public execution than Republicans (14 percent or 1 of 7 members; *Senate Journal of Tennessee* [1883], 634–35).

68. That is 40 percent of Republicans in the Louisiana House voting to retain public execution (the few calling themselves "Independent Democrats" also voted 40 percent against privacy). In Tennessee's House in 1883, 38 percent of Republicans (six out of sixteen) voted to keep public executions. In the Louisiana Senate, 12 percent of Democrats voted against private executions, compared with 33 percent of Republicans (*Journal of the Louisiana Senate* [1884], 372). In 1878, 38 percent of Democrats voted against privacy in executions in the South Carolina Senate (eight of twenty-one), compared with 57 percent of Republicans voting no (four of seven). In that case, four of the Republicans were African Americans, and they split their vote: two from counties on the coast voted yes to private executions; two from interior counties voted no (*Journal of the South Carolina Senate* [1877–78], 497–98). By the twentieth century, few Republicans remained in many state houses in the South, masking any further partisan divide. In both Mississippi in 1916 and Florida in 1923, not one of the voting legislators in either house was listed as a Republican.

69. The exception to this trend was a very particular—and very different—dynamic in terms of public and private executions: the return to local hangings for rapists in Kentucky in 1920. Here the context was not "normal" local public executions but rather the threat of lynching and the demand of whites to have rapists executed locally rather than electrocuted in the state penitentiary. Both Democrats and Republicans voted in favor of the bill, but a larger proportion of Republicans opposed this move. The state had centralized capital punishment in the previous decade, but in 1920, the legislature voted to reverse course, responding to an attempted (failed) lynching and a bloodbath as the sheriff resisted. The Kentucky House had broad bipartisan agreement to return executions for the crime of rape to the locality and to hanging, with thirty-four Democrats and thirty-four Republicans voting for it. But 11 percent of Democrats (four) compared with 26 percent of Republicans (twelve) voted against this measure (*Journal of the Kentucky House* [1920], 1776–79). The supercharged racial atmosphere and a threat of lynching in 1920 made this quite a different sort of vote from other public versus private ones where "public" meant "mixed race" and "private" meant "white." Here, "public" meant "caving to a white mob."

70. Masur, *Rites of Execution*; Lane, *Murder in America*, 99; Bowers, *Executions in America*, 5, 31; Bedau, *Death Penalty in America*, 12–14. Fitzhugh Brundage and Susan Jean have found that a similar discourse defined "legitimate" lynchings as solemn, sober, and earnest in contrast to "illegitimate" lynchings that were brutal, barbaric, and without community support ("Legitimizing 'Justice,'" 157–77). Christopher Waldrep likewise argues for the importance of shifting conceptions of lynching's legitimacy in his *Many Faces of Judge Lynch*.

71. *New Orleans Daily Picayune*, 6 June 1885.

72. *Atlanta Constitution*, 28 March 1878. See also editorials and articles in the *Constitution* on 23 May 1883; 25 January 1889; 13 May, 7 June, and 30 June 1891; 5 October, 10 October, 27 October, and 29 October 1893; 19 February 1894; 12 July 1909.

73. *Richmond Dispatch*, 12 February 1870.

74. *Nashville Daily American*, 21 February 1880. Large advertisements for "Perry Davis' Pain Killer" on the posts of the gallows might have confused the issue further in this particular hanging.

75. *National Police Gazette*, 6 March 1880; for another "holiday excursion" report of an execution, see *Atlanta Constitution*, 22 May 1883.

76. *Petersburg Index-Appeal*, 26 March 1879.

77. *New York Tribune*, 28 March 1879.

78. *Richmond Whig*, 27 March 1879; the *Richmond Dispatch*, while mentioning the holiday air of the crowd, likewise praised the sheriff for the order and propriety of the event.

79. *Petersburg Index-Appeal*, 2 April 1879. The *Richmond Dispatch* (2 April 1879) likewise printed the text of this bill with the preface, "In view of the recent exhibition at New Kent Courthouse, the General Assembly passed the following bill to prohibit public execution."

80. *Louisville Courier-Journal*, 22 February 1879.

81. *Louisville Courier-Journal*, 31 March 1880. The legislative debate was particularly interesting (and close), barely passing the House. Two House members offered what appear to be snide amendments which did not pass: "This act shall not be in force after Friday next" and instead of fifty witnesses allowed, another suggested the law should read 50,000. The first vote for the bill was tied. The amendment that yielded a positive vote stipulated that no witnesses to a private execution be charged admission for the privilege (*Journal of the Kentucky House* [1880], 1140–44).

82. *Louisville Courier-Journal*, 30 March 1880.

83. *Louisville Courier-Journal*, 3 April 1880. These were the early years after Reconstruction when fears of Black rescue were most acute.

84. Reminiscences in newspapers characterize public executions in this way: "N.C. Public Hangings Once Were 'Social Functions'" (*Durham Morning Herald*, 13 February 1949); see also "Old N.C. Custom Falls Victim to Science," *Durham Morning Herald*, 9 May 1954.

85. Pfeifer, *Rough Justice*.

86. For the broader rise in civility and a variety of middle-class and elite efforts to control public spaces, tame audiences, and contain the emotional outbursts of the

lower classes, see Kasson, *Rudeness and Civility*; Levine, *Highbrow/Lowbrow*; Elias, *Civilizing Process*; and Foucault, *Discipline and Punish*.

87. Kotch, *Lethal State*, 56.

88. *N. W. Ayer and Son's American Newspaper Annual* (1880), 323; Moore, "Black Militancy in Readjuster Virginia," 167–86. There may be other such partisan divides in the perspectives on public execution in the South, but I have not found them; most southern newspapers were supporters of the Democratic Party.

89. *Atlanta Constitution*, 7 June 1891.

90. Page, *Negro*, 98–99.

91. Sobel, *Trabelin' On*, 172; Harper, *End of Days*, 28–29.

92. Boles, "Forum," 176.

93. Tucker, *Relations of the Church*, 17.

94. Quoted in Litwack, *Been in the Storm So Long*, 469.

95. *New Orleans Daily Picayune*, 18 April 1891.

96. *Atlanta Constitution*, 30 June 1891.

97. *Atlanta Constitution*, 5 October 1893.

98. *Atlanta Constitution*, 5 October 1893. See also *Raleigh News and Observer*, 29 August 1879. This might be compared to the "alchemy" that Elaine Franz found in how the KKK (or, better, the idea or concept of the KKK—the story that circulated about them) would turn a specific violent act into an attack by abstract men on an abstract body. At least in the minds of whites, this alchemy would necessarily produce dread and terror in African Americans (Frantz [Parsons], *Ku-Klux*, 73).

99. *Atlanta Constitution*, 27 October 1891.

100. *Arkansas Democrat*, 26 July 1901; for a similar sentiment, see *Atlanta Constitution*, 28 March 1878, 19 February 1894.

101. *Atlanta Constitution*, 28 March 1878.

102. Quoted in Feimster, *Southern Horrors*, 194.

103. *Louisville Commercial*, 3 April 1880.

104. Barton, "Punishment of Crime" (1893), 179–80.

105. *New Orleans Daily Picayune*, 6 June 1885.

106. *Charleston News and Courier*, 24 August 1878.

107. *Atlanta Constitution*, 19 February 1894. This interest in the efficacy of the mystery of private executions can be found much earlier in the historical record. In 1852, a writer in the *Southern Literary Messenger* wrote, "Perhaps it would be better to have executions within jail-walls and in the presence only of those connected with the administration of the law. To invest an execution with the mystery of privacy would increase its deterring power to many" (C*****, "Death Punishment," 650).

108. *Atlanta Constitution*, 12 July 1909.

109. Seth Kotch argues that the presence and the behavior of black women at the gallows (especially their "shrieks and shouts") was a key element in the move toward eliminating public executions in North Carolina (*Lethal State*, 62–64).

110. *New York Times*, 9 April 1872. They are reporting a Tennessee execution.

111. *Nashville Daily American*, 3 June 1882; *Dallas Morning News*, 10 March 1900.

112. *Atlanta Constitution*, 29 October 1893. For more on this gendered dynamic at executions outside the South, see Linders, "Execution Spectacle," 622–25.

113. *Atlanta Constitution*, 8 June 1888. This is in reference to New York's proposed humanitarian introduction of electrocution. In addition to the range of sources above that reflect on the white South's desire to use its punishment regimes to curb and terrorize malefactors, particularly Black ones, see also *Atlanta Constitution*, 3 April 1893, 19 February 1894; *Arkansas Democrat*, 7 November 1911. George Wright found that in 1920, many Kentuckians believed electrocution to be "too humane" for rapists and called for the reintroduction of the rope (*Racial Violence in Kentucky*, 256).

114. Quoted in Coulter, "Hanging," 48–49. This is quite in contrast to the story of private execution told in the North, and quite in contrast to Foucault's vision of the evolution of punishment in the West. See Masur, *Rites of Execution*, and Foucault, *Discipline and Punish*. Public execution in the South was not considered to be the terrible, torturous affair Foucault stereotyped it to be, and the goal of private execution was to more effectively terrorize as much as it was to civilize. The growing use of torture-filled lynchings at the very same moment as these reforms likewise flies in the face of the pattern many chart for punishment in western societies. Mark Colvin came to the same conclusions: "What is striking about the case study of southern punishment is the absence of factors postulated by Foucault and Elias. Neither sophisticated, rational systems of punishment nor civilized sensibilities play significant roles in the transformation of punishment in the South" (*Penitentiaries, Reformatories, and Chain Gangs*, 264).

115. Bowers, *Legal Homicide*, 13; *Furman v. Georgia* (408 U.S. 238). By 1912, more southern states were using electrocution as a method for their capital punishment than were states outside the South.

116. In 1900, only two states, both in the North, used electrocution. By 1910, two southern states had turned to electrocution; by then, more than 40 percent of the nation's electrocutions were in the South. By 1930, despite having only one-third of the population (comparing the southern population with the total population of the collection of states with electrocution), southern states had an outright majority of the nation's electrocutions. From 1940 to the Furman decision in 1972, the South accounted for two-thirds of all of the nation's electrocutions (Espy file; Carter, *Historical Statistics*, 1:180–359).

117. Espy file. By this point, with centralization of execution in the hands of the state, the Espy file becomes dependable: Espy and Hearn and Laska are almost identical after that point. Each state's first electrocution, by date: 1908, Henry Smith (Virginia, for rape); 1910, Walter Morrison (North Carolina, rape); 1911, James Buckner (Kentucky, murder); 1912, John Cole (South Carolina, attempted rape); 1913, Lee Simms (Arkansas, rape); 1916, Julius Morgan (Tennessee, rape); 1924, Frank Johnson (Florida, murder-burglary); 1924, Howard Henson (Georgia, rape-robbery); 1924, Charles Reynolds, Ewell Morris, Melvin Johnson, George Washington, and Mack Matthews (Texas, murder); 1927, Horace Devaughan (Alabama, murder-robbery); 1940, Willie Bragg (Mississippi, murder); 1941, Eugene Johnson (Louisiana, murder-robbery).

This disproportion of African Americans condemned to the early chair persists when looking at the first three electrocutions in each state (all but one of which was a Black man), but thereafter the proportion of African Americans condemned returns to the "regular" level of (extraordinary) racial skew: 80 percent, around the Black proportion of condemned for the whole period under consideration here, if continuing to massively overrepresent the roughly 33 percent of the South's population who were Black in 1910.

Exaggerating a little more this odd additional skew of the first electrocutions, there were ten hangings in the South performed after a state's first electrocution had occurred, and these were racially skewed—in the opposite direction (only three of those ten were Black). If someone was condemned and the mode of execution in the state at that moment was hanging, a bill in the legislature to shift to electrocution would not necessarily change that decree, depending on the wording of the bill. And if that condemned man appealed the case, his execution might be delayed past the time when other condemned (either not appealing or not as successful with their appeals) whose judge decreed the newly mandated electrocution to be the method of execution were scheduled for execution. Seth Kotch found an example of a white condemned who attempted suicide to avoid being the first to die in North Carolina's electric chair (*Lethal State*, 205). (Espy file; Carter, *Historical Statistics*, 1:180–359).

118. Two states (Tennessee in 1909 and Louisiana in 1910; Louisiana rescinded this change eight years later) centralized private hangings in a state penitentiary separate from a shift to electrocution. With most states, however, it was with electrocution that they moved from local to state-sponsored capital punishment practiced in the bowels of a state penitentiary. This was a particularly effective means of avoiding crowds: far from the site of the crime and trial, typically, and buried in a large, guarded building. Two extraordinary exceptions from the Deep South are the use of a portable electric chair in both Mississippi and Louisiana in the 1940s: "The state's first 'modern' execution in the lamp-lit cell of a crumbling jail, soon to be abandoned, in the remote Livingston parish seat which has no power supply" (*New Orleans Times-Picayune*, 12 September 1941).

119. The connection of the technological sublime and electricity and particularly electrocution is convincingly made in Martschukat, "'Art of Killing by Electricity.'"

120. Perhaps it should not be surprising in the era of convict labor that many of the chairs were constructed by penitentiary prisoners.

121. *Dallas Morning News*, 8 February 1924.

122. *Arkansas Democrat*, 5 September 1915.

123. *Richmond Evening Journal*, 24 November 1911, Extra No. 2. This article was taken from Carrington, *History of Electrocution*.

124. Carrington, "Report of the Surgeon," *Annual Report of the Board of Directors of the Virginia Penitentiary* (1908), 33.

125. In addition to the several quotations using the word above, see *Charleston News and Courier*, 23 August 1912 and many others.

126. *Richmond Times-Dispatch*, 14 October 1908; *Richmond News Leader*, 13 October 1908; and several others. Other descriptors common to the reports and commentary on early electrocutions in the South were "mysterious" and "swift."

127. These states are Alabama, Arkansas, Florida, Georgia, Kentucky, North Carolina, South Carolina, Texas, and Virginia. Tennessee had a separate bill to centralize hangings in the state penitentiary, and Mississippi and Louisiana (the latter of which

centralized hangings for eight years [1910–18] before returning them to local parishes) adopted electrocution (1940 for both) and centralization (1955 and 1957, respectively) much later than the others.

128. In his study of North Carolina, Seth Kotch likewise finds electrocutions to be unsettling, delocalization as an issue, and arguments that its "incomprehensibility and mystery" would be a deterrent (*Lethal State*, 66–70).

129. *Richmond Times-Dispatch*, 6 March 1908.

130. *Richmond Times-Dispatch*, 14 October 1908. Editors of the *Richmond News Leader* (13 October 1908) agreed: "We have a very strong hope that the privacy and mystery of the execution of the death sentence will tend to make the law more terrible and to diminish crime." So did the man who would run Virginia's first electrocutions: Carrington, *History of Electrocution*, 2, 6.

131. *Atlanta Constitution*, 7 June 1891.

132. *Charleston News and Courier*, 23 August 1912. This is the only instance I've found of an electrocution with a condemned saying, "I see so many of my own color here," showing that, in South Carolina at least, African Americans were allowed to be among the thirty-five witnesses the law allowed. In most instances, however, it appears crowds were white and mostly made up of doctors, prison attendants, and in some states members of the press.

133. *Charleston News and Courier*, 14 August 1912.

134. *Arkansas Gazette*, 6 September 1915.

135. *Raleigh News and Observer*, 19 March 1910.

136. "Under the laws of the State nothing can be told of the details of the execution" (*Richmond News Leader*, 13 October 1908).

137. In those pages, Foucault describes the brutal 1757 torture and death of the regicide Damiens.

138. On more rare occasions, the noose loosened, and the condemned fell to the ground and had to remount the scaffold and be hanged again. With early electrocutions, not all condemned were clearly killed by the first burst of the current.

139. The *Richmond Dispatch* (7 August 1890), for instance, devoted nearly its entire front page to the execution, which it described as "bungling" and "brutal," reminding witnesses of the Inquisition, and making them physically ill. The *Dispatch* has another lengthy article on the arguments about its efficacy before Kimmler's execution; for instance, 21 July 1889. For more general response to Kimmler's execution, see Martschukat, "Art of Killing by Electricity," 918–20.

140. Carrington, *History of Electrocution*, 3–5.

141. *Nashville Banner*, 13 July 1916.

142. The *Atlanta Constitution* (11 March 1922) reported on an Arkansas bungled case: "After 11 attempts by an inexperienced electrician to electrocute James Wells, 18-year-old negro, had failed, the twelfth was pronounced a success."

143. Carrington, "Surgeon's Report," *Annual Report of the Board of Directors of the Virginia Penitentiary* (1909), 35.

144. For more on this dynamic outside the South, see Linders, "Execution Spectacle," 626–30; Masur, *Rites of Execution*.

145. *Atlanta Constitution*, 3 April 1893.

146. *Atlanta Constitution*, 11 March 1922.

147. *Richmond Times-Dispatch*, 14 October 1908.

Afterword

1. *Louisville Courier-Journal*, 15 August 1936; *Louisville Times*, 14 August 1936; Wright, *Racial Violence in Kentucky*, 257–58, images following p. 163.

2. *Louisville Times*, 14 August 1936.

3. *Louisville Times*, 14 August 1936.

4. *Louisville Times*, 17 December 1937.

5. At this point, Kentucky's legislature met biennially, and this was the first legislative session after the hanging of Bethea. A caveat: there may have been an execution in Louisiana or Mississippi—both states were tenacious in retaining local executions—that was public or had elements of a public execution after this date even though no executions were supposed to be so. Because other states moved to electrocution and centralization in a state penitentiary, I suspect no other public executions occurred in any other southern states after this date.

6. And at least in Virginia in 1879, Democratic and Republican newspapers followed suit.

7. *Richmond Daily Dispatch*, 11 September 1852.

8. Alexander, *New Jim Crow*, 7.

9. Furman v. Georgia, 408 U.S. 238 (1972); Gregg v. Georgia, 428 US 153 (1976).

10. "The Death Penalty in 2021: A Year End Report," Death Penalty Information Center, 16 December 2021 (www.deathpenaltyinfo.org). In 2021, five of the eleven executions were in the South (and three others in the border states of Missouri and Oklahoma; the other three were federal executions), the lowest number since the early 1980s.

11. *New York Times*, 25 March 2021.

Bibliography

Primary Sources

Local and State Periodicals

Alexandria Gazette
Arkansas Democrat
Arkansas Gazette
Atlanta Constitution
Atlanta Journal
Birmingham Age-Herald
Charleston News and
   Courier
Charlotte Observer
Daily Democrat
   (Mississippi)
Dallas Morning News
Durham Morning Herald
East Mississippi Times
Florida Times-Union
Galveston Daily News
Hattiesburg News
Houston Daily Post
Huntsville Gazette
Lexington Morning Herald
Louisville Commercial
Louisville Courier-Journal
Louisville Times
Mobile Daily Register
Montgomery Advertiser
Nashville Banner
Nashville Daily Advertiser
Nashville Daily American
New Orleans Daily
   Picayune
New Orleans
   Times-Democrat
New Orleans
   Times-Picayune
New Orleans Weekly
   Pelican
Norfolk Virginian
Petersburg Index-Appeal
Raleigh Gazette
Raleigh News and Observer
Raleigh Observer
Richmond Dispatch
Richmond Evening Journal
Richmond News Leader
Richmond Planet
Richmond State
Richmond Times
Richmond Times-Dispatch
Richmond Whig
Savannah Tribune
Southern Opinion
   (Virginia)
Vicksburg Herald
Virginia Law Register
Virginia Medical
   Semi-Monthly
Weekly Louisianan
Wilmington Morning News

Regional and National Periodicals

Alexander's Magazine
American Journal of
   Sociology
The Arena
Atlantic Monthly
Baltimore Afro-American
Chicago Defender
Christian Observer
Colored American
   Magazine
Contemporary Review
The Crisis
The Dial
Horizon: A Journal of the
   Color Line
Leslie's Weekly
McClure's Magazine
N. W. Ayer and Son's
   American Newspaper
   Annual
The Nation
National Police Gazette
New York Times
New York Tribune
North American Review
Outlook
Philadelphia Tribune
Putnam's Magazine
Sewanee Review
South Atlantic Quarterly
Southern Literary
   Messenger
Southern Quarterly Review
Voice of the Negro

Government Documents

ALABAMA
Acts of Alabama
Code of Alabama
General Laws of Alabama
Journal of the Alabama House
Journal of the Alabama Senate

ARKANSAS
Acts of Arkansas
Digest of the Statutes of Arkansas
Journal of the Arkansas House
Journal of the Arkansas Senate

FLORIDA
Acts of Florida
Digest of the Laws of Florida
Journal of the Florida House
Journal of the Florida Senate
Revised General Statutes of Florida

GEORGIA
Acts of Georgia
Code of Georgia
Journal of the Georgia House
Journal of the Georgia Senate
Park's Code of Georgia
Statute Laws of Georgia

KENTUCKY
Acts of Kentucky
General Statutes of Kentucky
Journal of the Kentucky House
Journal of the Kentucky Senate

LOUISIANA
Acts of Louisiana
Code of Criminal Procedure of Louisiana
Journal of the Louisiana House
Journal of the Louisiana Senate
Revised Statutes of Louisiana

MISSISSIPPI
Code of Mississippi
House Journal of Mississippi
Laws of Mississippi
Revised Code of Mississippi
Senate Journal of Mississippi

NORTH CAROLINA
Code of North Carolina
Journal of the North Carolina House
Journal of the North Carolina Senate
Laws of North Carolina

SOUTH CAROLINA
Acts of South Carolina
Journal of the South Carolina House
Journal of the South Carolina Senate
Statutes of South Carolina

TENNESSEE
Acts of Tennessee
Code of Tennessee
House Journal of Tennessee
Senate Journal of Tennessee

TEXAS
Complete Texas Statutes
Digest of the Laws of Texas
General Laws of Texas

Penal Code of Texas
Texas House Journal
Texas Senate Journal

VIRGINIA
Acts of Virginia
Annual Report of the Board of Directors of the Virginia Penitentiary

Code of Virginia
Journal of the Virginia House
Journal of the Virginia Senate

NATIONAL

Bureau of the Census, *Negroes in the United States*, Bulletin 8. Washington, DC: General Printing Office, 1904.

Carter, Susan B., ed. *Historical Statistics of the United States: Earliest Times to the Present.* Vol. 1, *Population.* New York: Cambridge University Press, 2006.

Coker v. Georgia, 433 U.S. 584 (1977).

Ex Parte Virginia, 100 U.S. 339 (1880).

Fourteenth U.S. Census, 1920. Vol. 3, *Population.* Washington, DC: General Printing Office, 1922.

Furman v. Georgia, 408 U.S. 238 (1972).

Gregg v. Georgia 428 U.S. 153 (1976).

Strauder v. West Virginia, 100 U.S. 303 (1880).

Twelfth U.S. Census, 1900. Vol. 1, *Population.* Washington, DC: General Printing Office, 1901.

Twelfth U.S. Census, 1900, Special Reports: Supplementary Analyses and Derivative Tables. Washington, DC: General Printing Office, 1906.

Virginia v. Rives, 100 U.S. 313 (1880).

Papers

Armistead C. Gordon Papers, 1705–1957, Virginia Historical Society, Richmond.

Davis, Allison. "The Negro Church and Associations in the Lower South." In *Problems of the American Negro.* Carnegie-Myrdal Study of the Negro in America research memoranda collection, Sc Micro F-13242, Schomburg Center for Research in Black Culture, Manuscripts, Archives and Rare Books Division, New York Public Library.

Du Bois, W. E. B. "Black Social Equals." W. E. B. Du Bois Papers, reel 82. Library of Congress.

———. Correspondence with Richard Jones of *Collier's Weekly.* 1904. The Papers of W. E. B. Du Bois. Microfilm, reel 7, Ann Arbor, MI: University Microfilm International.

Johnson, Guion G. and Guy B. Johnson, "The Church and the Race Problem in the United States." In *Problems of the American Negro.* Carnegie-Myrdal Study of the Negro in America research memoranda collection, reel 7, Schomburg Collection, Library of Congress.

Terrell, Mary Church. "Concerning Mr. Page's Article on the Race Problem in *McClure's Magazine*," undated [1907–8]. Mary Church Terrell Papers, Speeches and Writings, 1866–1953, box 32. Library of Congress.

———. "A Plea for the White South by a Colored Woman" [1905]. Mary Church Terrell Papers, Speeches and Writings, 1866–1953, box 29. Library of Congress.

———. "Who Are the Negro's Best Friends," undated. Mary Church Terrell Papers, Speeches and Writings, 1866–1953, box 32, Library of Congress.

Books and Articles

Baker, Ray Stannard. *Following the Color Line*. 1908; New York: Harper and Row, 1964.

———. "What Is a Lynching?: A Study of Mob Justice, South and North, I—Lynching in the South." *McClure's* 24 (January 1905): 299–314.

Barringer, Paul B. "The Negro and the Social Order." In *Race Problems of the South: Report of the Proceedings of the First Annual Conference of . . . the Southern Society for the Promotion of the Study of Race Conditions and Problems in the South*, 178–94. 1900; New York: Negro University Press, 1969.

Barton, R. T. "The Punishment of Crime." In *Report of the 5th Annual Meeting of the Virginia Bar Association*, 153–81. Richmond: Everett Waddey, 1893.

Bruce, Philip Alexander. *The Plantation Negro as a Freeman; Observations on His Character, Condition, and Prospects in Virginia*. New York: Putnam's Sons, 1889.

Burroughs, Edgar Rice. *Tarzan of the Apes*. 1914; Mineola, New York: Dover, 1997.

Carrington, Charles V. *The History of Electrocution in the State of Virginia*. Richmond: Williams Printing Co., 1910.

Davenport, F. M. "The Religion of the American Negro." *Contemporary Review* (September 1905), 369–75.

Douglass, Frederick. *Three Addresses on the Relations Subsisting between the White and Colored People of the United States*. Washington, DC: Gibson Brothers, 1886.

———. *Why Is the Negro Lynched?* Bridgewater: Whitby and Sons, 1895.

Du Bois, W. E. B. *The Correspondence of W. E. B. Du Bois. Vol. 1, Selections, 1877–1934*. Edited by Herbert Aptheker. Amherst: University of Massachusetts Press, 1973.

———, ed. *The Negro Church: A Social Study*. Atlanta, GA: Atlanta University Press, 1903.

———. *The Souls of Black Folk*. 1903; New York: Norton, 1999.

Faduma, Orishatukeh. "The Defects of the Negro Church." Occasional Papers #10. Washington, DC: American Negro Academy, 1904.

Griggs, Sutton. *Imperium in Imperio: A Study of the Negro Race Problem*. 1899; New York: Arno, 1969.

Holloway, W. H. "A Black Belt County, Georgia." In *The Negro Church: A Social Study*, edited by W. E. B. Du Bois, 57–63. Atlanta, GA: Atlanta University Press, 1903.

Julian, John. *Dictionary of Hymnology*. New York: Scribner's, 1892.

Lipscomb, Andrew, and Albert Ellery Bergh, eds. *The Writings of Thomas Jefferson*. Washington, DC: Thomas Jefferson Memorial Association, 1903.

Mickel, E. P., et al. *Triune Hymnal*. Dayton, VA: Ruebush, Kleffer, 1883.

Mitchell, Samuel C. "Nationalization of Southern Sentiment." *South Atlantic Quarterly* 7 (1908): 107–13.

Norwood, Thomas. *Address on the Negro*. Savannah, GA: Braid and Hutton, 1907.

Odum, Howard. *Social and Mental Traits of the Negro: Research into the Conditions of the Negro Race in Southern Towns, a Study in Race Traits, Tendencies and Prospects*. New York: AMS, 1910.

Page, Thomas Nelson. "The Great American Question: A Special Plea from a Southerner." *McClure's* 28 (1907): 565–72.

———. *The Negro: The Southerner's Problem*. New York: Scribner's, 1904.

———. "The Negro: The Southerner's Problem, Third Paper: Its Present Condition and Aspect as Shown by Statistics." *McClure's* 23 (1904): 96–102.

———. *Red Rock: A Chronicle of Reconstruction*. New York: Scribner's, 1903.

Ramsey, D. Hiden. "Negro Criminality." In *Lectures and Addresses on the Negro in the South*. Charlottesville, VA: Mitchie, 1915.

Redfield, H. V. *Homicide, North and South*. Philadelphia: J. B. Lippincott, 1880.

Richmond Police and Fire Department Directory. Richmond, VA: John T. West, 1896.

Terrell, Mary Church. "Lynching from a Negro's Point of View." *North American Review* 178 (1904): 853–68.

Thomas, William Hannibal. *The American Negro: What He Was, What He Is, and What He May Become*. New York: Macmillan, 1901.

Tucker, J. L. *Relations of the Church to the Colored Race*. Jackson, MS: Charles Winkley, 1882.

Watson, J. J. "Churches and Religious Conditions." *Annals of the American Academy of Political and Social Sciences* 49 (1913): 120–28.

Wells, Ida B. *Southern Horrors: Lynch Law in All Its Phases*. 1892; New York: Bedford, 1997.

Willcox, Walter F. *Negro Criminality*. Boston: George Ellis, 1899.

Work, Monroe N. "Negro Criminality in the South." *Annals of the American Academy of Political and Social Science* 49 (1913): 74–80.

Secondary Sources

Websites

Death Penalty Information Center. "The Death Penalty in 2021: Year End Report." www.deathpenaltyinfo.org. 16 December 2021.

Death Penalty Information Center. "Executions in the U.S.: 1608-2002; The Espy File." www.deathpenaltyinfo.org.

Death Penalty Information Center. "Facts about the Death Penalty." www.deathpenaltyinfo.org. 3 January 2022.

Project HAL: Historical American Lynching Data Collection Project. people.uncw.edu/hinese/HAL/HAL Web Page.htm.

Books and Articles

Alexander, Ann Field. "'Like an Evil Wind': The Roanoke Riot of 1893 and the Lynching of Thomas Smith." *Virginia Magazine of History and Biography* 100 (1992): 173–206.

———. *Race Man: The Rise and Fall of the 'Fighting Editor' John Mitchell, Jr.* Charlottesville: University of Virginia Press, 2002.

Alexander, Michelle. *The New Jim Crow: Mass Incarceration in the Age of Colorblindness.* New York: New Press, 2010.

Allen, Howard W., and Jerome M. Clubb. *Race, Class, and the Death Penalty: Capital Punishment in American History.* Albany: State University of New York Press, 2008.

Anderson, Margo J. *The American Census: A Social History.* New Haven, CT: Yale University Press, 1988.

Ayers, Edward. *Promise of the New South: Life after Reconstruction.* New York: Oxford University Press, 1998.

———. *Vengeance and Justice: Crime and Punishment in the 19th-century American South.* New York: Oxford University Press, 1984.

Bailey, Amy Kate, and Stewart E. Tolnay. *Lynched: The Victims of Southern Mob Violence.* Chapel Hill: University of North Carolina Press, 2015.

Baker, Bruce. *This Mob Will Surely Take My Life: Lynchings in the Carolinas, 1871-1947.* London: Continuum, 2008.

Baldwin, James. *Collected Essays.* New York: Library of America, 1998.

Banner, Stuart. *The Death Penalty: An American History.* Cambridge, MA: Harvard University Press, 2002.

Bardaglio, Peter. *Reconstructing the Household: Families, Sex, and the Law in the Nineteenth-Century South.* Chapel Hill: University of North Carolina Press, 1995.

Bedau, Hugo Adam. *The Death Penalty in America.* 3rd ed. New York: Oxford University Press, 1982.

Bessler, John D. *Death in the Dark: Midnight Executions in America.* Boston: Northeastern University Press, 1997.

Blackman, Paul H., and Vance McLaughlin. "The Espy File on American Executions: User Beware." *Homicide Studies* 15 (2011): 209-27.

Blum, Edward J., and W. Scott Poole, eds. *Vale of Tears: New Essays on Religion and Reconstruction.* Macon, GA: Mercer University Press, 2005.

Boles, John. "Forum: Southern Religion." *Religion and American Culture* 8 (1998): 166-77.

Bowers, William J. *Executions in America.* Lexington, MA: Lexington Books, 1974.

———. *Legal Homicide: Death as Punishment in America, 1864-1982.* Boston: Northeastern University Press, 1984.

Brundage, Fitzhugh. *Lynching in the New South: Georgia and Virginia, 1880-1930.* Urbana: University of Illinois Press, 1993.

Brundage, Fitzhugh, and Susan Jean. "Legitimizing 'Justice:' Lynching and the Boundaries of Informal Justice in the American South." In *Informal Criminal Justice,* edited by Dermot Feenan, 157-77. Burlington: Ashgate, 2002.

Carrigan, William. *The Making of a Lynching Culture: Violence and Vigilantism in Central Texas, 1836-1916.* Urbana: University of Illinois Press, 2004.

Carrigan, William, and Christopher Waldrep, eds. *Swift to Wrath: Lynching in Global Historical Perspective.* Charlottesville: University of Virginia Press, 2013.

Chesson, Michael. *Richmond after the War, 1865-1890.* Richmond: Virginia State Library, 1981.

Clarke, James. *The Lineaments of Wrath: Race, Violent Crime, and American Culture*. New Brunswick, NJ: Transaction Publishers, 1998.

Cohen, Daniel. "The Beautiful Female Murder Victim: Literary Genres and Courtship Practices in the Origins of a Cultural Motif, 1590–1850." *Journal of Social History* 31 (1997): 277–306.

Cohen, Patricia Cline. *The Murder of Helen Jewett: The Life and Death of a Prostitute in Nineteenth-Century New York*. New York: Knopf, 1998.

Colvin, Mark. *Penitentiaries, Reformatories, and Chain Gangs: Social Theory and the History of Punishment in 19th-Century America*. New York: St. Martin's, 1997.

Coulter, E. Merton. "Hanging as a Socio-Penal Institution in Georgia and Elsewhere." *Georgia Historical Quarterly* 57 (1973): 25–45.

Cox, David G. "'Half-Bacchanalian, Half Devout': White Intellectuals, Black Folk Culture, and the 'Negro Problem.'" *American Nineteenth Century History* 16 (2015): 241–67.

Crouch, Barry. "A Spirit of Lawlessness: White Violence; Texas Blacks, 1865–1868." *Journal of Social History* 18 (1984): 217–32.

Davis, Abraham L., and Barbara Luck Graham. *The Supreme Court, Race, and Civil Rights*. Thousand Oaks, CA: Sage Publications, 1995.

Davis, Allison, Burleigh Gardner, and Mary Gardner. *Deep South: A Social Anthropological Study of Caste and Class*. Chicago: University of Chicago Press, 1941.

Davis, Henry Vance. "The Black Press: From Mission to Commercialism, 1827–1927." PhD diss., University of Michigan, 1990.

Dixie, Quinton Hosford, and Cornel West, eds. *The Courage to Hope: From Black Suffering to Human Redemption*. Boston: Beacon, 1999.

Dorr, Lisa Linquist. *White Women, Rape, and the Power of Race in Virginia, 1900–1960*. Chapel Hill: University of North Carolina Press, 1904.

Dunlap, Leslie K. "The Reform of Rape Law and the Problem of White Men: Age of Consent Campaigns in the South, 1885–1910." In *Sex, Love, Race: Crossing Boundaries in North American History*, edited by Martha Hodes, 352–72. New York: New York University Press, 1999.

Edwards, Laura F. *Gendered Strife and Confusion: The Political Culture of Reconstruction*. Urbana: University of Illinois Press, 1997.

Elias, Norbert. *The Civilizing Process: Sociogenetic and Psychogenetic Investigations*. Malden, MA: Blackwell, 2000.

Emberton, Carole. *Beyond Redemption: Race, Violence, and the American South after the Civil War*. Chicago: University of Chicago Press, 2013.

Faust, Drew Gilpin. *This Republic of Suffering: Death and the American Civil War*. New York: Knopf, 2008.

Feimster, Crystal. *Southern Horrors: Women and the Politics of Rape and Lynching*. Cambridge, MA: Harvard University Press, 2009.

Foucault, Michel. *Discipline and Punish: The Birth of the Prison*. New York: Vintage, 1979.

Frantz [Parsons], Elaine. *Ku-Klux: The Birth of the Klan during Reconstruction*. Chapel Hill: University of North Carolina Press, 2015.

Fredrickson, George. *The Black Image in the White Mind: The Debate on Afro-American Character and Destiny, 1817-1914*. New York: Harper and Row, 1971.

Freedman, Estelle B. *Redefining Rape: Sexual Violence in the Era of Suffrage and Segregation*. Cambridge, MA: Harvard University Press, 2013.

Galliher, John F., Gregory Ray, and Brent Cook. "Abolition and Reinstatement of Capital Punishment during the Progressive Era and Early 20th Century." *Journal of Criminal Law and Criminology* 83 (1992): 538-76.

Geddes, R. Richard, and Sharon Tennyson. "Passage of the Married Women's Property Acts and Earnings Acts in the United States, 1850 to 1920." *Research in Economic History* 29 (2013): 145-89.

Genovese, Eugene. *Roll, Jordan, Roll: The World the Slaves Made*. New York: Pantheon, 1974.

Giggie, John M. *After Redemption: Jim Crow and the Transformation of African American Religion in the Delta, 1875-1915*. New York: Oxford University Press, 2008.

Gilmore, Glenda Elizabeth. *Gender and Jim Crow: Women and the Politics of White Supremacy in North Carolina, 1896-1920*. Chapel Hill: University of North Carolina Press, 1996.

Gonzalez-Day, Ken. *Lynching in the West, 1850-1935*. Durham, NC: Duke University Press, 2006.

Greenberg, Kenneth S., ed. *The Confessions of Nat Turner and Related Documents*. Boston: Bedford, 1996.

Hacker, J. David. "New Estimates of Census Coverage in the United States, 1850-1930." *Social Science History* 37 (2013): 71-101.

Hale, Grace Elizabeth. *Making Whiteness: The Culture of Segregation in the South, 1890-1940*. New York: Pantheon, 1998.

Hall, Jacquelyn Dowd. *Revolt against Chivalry: Jessie Daniel Ames and the Women's Campaign against Lynching*. New York: Columbia University Press, 1979.

Halttunen, Karen. *Murder Most Foul: The Killer and the American Gothic Imagination*. Cambridge, MA: Harvard University Press, 1998.

Harper, Ida Husted. *History of Woman Suffrage*, vol. 6, *1900-1920*. New York: J. J. Little and Ives, 1922.

Harper, Matthew. *End of Days: African American Religion and Politics in the Age of Emancipation*. Chapel Hill: University of North Carolina Press, 2016.

Harris, Lashawn. "The 'Commonwealth of Virginia vs. Virginia Christian': Southern Black Women, Crime and Punishment in Progressive Era Virginia." *Journal of Social History* 47 (2014): 922-42.

Harvey, Paul. *Redeeming the South: Religious Cultures and Racial Identities among Southern Baptists, 1865-1925*. Chapel Hill: University of North Carolina Press, 1997.

Hearn, Daniel Allen. *Legal Executions in Delaware, DC, Maryland, Virginia, and West Virginia: A Comprehensive Registry, 1866-1962*. Jefferson, NC: McFarland, 2015.

———. *Legal Executions in Georgia: A Comprehensive Registry, 1866-1964*. Jefferson, NC: McFarland, 2016.

———. *Legal Executions in Illinois, Indiana, Iowa, Kentucky, and Missouri: A Comprehensive Registry, 1866-1965*. Jefferson, NC: McFarland, 2016.

———. *Legal Executions in New York State: A Comprehensive Reference, 1639-1963*. Jefferson, NC: McFarland, 1997.

———. *Legal Executions in North Carolina and South Carolina: A Comprehensive Registry, 1866-1962*. Jefferson, NC: McFarland, 2015.

Higginbotham, Evelyn Brooks. *Righteous Discontent: The Women's Movement in the Black Baptist Church, 1880-1920*. Cambridge, MA: Harvard University Press, 1993.

Hodes, Martha. "The Sexualization of Reconstruction Politics: White Women and Black Men in the South after the Civil War." *Journal of the History of Sexuality* 3 (1993): 402–17.

Hogan, J. Michael, ed. *Rhetoric and Community: Studies in Unity and Fragmentation*. Columbia: University of South Carolina Press, 1998.

Hunter, Tara. *To 'Joy My Freedom: Southern Black Women's Lives and Labors after the Civil War*. Cambridge, MA: Harvard University Press, 1997.

Kahneman, Daniel. *Thinking, Fast and Slow*. New York: Farrar, Straus, and Giroux, 2013.

Kasson, John. *Rudeness and Civility: Manners in Nineteenth-Century Urban America*. New York: Hill and Wang, 1990.

Kotch, Seth. *Lethal State: A History of the Death Penalty in North Carolina*. Chapel Hill: University of North Carolina Press, 2019.

———. "Making of the Modern Death Penalty." In *Crime and Punishment in the Jim Crow South*, edited by Amy Louise Wood and Natalie J. Ring, 192–214. Urbana: University of Illinois Press, 2019.

Lane, Roger. *Murder in America: A History*. Columbus: Ohio State University Press, 1997.

Laska, Lewis L. *Legal Executions in Tennessee: A Comprehensive Registry, 1866-1962*. Jefferson, NC: McFarland, 2011.

Lears, T. J. Jackson. "The Concept of Cultural Hegemony: Problems and Possibilities." *American Historical Quarterly* 90 (1985): 567–93.

Lebsock, Suzanne. *A Murder in Virginia: Southern Justice on Trial*. New York: W. W. Norton, 2003.

Levine, Lawrence W. *Highbrow/Lowbrow: The Emergence of Cultural Hierarchy in America*. Cambridge, MA: Harvard University Press, 1988.

Linders, Annulla. "The Execution Spectacle and State Legitimacy: The Changing Nature of the American Execution Audience, 1883-1937." *Law and Society Review* 36 (2002): 607–56.

———. "'What Daughters, What Wives, What Mothers, Think You, They Are?': Gender and the Transformation of Executions in the United States." *Journal of Historical Sociology* 28 (2015): 135–65.

Linders, Annulla, and Alana Van Gundy-Yoder. "Gall, Gallantry, and the Gallows: Capital Punishment and the Social Construction of Gender, 1840-1920." *Gender and Society* 22 (2008): 324–48.

Litwack, Leon. *Been in the Storm So Long: The Aftermath of Slavery*. New York: Vintage, 1979.

———. *North of Slavery: The Negro in the Free States, 1790-1860*. Chicago: University of Chicago Press, 1961.

———. *Trouble in Mind: Black Southerners in the Age of Jim Crow*. New York: Knopf, 1999.

Lowry, Beverly. *Her Dream of Dreams: The Rise and Triumph of Madam C. J. Walker*. New York: Knopf, 2003.

Martschukat, Jürgen. "'The Art of Killing by Electricity': The Sublime and the Electric Chair." *Journal of American History* 89 (2002): 900–21.

Masur, Louis P. *Rites of Execution: Capital Punishment and the Transformation of American Culture, 1776-1865*. New York: Oxford University Press, 1989.

Mathews, Donald. *At the Altar of Lynching: Burning Sam Hose in the American South*. New York: Cambridge University Press, 2018.

———. "Lynching Is Part of the Religion of Our People: Faith in the Christian South." In *Religion in the American South: Protestants and Others in History and Culture*, edited by Beth Barton Schweiger and Donald G. Mathews, 153–94. Chapel Hill: University of North Carolina Press, 2004.

McHenry, Elizabeth. "Toward a History of Access: The Case of Mary Church Terrell." *American Literary History* 19 (2007): 381–401.

Miller, Vivien. "Hanging, the Electric Chair, and Death Penalty Reform in the Early-Twentieth-Century South." In *Crime and Punishment in the Jim Crow South*, edited by Amy Louise Wood and Natalie J. Ring, 170–91. Urbana: University of Illinois Press, 2019.

Montgomery, William E. *Under Their Own Vine and Fig Tree: The African American Church in the South, 1865-1900*. Baton Rouge: Louisiana State University Press, 1993.

Moore, James T. "Black Militancy in Readjuster Virginia, 1879-1883." *Journal of Southern History* 41 (1975): 167–86.

Morris, Thomas. *Southern Slavery and the Law, 1619-1860*. Chapel Hill, University of North Carolina Press, 1996.

Muhammad, Khalil Gibran. *The Condemnation of Blackness: Race, Crime, and the Making of Modern Urban America*. Cambridge, MA: Harvard University Press, 2010.

Myers, Lois E., and Rebecca Sharpless. "'Of the Least and the Most': The African American Rural Church." In *African American Life in the Rural South, 1900-1950*, edited by R. Douglas Hunt, 54–80. Columbia: University of Missouri Press, 2003.

Odem, Mary. *Delinquent Daughters: Protecting and Policing Adolescent Female Sexuality in the U.S., 1885-1920*. Chapel Hill: University of North Carolina Press, 1995.

Pfeifer, Michael J., ed. *Lynching beyond Dixie: American Mob Violence Outside the South*. Urbana: University of Illinois Press, 2013.

———. *Rough Justice: Lynching and American Society, 1874-1947*. Urbana: University of Illinois Press, 2002.

Piketty, Thomas. *Capital in the Twenty-First Century*. Cambridge, MA: Harvard University Press, 2014.

Pitts, Walter. "Keep the Fire Burnin': Language and Ritual in the Afro-Baptist Church." In *Embodying the Spirit: New Perspectives on North American Revivalism*, edited by Michael McClymond, 196–210. Baltimore: Johns Hopkins University Press, 2004.

Poole, W. Scott. "Confederate Apocalypse." In *Vale of Tears: New Essays on Religion and Reconstruction*, edited by Edward J. Blum and W. Scott Poole, 36–52. Macon, GA: Mercer University Press, 2005.

Prince, K. Stephen. *Stories of the South: Race and the Reconstruction of Southern Identity, 1865–1915*. Chapel Hill: University of North Carolina Press, 2014.

Rabinowitz, Howard. *Race Relations in the Urban South, 1865–1890*. Urbana: University of Illinois Press, 1980.

Rable, George. *But There Was No Peace: The Role of Violence in the Politics of Reconstruction*. Athens: University of Georgia Press, 1984.

Raboteau, Albert. "The Blood of Martyrs Is the Seed of Faith." In *The Courage to Hope: From Black Suffering to Human Redemption*, edited by Quinton Hosford Dixie and Cornel West, 22–39. Boston: Beacon, 1999.

Randle, Judith. "Cultural Lives of Capital Punishment in the United States." In *The Cultural Lives of Capital Punishment*, edited by Austin Sarat and Christian Boulanger, 92–111. Stanford, CA: Stanford University Press, 2005.

Rise, Eric. *The Martinsville Seven: Race, Rape, and Capital Punishment*. Charlottesville: University of Virginia Press, 1995.

Roth, Randolph. *American Homicide*. Cambridge, MA: Harvard University Press, 2009.

Sarat, Austin, and Christian Boulanger, eds. *The Cultural Lives of Capital Punishment: Comparative Perspectives*. Stanford, CA: Stanford University Press, 2005.

Schor, Paul. *Counting Americans: How the US Census Classified the Nation*. New York: Oxford University Press, 2017.

Schwarz, Philip. *Slave Laws in Virginia*. Athens: University of Georgia Press, 1996.

———. "The Transportation of Slaves from Virginia, 1801–1865." *Slavery and Abolition* 7 (1986): 215–40.

———. *Twice Condemned: Slaves and the Criminal Laws of Virginia, 1705–1865*. Baton Rouge: Louisiana State University Press, 1988.

Schweninger, Loren. *Black Property Owners in the South, 1790–1915*. Urbana: University of Illinois Press, 1990.

Shapiro, Herbert. "Muckrakers and the Negroes." *Phylon* 31 (1970): 76–88.

———. *White Violence and Black Response: From Reconstruction to Montgomery*. Amherst: University of Massachusetts Press, 1988.

Silber, Nina. *The Romances of Reunion: Northerners and the South, 1865–1900*. Chapel Hill: University of North Carolina Press, 1993.

Smith, Hubert F., ed. *Richard Watson Gilder*. New York: Twayne, 1970.

Smith, John David, ed. *Anti-Black Thought, 1863–1925*. Vol. 4, "The Benefits of Slavery." New York: Garland, 1993.

Smith, Suzanne. *To Serve the Living: Funeral Directors and the African American Way of Death*. Cambridge, MA: Belknap Press, 2010.

Sobel, Mechal. *Trabelin' On: The Slave Journey to an Afro-Baptist Faith*. Princeton, NJ: Princeton University Press, 1988.

Sommerville, Diane Miller. *Rape and Race in the Nineteenth-Century South*. Chapel Hill: University of North Carolina Press, 2004.

Southern, David. *The Malignant Heritage: Yankee Progressives and the Negro Question, 1901–14*. Chicago: Loyola University Press, 1968.

Taylor, Marshall. *The Fastest Bicycle Rider in the World*. Worcester, MA: Wormley, 1928.

Tolnay, Stewart E., and E. M. Beck. *A Festival of Violence: An Analysis of Southern Lynchings, 1882–1930*. Urbana: University of Illinois Press, 1995.

Trotti, Michael. *The Body in the Reservoir: Murder and Sensationalism in the South*. Chapel Hill: University of North Carolina Press, 2008.

———. "The Scaffold's Revival: Race and Public Execution in the South." *Journal of Social History* 45 (2011): 195–224.

———. "What Counts?: Trends in Racial Violence in the Postbellum South." *Journal of American History* 100 (2013): 375–400.

Vandiver, Margaret. *Lethal Punishment: Lynchings and Legal Executions in the South*. New Brunswick, NJ: Rutgers University Press, 2006.

Vivian, Tim. "Wake the Devil from His Dream: Thomas Dudley, Quincy Ewing, Religion, and the 'Race Problem' in the Jim Crow South." *Anglican and Episcopal History* 83 (2014): 371–416.

Waldrep, Christopher. *The Many Faces of Judge Lynch: Extralegal Violence and Punishment in America*. New York: Palgrave, 2002.

Ward, Geoffrey. *Unforgivable Blackness: The Rise and Fall of Jack Johnson*. New York: Knopf, 2004.

Williams, Kidada. *They Left Great Marks on Me: African American Testimonies of Racial Violence from Emancipation to World War I*. New York: New York University Press, 2012.

Williamson, Joel. *The Crucible of Race: Black-White Relations in the American South since Emancipation*. New York: Oxford University Press, 1984.

Wood, Amy Louise. *Lynching as Spectacle: Witnessing Racial Violence in America, 1890-1940*. Chapel Hill: University of North Carolina Press, 2009.

Wright, George. *Racial Violence in Kentucky, 1865-1940: Lynchings, Mob Rule, and "Legal Lynchings."* Baton Rouge: Louisiana State University Press, 1990.

Wyatt-Brown, Bertram. *Southern Honor: Ethics and Behavior in the Old South*. New York: Oxford University Press, 1982.

Index

African Americans: demographic trends outside South, 90; experience in North, 90; falling percentage of South's population, 94-95; improvements for, 3, 67; public authority of, 10, 12, 17, 60, 81, 129, 146-50. *See also* churches, African American; execution; racism; religion, African American
Agassiz, Louis, 64
age of consent laws, 123-25. *See also* rape
Alabama, 93, 118, 125; capital punishment law changes in, 41, 122-24, 154
anthropology, contemporary views of, 64
Arkansas, 45, 112, 125; capital punishment law changes in, 40, 41, 123-24; return to public execution in, 136-39
Arp, Bill, 151
arson, 39, 41, 44
Atlanta riot of 1906, 114
attempted murder, 39, 41, 44
attempted rape, 36, 39, 41, 45, 123
Ayers, Edward L., 67

Baker, Ray Stannard, 76, 80, 108
Baldwin, James, 161
Baptists, 21, 24. *See also* religion, African American
Beck, E. M., 36
Bethea, Rainey, 38, 161-62
Bible passages: at executions, 12, 27-29; white conservative use of, 19; in support of African American religion, 20-25
Birth of a Nation, 80
Blackman, Paul H., 87-88, 100

Brundage, W. Fitzhugh, 92, 126
burglary, 34, 39, 40, 41, 45, 55
Burroughs, Edgar Rice, 64-65

capital punishment: abolition in North, 36, 41; abolition in South, 84, 125, 167; scholarship on the South's history of, 4, 85. *See also* electrocution; execution
Carrigan, William D., 106
Carrington, Charles V., 154
Catholic execution services, 15, 29, 161
Chesnutt, Charles W., 71, 73, 76
Christian, Virginia, 45, 50-51
churches, African American: formation of 21, 60; importance as community center, 24-25, 31; influence of the congregation upon, 24
Cluverius, Thomas, 53-54
constitutional amendments, post–Civil War, 40
convict lease, 40, 69, 96, 164

Danforth, Frank, 1-2, 6-7, 12, 18
death penalty. *See* capital punishment; electrocution; execution
Dixon, Thomas, 64, 75
Dorr, Lisa Lindquist, 119
Douglass, Frederick, 80-81
Du Bois, W. E. B., 56, 71, 73, 75, 76, 161

electrocution, 11, 45, 50-51, 135, 138, 139, 152, 157; press restrictions of, 156-57; rationale for, 153-55; religion, changed place of, 156; trends in, 153. *See also* execution

Espy file, 39, 84, 86–87, 92, 120, 170n7, 181n8; additions of Hearn and Laska to, 82, 88, 94, 100; undercount of African Americans and the South in, 84, 87–89, 94, 98, 100, 185n37

execution
— Black crowds at, as a problem, 143–46; rescue or riot, fear of, 112–13; timing of these fears, 113–14
— centralized under state authority, 82, 87, 131, 136–39, 153–56
— condemned at: desiring public, 18, 32; in African American press, 14–15; speeches of, 13–14
— crowds at: and gender, 15–16, 32, 150–51; and race, 10, 12, 13, 34, 88–89; changes in, with privacy, 133–34, 146–51, 158; outside walls, 30, 133
— for minor crimes, 39–45; nature of, 43–44; racial disparity in, 44–45
— for rape, 35–39, 103–27; nature of, 37–39, 114–17, 136–39; rare for whites, 37; trends in, 118–26
— lynching comparison, 37, 82, 103–27 passim. *See also* lynching
— of white men, 34, 35, 37, 51–56; as likely public as Black men, 52; more press coverage of, 53–55; nature of, 52–53
— of women, 45–51; nature of, 46–47; of white women, 46–50
— political parties affecting, 96, 98–99, 100, 101, 139–42, 162; and press coverage of, 146
— private, arguments for, 142–52; consolidating white authority, 130; justified as provoking terror, 129; laws shifting to 127–39; North and West shift to, 130; transitional mix of public and private, 131–33; race and gender in the crowds, 133
— public: arguments for, 134–35, 137, 138; calling out of crowds in, 109; failing to teach lesson, 128–29, 139; interpreting the nature of 103, 114, 117–18, 151–52; reintroduction of, 136–39; relics/souvenirs of, 110; traditional view of, 130
— racial skew in, 12, 34, 83, 86, 88–89, 93–94; decline of, during Republican regimes, 96, 100
— trends in, geographic: prominence in South, 83, 84–94; settled areas v. frontier, 90, 102; in North and West, 84, 90, 93; whites executed more in South, 85–86
— trends in, interpreting, 82–102, 199n22; counts vs. rates, 86. *See also* execution — racial skew in; lynching, trends in
— trends in, over time, 94–100, 205n50; before the Civil War, 66, 84; falling in the 20th century, 82, 83, 100, 106–7; high point, 82, 99–100, 102; since 1976, 83, 167. *See also* execution — for rape, trends in
— white crowds acting like lynch mobs at, 103, 114–17; religion foreshortened at, 116–17; timing of, 117–18; when condemned was white, 110–11, 116

Felton, Rebecca Latimer, 36
Florida, 45, 84, 90, 102, 112, 120, 125; capital punishment law changes in, 41, 123–24, 154
Foucault, Michel, 145, 156
Freedmen's Bureau, 67, 77–78

Georgia, 86, 92–93, 107, 112, 114, 115, 120, 125, 130, 131, 150, 159; capital punishment law changes in, 41, 122–24
guns, superabundance of, 85

Haiti, 79
hanging. *See* execution
Hearn, Daniel Allen, 39, 82, 92–93, 213n74
Hoffman, Frederick, 78–79

Hose, Sam, 69, 107, 109, 110
hymns sung at executions, 8, 13, 27-29, 32; crowds and, 30-31; themes in, 26-28; written by condemned, 26-27

immigrant communities: affecting northern views of race, 77, 80; compared to African Americans, 90
Indiana, 149

Jesus, 9, 20, 32; mentioned in gallows services, 18, 25; own public execution, 25, 27-28
judges, 98-99, 125, 164
juries, 125, 164; all white as constitutional, 98-99; discretion in sentencing of, 39, 40, 122
justice 128; African American view of, 17, 58; white view of, 58-60, 128-29

Kentucky, 113, 115, 118, 120, 125, 134, 161-62; capital punishment law changes in, 41, 122-24, 143-46, 149, 162; return to local (public) executions in, 137-39
Kotch, Seth, 145

Laska, Lewis L., 39, 82, 88, 213n74
law enforcement, changes in, 120-21. *See also* justice
laws, changes in. *See* age of consent laws; execution—private, laws shifting to; rape, changes in laws of
Louisiana, 113, 116, 120, 125, 147-48, 149; capital punishment law changes in, 41, 124, 142, 152
lynching, 74, 104-9; and public execution's failures, 108; Black counterarguments to, 74-75; Black participation in, 106; comparison with public execution, 4, 106-9, 120, 126-27, 128, 152, 159-66 passim;

motivated by rape, 35-36; replaced by executions, theory debunked, 82; trends in, 104-6. *See also* racism

Massachusetts, 85
Mathews, Donald G., 109, 111
McLaughlin, Vance, 87-88, 100. *See also* Espy file
Methodists, 15, 21
minstrelsy, 77, 180n144
Mississippi, 45, 118, 120, 125; capital punishment law changes in, 41, 122-24
Mitchell, John, 50, 72, 73
Mitchell, Samuel Chiles, 80-81
Muhammad, Khalil Gibran, 75

narratives, understanding the world through, 58, 67, 68, 72-79, 130
National Association for the Advancement of Colored People, 50
National Association of Colored Women, 50
New York, 152, 156
North Carolina, 44, 100, 112, 118, 120, 125, 135, 156; capital punishment law changes in, 40, 41, 123-24
northern states: African American rights seen as experiment in, 77-78; as dominating the federal government, 67; context of Empire and immigration on, 77, 80; effect of southern racist notions on, 57, 59, 72-79. *See also* capital punishment, abolition in North; press, northern

Page, Thomas Nelson, 35, 56, 57, 62, 68-79 passim, 147
Pfeifer, Michael J., 126, 145
Philippines, colonial comparison, 69
political echo chambers, 166-67. *See also* press, northern

Index 249

press: and disruptive executions, 104; and sensationalism in era of private executions, 135–36; Black, building a counter public sphere, 75, 79; Black, covering executions, 14–15; interpreting as a source for executions, 171nn13–14, 173nn28–29, 174n46; northern, 56, 73, 74–77

prison, 69; shift to from white to Black populations in, 96, 166

prosecutors, 44, 55, 122, 125, 164

public defenders, 166

punishments, 2, 4, 158, 163; as deterrent, 8–9; racist system of, 66–72, 159, 165; whipping post, 66, 193n75. See also capital punishment; electrocution; execution; justice

Racist perspectives: African American counterarguments to, 71–72, 74–77; and challenges to white monopolies of power, 67, 129; and data, 70, 82; and fear, 3, 6; elements left out of, 81; informing the stories South told the nation, 73–74, 77; on African American nature, 57, 58, 59, 63, 65; on education ruining Blacks, 63, 70; on mobility and vagrancy, 68

rape: changes in laws of, 122; changes in understanding of sexual violence, 121–22; excuse for lynching, 35–36, 58; punishments for, 36–37, 118. See also age of consent laws; attempted rape; execution—for rape

Republican party: racism of, 77–78. See also execution—political parties affecting

religion, African American, 3, 5; and history, 10–11; baptism, 22; class differences within Black communities about, 20; chosen people, 20–21, 23, 24; conversion, 23; emotional expression of, 15–16, 21–22; equality stressed, 11, 24, 27–28, 31; faith as central 21; good works, 23; importance of salvation, grace, and forgiveness, 9, 18, 23, 28–30, 32; interpreting the evidence of, 12–13, 29, 31; original sin, 9; sacrifice, Christian history of, 9, 25, 28, 32; slavery, end of, and Exodus, 24; subversive effects of, 11, 17–18, 24, 26, 31, 146–51, 158–60, 163; suffering, 28; traditional beliefs, 24; white views of, 19, 59, 60–66, 147–51. See also churches, African American

religion at executions, 1–2, 4–5, 8–33; in cell, preceding, 15; ministers at, 29, 30; public role ended, 147–50, 156, 157–58. See also Bible passages at executions; execution; hymns sung at executions

Richmond, Virginia, competing police forces in, 98

robbery, 39, 41, 44, 55

Schwarz, Philip J., 84

segregation, 16, 164, 166

sheriffs, 12,13, 133; woman as, 134

Silber, Nina 77

Sommerville, Diane Miller, 118

South, distinctive history of, 2. See also execution—trends in, geographic; rape, punishments for

South Carolina, 85, 120, 125, 155–56; capital punishment law changes in, 41, 122–24, 142

Tarbell, Ida, 77

Tennessee, 45, 111, 125; capital punishment law changes in, 41, 122–25, 135, 142

Terrell, Mary Church, 36, 50, 57, 67, 71, 76, 79

Texas, 45, 83, 93, 102, 106, 118, 120, 125; capital punishment law changes in, 41, 122–24, 154, 155

Thomas, William Hannibal, 35, 62, 70

Tillman, Benjamin, 64, 73, 75

Tolnay, Stewart, 36

Turner, Nat, 62, 66

vagrancy, 40, 96, 164
Vardaman, James, 73, 82
Vesey, Denmark, 62
violence in South 84–85; in scholarship, 10
Virginia, 87, 92–93, 100, 118, 119, 120, 125, 131, 154, 156, 157; abolition of the death penalty in, 84, 167; capital punishment law changes in, 40, 41, 122–24, 130, 143–46, 152, 155, 167

Wells, Ida B., 36
Williams, Kidada E., 75
women: assumed to be notorious, 124; in churches, 16. *See also* execution—crowds, and gender; execution—of women
Women's Christian Temperance Union, 123–24
Wood, Amy Louise, 126
Wyatt-Brown, Bertram, 85, 126

www.ingramcontent.com/pod-product-compliance
Lightning Source LLC
Chambersburg PA
CBHW030535230426
43665CB00010B/903